World Tanks and Reconnaissance Vehicles Since 1945

NOEL AYLIFFE-JONES

HIPPOCRENE BOOKS
New York

First published 1984

Published in the United States by
HIPPOCRENE BOOKS, Inc.,
171 Madison Avenue,
New York, N.Y. 10016

ISBN 0-88254-978-2

Printed in Great Britain

Contents

Cover: Head-on view of a Chieftain Mk 7 of The Royal Scots Dragoon Guards at Bergen-Hohne during the Canadian Army Trophy competition in June 1983. *Simon Forty*

Title page: T-54/55s on exercise — now outdated, the T-54/55 was one of the most significant AFVs of its period if only because it served in the armies of 33 countries. *via C. Foss*

Left: British Battle Tanks from 1945 to the present day, represented (r to l) by Centurion Mk3 with 20pdr, Chieftain with 120mm and Challenger with 120mm and Chobham armour. *MoD*

Preface

It was originally intended to cover, in this book, all types of Armoured Fighting Vehicles since 1945. However, this period is more than half the whole life, to date, of the tank and contains the period of greatest development and proliferation, so we have restricted ourselves to Main Battle Tanks and Reconnaissance Vehicles.

Without pretending to be either a definitive history or a technical manual, we have tried to tell the story of how and why technology, tactics, strategy and politics have all had a hand in the development of the AFVs of today. If it is not 100% up to date when you read it, blame the pace of history, and don't shoot the typist. The other half of the story, about all the types of AFVs spawned by the tank, remains to be told.

Acknowledgements

I should like to thank all those who have helped me by providing information and pictures for this book, individually and as organisations. In particular I have received help from: Robert Bos; Simon Dunstan; Michael Foncannon; Christopher Foss; Fred Garner; Helmoed-Roeder Heitman; Philip Lilleyman; Richard Ogorkiewicz; Toby Wrigley; from the following Regiments, Establishments and Ministeries: 4th/7th Royal Dragoon Guards; MVEE; RAC Tank Museum; Royal Ordnance Factories; Ministry of Defence of Great Britain, Australia, Canada, France, Italy, Japan, Switzerland, West Germany, United States of America; and Companies: AAI Corporation; Alvis Ltd; Bernardini sa; British Leyland; Cockerill-Sambre; GKN Ltd; General Motors of Canada Ltd; General Defense Corporation; Engesa; Krauss-Maffei gmbh; Lohr sa; Marconi Radar Systems Ltd; Pains-Wessex Ltd; Sibmas sa; Vickers Ltd.

Bibliography

Design and Development of Fighting Vehicles, Richard Ogorkiewicz; *Centurion*; Simon Dunstan; *Chieftain*, George Forty; *Leopard*, A. J. Barker; *M48*, Geoffrey Tillotson; *Modern American Armour*, Steve Zaloga & James Loop; *Modern Soviet Armour*, Steve Zaloga; *The Business of Tanks*, G. MacLeod Ross; *Janes World Armoured Fighting Vehicles*, Christopher Foss; *Armour of the West*, R. Adshead & N. Ayliffe-Jones; *AFV Profiles*, Profile Publications; *The Guinness Book of Tank Facts and Feats*, Kenneth Macksey; *Encyclopaedia of Tanks*, Duncan Crow and Robert Icks.

Scorpion of the 17/21 Lancers during Exercise 'Atlantic Lion' 1983. *Michael C. Klaver*

4

Abbreviations

AA	Anti-aircraft	IDF	Israeli Defence Force
AEV	Armoured engineer vehicle	IR	Infra-red
AFV	Armoured fighting vehicle	ICV	Infantry combat vehicle
AIFV	Armoured IFV	IFV	Infantry fighting vehicle
AMX	Ateliers de Moulineaux	JSDF	Japanese Self-Defence Force
AOS	Add-on stabilisation	KE	Kinetic energy
AP(HE)	Armour-piercing (high explosive)	LAV	Light armoured vehicle
APC	Armoured personnel carrier	LCC	Life cycle cost
AP(FS)DS	AP (fin-stabilised) discarding sabot	LOS	Line of sight
AR/AAV	Armoured reconnaissance/airborne assault vehicle	LRF	Laser rangefinder
		MBT	Main battle tank
ARSV	Armoured reconnaissance scout vehicle	MG	Machine gun
ARV	Armoured recovery vehicle	MICV	Mechanised ICV
AVRE	Armoured vehicle Royal Engineers	MMBF	Mean miles between failures
ATGW	Anti-tank guided weapon	MoD	Ministry of Defence
AVLB	Armoured vehicle launched bridge	MRS	Muzzle reference system
C&R	Command & Reconnaissance	m/v	Muzzle velocity
CE	Chemical energy	MVEE	Military Vehicles Experimental Establishment
CEV	Combat engineer vehicle	NBC	Nuclear, biological, chemical
CFV	Cavalry fighting vehicle	OPFOR	Opposing forces
CI	Compression ignition	pdr	Pounder
CLGP	Cannon-launched guided projectile	PLA	People's Liberation Army (China)
CVR(T)(W)	Combat vehicle reconnaissance (tracked) (wheeled)	PRC	People's Republic of China
		PV	Private venture
DU	Depleted uranium	RAC	Royal Armoured Corps
EPC	Engin Principal de Combat	RAM-D	Reliability, Availability, Maintainability — Durability
ESR	Electro-slag refined		
FCS	Fire control system	RARDE	Royal Armament Research and Development Establishment
FEBA	Forward edge of battle area		
FN	Fabrique National (Belgium)	RDF	Rapid Deployment Force
FRG	Federal Republic of Germany (West)	RMG	Ranging MG
FS	Fin-stabilised	ROF	Royal Ordnance Factory
FVRDE	Fighting Vehicles Research & Development Establishment	RSAF	Royal Small Arms Factory
		SP	Self-propelled
GAO	General Accounting Office	-T	-Training
GPMG	General purpose MG	TACOM	Tank Automotive Command (US Army)
HE	High explosive	TBO	Time between overhauls
HEAT	HE anti-tank	VCR	Variable compression ratio
HESH	HE squash head	WP	White Phosphorous
HVAP	High velocity AP	WW(1) (2)	World War (1) (2)

M60A1 of US 1st Cavalry Division on Exercise 'Aquamarine' crossing the River Maas. *NATO*

Introduction

When WW2 ended in 1945 the Allies had just started to bring into service the tanks that matched, in firepower and protection, those of their enemies. They had won the armoured battle by weight of numbers and by mobility and the majority of the surviving tanks were outworn and outdated.

Just as WW1 had seen the birth of the tank, so WW2 had seen it come of age, becoming master of the battlefield instead of the supporting weapon at first envisaged. The tank also spawned a huge family of other armoured fighting vehicles for a multiplicity of roles. Though Liddell Hart's 'all-tank-army' had not materialised, the Armoured Division had come to stay.

The end of the war gave a breathing space, and those who cared to think about the future of armour took the opportunity to take stock and to consider philosophies and policies for the development of the AFV and its use. At last there was a pause in which to evaluate, and learn from, the lessons and mistakes of 1939-45.

Technical Situation 1945

Although improved equipments had been requested by the users and design started as far back as 1942, few of these were in service by the end of the war. The reason for this apparent disregard for the lives of the tank crews was neither callousness nor parsimony, but the realisation that, if the quantity of production was not maintained, replacements at the front would be in short supply and the whole momentum of the Allied attack would run down.

It was more important, therefore, to ensure the uninterrupted supply of Shermans, Churchills and Cromwells than to turn the factories over to building A41 (Centurion), Comets and M26 Pershing (though some of the last two did see service in 1945) with the inevitable hiatus in production, teething troubles and training problems.

A part answer to the problem was to improve existing vehicles where possible. Many British Shermans were rearmed with the 17pdr gun and renamed Firefly. The Americans, though offered the 17pdr by Britain, turned it down in favour of their own, less powerful 76mm gun.

In America improvements were mainly in engines. The clumsy, aircraft type, radial engine had been replaced with a stopgap five-bank Chrysler petrol engine, then a twin GMC diesel installation, before the purpose-built Ford V8 GAA petrol engine of 500hp came out. There was almost no advance in transmissions, most American tanks having a five-speed synchromesh gearbox and Cletrac double differential steering, both requiring harder work on the part of the driver than the regenerative Merritt-Brown combined transmission and steering units in the contemporary British tanks. The exceptions were the M5 Stuart and M24 Chaffee light tanks which had automatic transmissions.

It was the M26 Pershing which changed the style of American tanks. With a 90mm gun, rear drive, torsion bar suspension, and in later models an automatic transmission, it was a complete breakaway from previous designs and one which set a trend for the next 30 years.

The Russians were the only country among the Allies to produce a tank, which saw service in significant numbers, that was a radical change in design from previous tanks in service. The T-34, with well sloped armour, simple and robust diesel engine and Christie suspension was itself the inspiration for the German PzV Panther. Only at the very end of the fighting in 1944-45 did the Russians introduce the IS-2 and IS-3 with the 122mm gun, the biggest tank gun of the war and for the next three decades. This, too, was a significant change of design, with a low silhouette and well-shaped, almost hemispherical turret which set the trend for

Cromwells of a recce unit wait to advance. Fast and manoeuvrable, they were armed with a 75mm gun and all armour except the glacis plate was vertical. Vehicles further back in the column are Stuart light tanks.
MoD

Soviet tanks for the future, providing some of the best looking (if least comfortable) MBTs in the world.

'Over the hill', in Germany, there had been a continuous improvement, development and compromise, which kept German AFVs ahead of the Allies in firepower and protection. However they suffered from 'Fuhrer-directivs' which insisted on diverting effort from the excellent, proven designs of PzIV, PzV and PzVI, to the huge, unwieldy, far from mobile, heavy tanks which Hitler loved. The result was disruption in the factories and delivery of very small numbers of King Tigers.

By 1945 Europe, having been the major battlefield of the war, was littered with armoured vehicles, most of them out of date and worn out. Britain was about to field the first of its new A41 Centurions: a few M26 Pershing were the US battalions in the Zone of Occupation: and the USSR showed the IS-3 at a parade in Berlin, sending a shiver of apprehension among Western observers and starting a race of tank development that is the main subject of this book.

Fighting vehicle concepts

Before WW2 tank operations in most countries were subordinate to and in the hands of infantrymen. Tactics, such as there were, called for little more than the ability to carry some sort of firepower around the battlefield at the pace of the horse and foot and protection was minimal. Tank design was influenced more by considerations of cost than effectiveness and were in the hands of commercial rather than military interests.

Practical considerations, born of experience in the field and the factories shaped the AFVs of WW2, a matter of expediency and reaction to events. It was not until the combatants had time to settle down and digest the lessons learned between 1939 and 1945 that tank design got the full attention of either the users or the builders. At last each country could consider its own requirements for the AFVs it would build. As a result designs began to reflect national needs and strategies, and also national characteristics.

Instead of relying on supplies from allies, nations trying to rebuild shattered industries and economies found the arms industry a useful way of spending money and of creating jobs, all with the high moral purpose of national defence. In the early post-war years no-one quite envisaged the extent to which the armoured vehicle would proliferate.

France

France had some prewar ideas which they longed to try out, and these generally followed the usual path of bigger and bigger guns on larger and heavier tanks. It was not until 1957, when France and Germany agreed jointly to develop a new tank, that the philosophy of agility as a form of defence began to evolve. The destructive power of the anti-tank gun and missile had, it was reasoned, over-matched the ability of armour plate to protect the crew to the point where thicker and heavier armour was counter-productive.

By shedding as much weight as possible the tank could increase its agility (acceleration and cross-country performance) so that it would be a very difficult target to hit. By adding only as much armour as would give the tank immunity from artillery, cannon-armed APCs and light weapons, the designer could improve speed, range and weight. These characteristics became embodied in all French designs, both for tanks and reconnaissance vehicles. The lack of protection necessitated by the shedding of surplus weight caused serious potential combatants to think

twice about the AMX30 and it was not taken up by any major power. When, in 1977, the design was updated in an attempt to compete with more modern vehicles, a higher level of protection was specified.

Germany

This was almost a parallel to the German philosophy. When the German army was reformed in 1955 it was largely American-equipped, tanks being M47s. The Germans, with their great experience of tank design, decided in 1956 to build a new one to their own specification. Feeling that it had been weight and poor mobility that had let them down in 1944-45, they decided on a battle weight of about 30 tonnes, with a power/weight ratio of 30hp/tonne and a 105mm gun, which at that time was an overmatch for the current Soviet armour.

Since the French had a very similar requirement it was agreed that they should work to a common end. However, as with so many collaborative agreements, it foundered on the reef of chauvinism. The French went ahead with the AMX30 and Germany developed the Leopard.

As in the AMX30, protection was sacrificed to mobility and firepower. With typical thoroughness a complete family of ARV, AVLB, AA tank, armoured engineer vehicle and training vehicle was developed at the same time as the MBT. The result was so successful that it was adopted by five NATO countries and by Australia.

Although, from the start, a programme of improvement was initiated so that production vehicles can be classified and recognised by different marks, it was quickly realised that Leopard 1 was not going to be good enough for the 1980s. Germany entered, in 1963, upon the joint development with the USA, of the MBT70. This should have answered all foreseeable problems and have been the first practical example of standardisation in NATO of a major piece of equipment.

But while Germany wanted a tank for the defence of the central sector of NATO, with foreign sales as an added bonus if possible, the USA determined on the best design for all theatres and so, in January 1970, the Americans and Germans parted ways and in both countries MBT70 was relegated to the status of a study for future hardware.

Germany pulled out of the MBT70 programme and pulled out of its pigeonhole the design for a successor to Leopard which, in their careful way, they had started back in 1967. Crew survivability was given greater priority and a 120mm gun with the latest fire control equipment extended the killing range so that the new Kampfpanzer 2 could engage attacking Soviet armour before the latter got within effective range.

By this time the Germans had been informed by Britain of their newly developed 'Chobham armour', a combination of new materials and spaced armour that reduced the effects of both chemical and kinetic energy attack. Under an agreement between NATO partners such information was to be shared. Now the frontal arc of the new MBT was given the latest protection.

Although the Leopard 2 was to come out at 50.5 tonnes (very close to the 55 tonnes of the British Chieftain), it retained its agility, with a power/weight ratio of 29.7hp/tonne.

West Germany is intersected by many rivers, providing defensive positions and obstacles in profusion. This was a prime consideration when the operational requirements for a new reconnaissance vehicle were established. It must swim without any preparation — no waiting about like the British while they erected flimsy buoyancy screens — and it must

An attempt at a Franco-German collaborative venture, the German Leopard was remarkably successful on the export market with major European and NATO sales. Illustrated is the Leopard 1A1A1, the reference given to improved Leopard 1A1s. Note applique armour on turret sides and mantlet.
Bundesministerium der Verteidigung (BdV)

have positive screw propulsion to cope with fast flowing rivers.

The Spähzpanzer 2, when it appeared, was strongly reminiscent of the WW2 eight-wheeled Sdkfz 242 Puma. Its bulk gives it sufficient volume to be inherently buoyant, but although its swimming capability and cross-country performance make it one of the most mobile units in NATO, its armament of one 20mm cannon seems ludicrously impotent for its size. It seems to be intended that reconnaissance will normally take place within supporting range of the higher formation, and that only light firepower and smoke is necessary to get out of trouble.

Another apparent throwback to WW2 in German thinking is the use of a specialised tank-hunting AFV. The outline of the Kanonejagdpanzer is very like the WW2 Jagdpanzer IV. In the defensive situation of NATO, and in particular of West Germany, the armoured, low silhouette, mobile anti-tank gun is sure to be a potent weapon, and it is less costly than killing tanks with another tank.

West Germany lives under the constant threat of nuclear war, in particular tactical nuclear weapons rather than the larger strategic type. They have, therefore, given great thought to mobility in the nuclear environment and are providing a family of Transportpanzer as widely as possible.

There is a school of thought that envisages an attacking strike into East Bloc territory as an immediate counter, if not pre-emptive, attack and if Germany subscribes to this, as a method of avoiding combat on their home territory, they would need all the mobility and agility that they have provided for their armoured forces.

Israel

The nation with perhaps the greatest, and most successful, experience of armoured warfare in the last 30 years is Israel. The Israelis have progressed from using out-dated and home-made equipment, to being designers and builders of a sophisticated MTB. For a long period in their history they used fairly modern vehicles built elsewhere. In their original state, these never quite matched up to the requirements of the day. This caused the Israelis to become masters of improvisation and improvement — if the vehicle was mechanically sound it could be made to be of use, and there proliferated in the IDF an extraordinary range of modifications and rebuilds.

In the 1950s and 1960s necessity led them to adopt simple, head-on tactics which brought them great success in battle. It also made them think that they knew it all, as far as equipment was concerned. They felt that what they had was what they needed; and if they didn't have it, they didn't need it. The October war of 1973 caused a change of thought. Their casualties, not great in number, were a terrible loss to a small nation, and for the first time they turned to greater sophistication as means of survival. They designed and built their own MBT, a tremendous achievement for a country with such meagre resources. They had already designed an armoured scout car for their own special circumstances, but it has not proved very attractive to other countries, being unsuited to European conditions.

Wherever possible the Israelis will let the enemy armour come to them. They plan defensive positions of great strength, with the MBTs in prepared fire positions, and with several alternative positions for each tank when possible. The Israeli MBT Merkava is designed with this sort of positional warfare in mind. They want their enemy to hurl themselves upon the prepared positions and are prepared themselves to wait until the range is down to less than 500 m before engaging, to ensure a kill.

United Kingdom

In WW2 British tank crews suffered severe casualties due to the under-gunning and under-armouring of their tanks, the price paid for good (though not too reliable) mobility, and stemming from the split requirements for both 'infantry' and 'cruiser' tanks. This design trend started to swing the other way in 1943 when the General Staff Requirement for the A41 Cruiser emphasised that durability and reliability were of particular importance, and specified protection against the much-feared German 88mm and against hollow charge weapons.

By the time of WW2, the general principle was established that the three main characteristics of tanks should be fire-power, protection and mobility, in order of priority. Just as important was the abandonment of the Cruiser and Infantry tank classification in favour of the Universal tank. This was to be capable of carrying out the tasks of both previous types, and of conversion to specialist roles such as AVRE, ARV, bridgelayer, etc. By having one basic hull and automotive train, considerable economies could be made in production, spares, training and, above all, in development time.

Tactical thinking, too, underwent a change in the late 1940s as the forces of the East and West settled down facing each other across the newly drawn frontiers of central Europe. Instead of 'mixing it' in close combat, as previously necessitated by the short effective range of their guns, the principle of long range attrition was established. In the face of the larger calibres of Russian tank guns it became vital to hit further away and this gave rise to a line of super heavy tanks and SP guns.

As the army became a totally volunteer force and, therefore, smaller, the philosophy of crew survival became more important. It takes longer to train crew men than to build a tank. Armour protection became thicker and greater attention was given to the angle of the plates. The vertical plate in front of the driver disappeared with the Comet. Hitting targets at greater ranges gave an impetus to the development of another significant factor, the ATGW. The short-range man-portable Panzerfaust or bazooka had been around for some time and the doctrine of prophylactic MG fire had evolved to discourage their uses. But the ATGW, even in the improved versions of the late 1970s, is only a long range support weapon for the cannon-armed tank. It is of great tactical value but only when carried under armour itself and integrated with armoured vehicles.

Another major change in British armoured thinking was the return of the use of light tracked vehicles for reconnaissance. Until the early 1970s this had been the traditional province of the wheeled armoured car. The light tanks of the 1930s had been intended as fighting vehicles and not merely for reconnaissance.

The decision to adopt tracked vehicles for recce came about because the bulk of the British Army was (and still is) concentrated in Europe, on the NATO Centre Front. Here it was felt, there would be little or no opportunity for long range recce, but a great need for close recce and the associated roles of flank guards, anti-airborne operations etc. Most movement would be cross-country, so it made sense to have tracked mobility; hence the family of Combat Vehicles, Recconnaissance was born. Since it was envisaged that there would be a minor role for wheels in the UK and rear areas, armoured cars would remain and the family was divided into CVR(T) for tracked and CVR(W) for wheeled.

Although there has been a great deal of useful debate about the future of the tank and its configuration, the British Army seems determined to retain its order of priorities of characteristics for MBT's. So far there has been no convincing argument against the conventional turreted vehicle, nor against the high velocity gun as its main armament. Changes, it seems, wait upon improvements in technology.

A change in general staff thinking, rather than in armoured philosophy, was the gradual tendency to put as much as possible of the army in the field under armour and on tracks. This was brought about by the nuclear strategy of both sides, necessitating protection against flash, blast and fallout, and by the tactical requirement for all arms to have the same cross-country ability as the MBT. Thus infantry, gunners and engineers found themselves provided with AFVs of one sort or another and in all armoured formations the proportion of AFVs increased.

The definition of armoured warfare has changed, over the last three decades, from meaning a tank battle supported by the other unarmoured arms, to encompassing all the teeth arms and their supporting engineer and signals units. As the threat of nuclear war looms larger, given the means, almost entire armies will find themselves in AFVs of one sort or another, and armoured warfare will come to mean any engagement that is not mounted from sea or air.

USA

The US Army had generally agreed with the relative priorities of tank characteristics, and tried, in the same way as the British, to match the increasing gun-power of the Soviets. However, an increasing priorty was to simplify operation and maintenance and to enable training time to be reduced. So while the automotive side tended towards automatic transmission, single stick control and component replacement, the gunnery department tried to enhance effectiveness using the same gun. The Americans were the first to introduce the ballistic computer and made the widest use of the optical rangefinder, but fell behind in striking power while they adhered to the 90mm gun. Having observed the usefulness of specialised armour in Normandy, and beyond, the US Army adopted the CEV and the AVLB.

In the late 1960s the Americans realised that they were falling behind in the AFV race and decided on a completely new tank, incorporating all the most advanced and revolutionary ideas. The MBT70, designed in conjuction with Germany, was an expensive disaster and never got off the ground. The Germans, being cost conscious and realistic, abandoned it first, then the Americans, recoiling from a projected unit cost of over a million dollars in 1970, relegated it to the status of a study for a future vehicle.

The same story was followed in the development of ARSV (armoured reconnaissance scout vehicle). This was to take over the 'recon' role for all arms and, in consequence, had to do a bit of everything. Started in the early 1960s, ARSV went back to the drawing board several times until it was finally dropped in 1974.

It was the Americans, however, who initiated and then dominated the modern APC and SP artillery market. Most of the world outside the Soviet bloc adopted American equipment in the 1950s simply because it was readily available at good prices, but since then the M113 APC has become the most widely used AFV in the west with over 70,000 having been built.

American armoured thinking suffered greatly from the misuse and abuses of the Vietnam war. Convoy duty and static strong points became the norm and as tanks were less used in their proper role so the skills of their crews were eroded and emphasis became placed on other functions. Thousands of AFVs were used in Vietnam, but it was not armoured warfare.

The close, jungle war seemed to call for terrific all-round small arms fire as a prophylactic measure. Every vehicle mounted one or more machine guns on the roof or turret, to fire which the gunner had to expose half his body. When casualties rose because of this exposure so did the ramparts of cupolas, gun-shields and sandbags, and the height of the AFV crept higher.

These excesses of design and development were brought into perspective in the late 1970s with the second attempt to design the battle tank of the 1980s. Survivability and reliability were recognised as of equal importance to striking power. This time it had to be right, since the Pentagon decided it was necessary to acquire 7,058 of the new tank. With the Soviet preponderance of MBTs in Europe approaching 6:1, even the cost became less frightening; though at the time of acceptance, the price of a single XM1 was a staggering $1,820,000 (*Defence*, Report from the Pentagon). Survivability of both tank and crew led to the reduction of height, new armour and improved agility but

Left: This sectioned drawing of the Comet shows how the engine and transmission took up half the hull. The thickest armour was the mantlet, which was 101mm thick, almost as much as the Churchill. *Leyland Motors*

Top right: M113s of the 1st Squadron, 4th Cavalry, in the reconnaissance role. *US Army*

Right: M551 Sheridan of the 2nd Armored Cavalry in Germany. The additional armour protection for the commander adds almost 100% to the turret height. *US Army*

the new tank carries the same gun as its predecessors. This will be uprated when a new gun is available and there is a built-in capability to receive the larger weapon.

At the same time the Army went ahead with plans to put as many soldiers as possible under armour, for protection against the huge bombardment capability of the Soviet Army and the threat of NBC warfare. The US Army is committed to operations under armour in a wider sense than ever before and should have great flexibility and mobility.

USSR

Soviet armour accords with the requirements of a doctrine of overwhelming firepower followed by rapid advance of massed armour. All equipments are kept relatively simple so that the largely conscript army can absorb both technical and tactical training in the two-year span of service.

This does not mean that Soviet armour as a whole is less effective than that of NATO. It does mean that they are prepared to accept huge losses, both kill and breakdown, as they launch their masses of AFVs in a steamroller assault.

The Russians expect a superiority of at least 4:1 for any attack, and 8:1 for an attack on a major axis.

Tanks have been kept down in weight so that they can be more easily moved by road and rail and retain a good cross-country mobility. Ballistic shapes are excellent so that only a direct hit is likely to kill a tank, but protection is necessarily limited and when hit by HEAT or HESH damage is extensive and usually fatal.

To play a part in the massed firepower phase, Soviet tank guns retain a useful HE and indirect fire capability. It is hoped that their huge numbers will enable them to close tank vs tank combat ranges to under 1,500m, so the use of crude range estimating techniques was accepted, until the advent of the laser rangefinder, which gives a simple digital readout. Russia was the first to fit a smoothbore main gun as standard, sacrificing accuracy at longer distances for superior penetration at the engagement ranges they wanted.

Although the performance has been improved, the engine and transmission of modern Soviet tanks has been virtually the same since 1939-40; the V55 diesel of 580hp is merely an updated version of the V2 which powered the T-34. But

The Soviet T-34, progenitor of a series of vehicles that have seen service for over three decades. *via G. Forty*

the latest development, the T-72, has a 750hp V12 diesel, probably again an uprated version of the V-55. This reflects the Soviet system of developing the potential of an equipment as far as possible. The T-54, T-55 and T-62 are visibly of the same lineage, descended from the T-44, and covering over three decades of service. Nevertheless, if new technology or a new operational requirement appears, new equipment is swiftly accepted. Chobham style armour is used on the latest Soviet tank, identified as the T-80 by NATO, but of which little else is known.

One such operation requirement is that of a good night fighting capability. Soviet armour adopted infra-red night vision devices as standard in the late 1950s and still use it, though passive equipment is fitted to the latest vehicles and is gradually being retro-fitted to older models.

Because of the great number of rivers crossing the main axes of Soviet advance (at least one per day on German front), they take river crossing techniques very seriously. Battle tanks are equipped to enable them to schnorkel and cross on river beds while the T-76 light tank and BRDM recce vehicles are fully amphibious, as are the BMP and BTR-60, BTR-50 APCs.

All Soviet troops are trained in NBC warfare and all fighting formations have Chemical Defence Companys. Most tanks, certainly all those in front line formations, have NBC packs similar to those in western tanks.

A feature of the Soviet NBC system is that when the sensors detect abnormal radio-activity the engine automatically shuts down to warn the crew. The latest designs T-62 and T-72 incorporate an automatic system which, on detecting any NBC attack, seals the hull and creates an over-pressure to exclude contaminants.

The great advantages of the Soviet method are that they are able to convert tank crews to new vehicles more easily as there are so many similarities within the family and that older vehicles can be kept in use for training and reserve units.

1 MBT Development and Evolution

China, People's Republic of

The People's Republic of China (PRC) has the largest army in the world, of about 3,900,000 men. It is formed into some 40 armies, each of three divisions and supporting troops. Most of these are infantry units, with unarmoured supporting arms, but there are 11 armoured divisions. An armoured division of the People's Liberation Army (PLA) has three armoured regiments, a mechanised infantry regiment and an armoured recce company, with the usual supporting arms and services. There are about 300 tanks on the strength of a division, and under 100 APCs, enough to lift one battalion of the three in the mechanised infantry regiment. Probably the artillery regiment has at least one sub-unit (corresponding to a British artillery regiment) equipped with a SP howitzer. Tanks are also deployed in infantry divisions with about 32 tanks in the divisional tank regiment. Latest reports indicate that the PLA has about 11,000 tanks in service which can be classified as MBTs. There are also some 600 recce and light tanks.

All Chinese MBTs are obsolete and many date from the 1940s. Many Soviet T-34 and heavy IS-2 tanks were passed to China in the 1950s, when the friendship between the USSR and the PRC was less strained, and these were followed by some thousands of T-54. As the attrition of age takes effect fewer and fewer of these veterans are seen in the front line divisions. However, since 1961 the PLA has been supplementing its tank strength with its own version of the T-54. The Chinese copy of the T-54 is the T-59, and they are virtually indistinguishable with the naked eye. Only in the finish of the vehicle and the lack of even the least sophisticated equipment could the local product be discovered.

Most surprising was the lack of a power traverse, but in early models of the T-59 both loader and gunner had manual traverse handles. It must have been very tiring traversing the heavy barrelled D-10 gun (also copied from the Soviets) 'uphill', and could lead to some confusion when the gunner took over for the fine lay. It is probable that this particular deficiency has been rectified by a retro-fit of a simple electric power traverse, but it is indicative of the Chinese attitude to equipment.

Since the early T-59s lacked a power traverse it is hardly surprising that there was no stabiliser, nor any of the simple IR night fighting and driving equipment. These deficiencies, too, have probably been put right in the later models, sometimes called T-69. These tanks have been exported to Pakistan and Vietnam, where they saw action and to Albania, Tanzania, Sudan and North Korea, where they have not. The reaction of the Pakistanis, who acquired 250 of the T-59 in time to lose most of them in the 1971 Indo-Pakistan war, may well have contributed to the modernisation programme which has since improved the T-59 in these areas. Pakistan acquired more tanks and now has about 1,000 in service, but this is most likely because they were cut off from other sources than for a liking of the T-59.

The defence industry of the PRC is capable of producing about 1,000 tanks a year and is continuing to make improved versions of the T-59, with the aid of western technology and expertise. Interest has been shown in making western tanks under licence, but although the AMX30 has been mentioned as a possibility, nothing positive has been reported.

France

In 1945 the French Army was almost completely equipped with American vehicles. The main tank was the M4 Sherman, in its many versions, and this was later superseded by the M47. After WW2 the French were anxious to pick up the pieces of their defence industry and to start work on, among other things, armoured vehicles. The tank design section was at the industrial facility of Ateliers d'Issy les Moulineaux, at Satory near Versailles, and many of the people who had been working on the successor to the Char B at the time of the fall in France in 1940 had been collected there.

In fact there were already plans in existence for a heavy tank — the ARL44 — designed surreptitiously during the war. The hull of this 48tonne monster had a very thick glacis, and the tracks were similar to the Char B's including the way they ran all round the sponsons. The 700hp engine gave it a speed of 40kph on the road and the main armament was a 90mm gun, mounted in a high, slab-sided turret. This vehicle was already out of date when it went into production in 1946, for a quantity of 60 only, and work had started on its successor even before this date. The one battalion which received ARL44s served until they were phased out in the early 1950s.

AMX50

The French army decided that it would need three types of AFV for its operations in future; an armoured car, an airportable light tank and a battle tank. For the latter the French thought to take the best features of the German tanks which had caused them so much trouble in WW2. The new tank was called AMX50, and had a design weight of 50 tonnes. The hull bore more than a passing resemblance to the Panther as did the sloping glacis sides and the overlapping roadwheels which appeared on some of the prototypes. There were some original ideas too. On one model the five large roadwheels were fitted with large pneumatic tyres which ran inside the tracks.

The most important innovation was the oscillating turret, in which the top half of the turret pivoted on trunnions at each side of the lower part. The gun was fixed in the top half and was aimed by traversing the whole turret in the ordinary way and by tilting the upper part up or down for elevation. Since in this design the gun does not have to move relative to the part of the turret in which it is mounted, it can be fixed just under the roof. This saves a lot of space in the upper half

Left: The AMX50 was the first heavy tank built by France after World War 2. This view shows how much the design owes to the German PzKpfw V Panther, even to the louvres and horizontal fan inlets on the engine deck. The overlapping wheels and exhaust outlets are also copied from the German tank. The main difference is the long-barrelled 120mm gun in a fixed mounting in the top half of the oscillating turret, making the AMX50 the most powerful western tank of its day. A machine gun is mounted coaxially to the right of the main armament and there are two more 7.5mm M1931A MGs with drum magazines at the roof hatch. Although the AMX50 carries a co-driver, there is no sign of a bow machine gun. *ECP Armées*

Right: After initial plans to produce a vehicle in collaboration with Germany and Italy, France went it alone to produce the AMX30. Note 20mm coaxial cannon and remote-controlled commander's MG. *ECP Armées*

and permits the use of an automatic loading device. Ammunition can be contained in a magazine in the turret bustle and fed to the breech automatically. The loader can thus be saved and the turret made smaller. Since the gun can be mounted directly under the turret roof, less of the turret is exposed when in a hull down position.

On the debit side, the effort needed to elevate the mass of the gun and upper part of the turret is much greater than for the gun on its own, and greater strain is placed on the gun control system. The gap between the two halves of the turret can be sealed against dirt to some extent by fitting a canvas cover, but it cannot be sealed against gases or liquids, so wading is restricted to the level of the hull top. There is also the danger of the turret becoming jammed by shot, even of small calibre.

The AMX50 was armed at first with a 90mm gun, but in the second prototype this was replaced by a 100mm, and latter by a 120mm gun firing the same ammunition as the American M103 heavy tank. All these were mounted on oscillating (or gimballed) turrets. This made it of the same stock as the British Conqueror and the M103, and it suffered the same fate. In fact the AMX50 did not even get into service because the philosophy which had required these heavy weights as 'overwatch' and support tanks for the medium gun tank changed abruptly. Authority had been given for production of a limited number, but at the same time France was joining a co-operative plan with her allies to produce a tank that could be standardised in NATO. It would have been a waste of money to continue, so AMX50 was relegated to the scrapyard and the gap was filled by M47s.

It is interesting to note that though the oscillating turret was a feature of all three vehicles produced under the 1946 requirements, none of the multitude of AFVs produced in France subsequently had a turret of this type.

AMX30 and AMX32

In the mid--1950s it seemed as though the killing power of the gun and ATGW had leaped ahead of the protective powers of armour plate and that, consequently, it was a waste of time and money to provide armour heavier than that necessary to keep out small arms, splinter and blast from artillery and mortars and shot from vehicles in lighter categories than battle tanks. By dispensing with a great weight of armour the tank could be lighter and faster and use its speed and agility to dodge enemy fire. The Germans certainly felt that the great weight and immobility of their tanks was a major cause of their defeat, while the dash and elan of the lighter tanks appealed to the French character. So when, in 1956, France, Germany, and Italy agreed the principles of their co-operation, the priorities were firepower, mobility and protection — in that order. The outline requirement called for a 105mm gun, a high power/weight ratio, weight of 30 tonnes and a low silhouette. Both Germany and France were to build prototypes and submit them for comparative trials in 1961.

At these trials the French declared themselves unsatisfied with the arrangements and decided to continue on their own, though more trials were agreed upon, mainly to see if agreement could be reached on components.

The main characteristics required in their new tank were the firepower to bring effective fire to bear at ranges out to 3,000m, strategic mobility to bring the tanks to the most effective point of attack and ability to survive the effects of nuclear attack. The AMX30 did come out pretty close to its design weight; at 32.5 tonnes it was the lightest main battle tank of comparable power. Its dimensions allowed it unrestricted rail movement and its ability to cross rivers under water by using a schnorkel made it more strategically mobile than most other tanks. Provision of an NBC filtration pack and a turret over-pressure system gave the ability for the crew to survive in a nuclear environment.

The AMX30 is conventional in layout and in most of its components. The prototypes were powered by gasoline engines, but in the period when they were designed there was a general move among NATO forces towards the multi-fuel concept. Engines were supposed to be able to operate on a range of fuels from diesel oil to gasoline, with little more than a minor adjustment. In practice they were diesels which operated at less efficiency than usual when on the lighter fuels. The original gasoline engines developed 720hp, giving the tank an enviable 22hp/tonne. All production models were powered by an Hispano-Suiza diesel with the same output, but with better torque in the lower rpm ranges. Transmission is by a gearbox and steering unit with five speeds in each direction. The gears are preselected with a visual indicator for the driver. Steering is a triple differential

system, with turning radii in proportion to the gear selected; the lower the gear the tighter the turn. The driver has a small steering wheel, adjustable for height and pitch, in the driving position, with a wheel position indicator, so that the driver knows how much 'lock' is on. The engine cannot be started unless the wheel is in the 'straight ahead' position. A test drive described in *IDR* of 12/81 noted that the steering was stiff and had a poor minimum turning circle, though a pivot turn is available when the gearbox is in neutral.

Suspension is by torsion bars which are placed in novel fashion to make best use of space in the hull. The first, third and fifth wheels each side are on leading arms, while the second and fourth are trailing arms. This means that the torsion bars for the leading pair of wheels are close together, and then the bars for the second pair, the bar for the fifth wheel being close to the rear of the hull. The spaces between the pairs of torsion bars are usable, instead of useless if the bars are spaced out.

In line with the requirement for mobility, AMX30 carries 970 litres of fuel, sufficient to give it a road range of over 500km, or 18 hours of a constant combat day. It can ford, unprepared, to a depth of 1.3m and to 2m with very little work. By fitting a schnorkel tube to the loader's hatch it can wade to a depth of 4m, enough to make river crossings in most areas.

For tank-killing firepower the French have found a most unusual compromise. They have based their attack on the hollow charge effect and created a method of delivery which overcomes the main disadvantages of this type of round. If a hollow charge (*Charge Creuse*) round is spin-stabilised by means of rifling in the barrel, the centrifugal force engendered by its rotation tends to dissipate the strength of the jet of gas created by its detonation. One method of avoiding this is by firing from a smoothbore gun and using fins for stabilisation, but this had its own disadvantage in that the accuracy of a fin-stabilised round falls off after ranges of 1,800-2,000m. But, the French reasoned, it is only the explosive charge that should not be spun. It makes no difference if the outer casing revolves as long as the charge is almost stable in flight. They designed the Obus G, in which the outer casing is spin-stabilised by rifling in the barrel, but the explosive inside is mounted in ball bearings and does not spin at more than about 20-30rpm, which has little or no effect on its penetration performance.

It is claimed that the Obus G can penetrate to a depth of over 360mm, enough to kill all battle tanks armoured with conventional steel plate; it remains to be seen how it performs against compound and laminated armour. The Obus G has equal effect at all ranges at which a hit is obtained, regardless of velocity, so it is fired at 1,000m/sec, reducing bore wear. It does not have as good an effect as a conventional HE shell on soft targets, so other natures of ammunition are available, including HE, smoke, illuminating and practice.

Secondary armament is also unusual. There is no coaxial machine gun, though the commander has one on a remote control mounting on his cupola. Instead there is a 20mm cannon alongside the 105mm gun, in a mounting which can be aligned with the main armament or disengaged and elevated up to 40° (20° above the main armament) to fire in an anti-helicopter role. Only 480 rounds for the 20mm are carried, so the gunner and commander must be careful in what targets they engage with the secondary weapons.

The turret and gun control is electro-hydraulic and fire is controlled mainly by the commander, who has a cupola with 10 fixed periscopes and a x10 binocular telescope. The turret can contra-rotate to allow the commander to acquire a target and bring the main armament to bear without losing sight of it by means of an override control. In the early versions the AMX30 had a 2m base coincidence rangefinder mounted across the turret. This was also operated by the commander, who could use it as an observation device. So that all members of the crew can assist in the observation task, the gunner is provided with two periscopes in addition to his main sight, and the loader has three periscopes.

In the updated versions, which the army call the AMX30B2, and the export salesmen the AMX32, the commander is provided with a stabilised sight to which the gun and the gunner's sight are slaved. The gunner has the LRF integrated with his x10 telescopic sight. The commander also has the task of putting into the ballistic computer data on the nature of round to be fired, and cross wind and temperature where applicable. On the later models the optical rangefinder as been deleted; so has the infra red night vision equipment, superseded by new passive systems. The gunner now uses a low light TV camera which is mounted externally to the right of the mantlet, and which gives displays to both gunner and commander, who also has an image intensification viewer in his own sight.

The AMX30 has well-angled armour and a low silhouette, but at only 34 tonnes it does not promise much in the way of protection against armour piercing attack. The ammunition stowage, too, is vulnerable by modern standards. Of the 50 rounds of 105mm carried, four are stowed in the turret, near the loader, as ready rounds and 28 to the right of the driver in the hull front, but 18 are carried in the turret bustle, well above the turret ring, and there are no special provisions for blow-out panels in the roof, or safety doors to the fighting compartment.

In the B2 or AMX32, protection has been increased by adding Chobham armour to the front of the hull and turret, and by adding skirting plates to the sides. However, the amount of additional armour which can be applied to AMX30 is limited by the permitted all-up weight. Even on the AMX32 the combat weight is only 38 tonnes, two tonnes more than on the original tanks.

While there is little more that can be done in passive protection, the designers have left room for improvement in firepower. The turret is capable of taking a French 120mm smoothbore gun which can fire the same ammunition as the German gun in Leopard 2. In this case the ammunition stowage would be reduced to 38 rounds.

With their keen eye for an export market the French have produced a tank which can be adapted to the requirements of many overseas countries. The original basic model had a simplified commander's cupola and no IR equipment, NBC or heater. The AMX30s (Pays Chauds) was given sandshields and modifications to the power train, with improved air filters and cooling. The fire control system can be uprated in steps, adding LRF and night fighting equipment according to the purse and requirements of the customer. This means that, while other countries try to sell their tank with all its equipments in the original deal, the French offer the AMX30 cut down to an agreed price, with the optional extras to follow. Saudi Arabia, Qatar, the United Arab Emirates, Iraq, Morocco, Spain, Greece and Venezuela have all bought AMX30, but as yet it has not been into battle. Only then will the concept of mobility and agility as a prime method of protection and survivability be proved . . . or not.

Apart from the battle tank role, AMX30 has been adapted for the usual range of duties. The ARV has a dozer blade and hydraulic crane and can exert a 35tonne pull with its main recovery winch. It also has an auxiliary winch for light duties and for drawing out the heavy cable of the main winch. There is space on the rear engine deck to carry a complete reserve power pack. The bridgelayer carries a 22m long scissors bridge than can take tanks up to 40 tonnes and that can be laid or taken up in 10 minutes. This is quite a long time compared with the two or four minutes taken by other AVLB. For anti-aircraft defence of armoured formations the AMX30 mounts a SAMM turret with twin 30mm cannon

and a fire control radar. It carries 1,200 rounds of 30mm ammunition, which is a respectable number for an AA tank (the Gepard carries 680 rounds of 35mm).

France developed its own tactical nuclear missile, the Pluton, under its policy of an independent nuclear deterrent, and adapted the AMX30 to act as launcher vehicle. In the more conventional role, a fast firing 155mm artillery piece is mounted in a full 350° traverse turret, with 42 rounds, for immediate fire support.

The first AMX30B2 were scheduled to be delivered in January 1982 to the 503rd Tank Regiment. These would be some of the 271 new build vehicles ordered. The army would then commence a programme of retro-fitting 730 AMX30s to the B2 standard, so that they will have enough modernised vehicles to see them through into the 1990s, when they will have the new EPC, or the result of another Franco-German cooperative project, in service. In February 1980 the two governments signed a 'declaration of intent' to design a new MBT for the 1990s. It was agreed that the three main characteristics of firepower, protection and mobility would be of equal importance, and that as much attention would be given to reliability, ease of maintenance and repair.

It was also recognised that there were two courses open: one to improve an existing design (the Germans meant to develop the Leopard) or to start from the beginning and design and produce a new tank. This would be more favoured by France, since it would allow greater initial participation by their industry, especially the electronic side, which would account for about 40% of the vehicle cost. There are differences of opinion on many basic items which could cause dissent or lead to a compromise, satisfying neither party. France favours a tank of 40-45 tonnes suitable for road networks with limited bridge classes, while Germany would prefer a heavier vehicle, up to the 60tonne range, with much more protection. This problem may be partially solved by the use of compound armour.

Although both countries want a 120mm gun, each has developed its own weapon. However, here at least is the bonus that both can fire the same ammunition. The requirements for the FCS are almost identical in that they include LRF and thermal imagers, but the Germans prefer the gun to be stabilised while the French like stabilised primary sights with the gun slaved to the sight.

While certain differences are inevitable, there is broad

agreement on most facets of the concept. A low silhouette and reduction in IR, acoustic and radar signatures, together with a high-speed fire extinguisher system, are fundamental to survival. A high power/weight ratio and a very good suspension are of prime importance to give the agility which both France and Germany see as affording extra protection, while improved availability and reliability would reduce the overall cost considerably.

The time frame for this project is critical. The development phase will run from about 1985 to 1990 and production would not start until two or three years later, at best. By then Germany will want to replace some 1,500 tanks and the French 1,000 or more. At the same time other countries will have the need to replace old vehicles such as Belgium, Denmark, Norway and the Netherlands, with their, by then, outclassed Leopard 1s. The French appear more anxious than Germany to get the project moving. At a meeting with his German counterpart in March 1982, the French minister of defence said: 'I will not allow dithering about either the substance or the time scale of this cooperation to go on indefinitely'. So far the Germans had worked out the idea of a new, two-man turret with a 120mm smoothbore gun and automatic loader. This is to go on a Leopard 2 hull, at least for the concept study. However, though the French have agreed to this, they would definitely prefer to start with a new hull, on which they would hope to lead development.

AMX13

For the light, airportable tank which was to be designed alongside the MBT, the French designation was Char 13t-75 Modèle 51, but it has been known as the AMX13 since production started in 1951. The design weight of 13 tonnes was, in the late 1940s, merely a guess at what a large transport aircraft might be able to carry in five or 10 years' time. In any case, even the first version with the smallest gun came out at 15 tonnes. It has never been used as an airborne tank but has served in nearly every corner of the world, in some 26 countries.

The idea of the oscillating turret, with an automatic loader for the main armament, has found its best expression in the AMX13, possibly because it was working at a lower weight than in the MBT and was easier to apply control. The first version of AMX13 carried a 75mm gun adapted from that in the German Panther tank, but only 61.5 calibres long instead of 70. It is mounted directly under the turret roof, since there is no need for space in which the breech can swing for elevation and depression. The recoil mechanism is fixed directly to the turret and the gun recoils in a straight line which never varies, so the breech can always be aligned with a magazine in the turret bustle. The gun had a muzzle brake which helped reduce recoil and empty cartridge cases were disposed of automatically on ejection, through a small hatch in the back of the turret.

Despite its weight the turret handled easily; hydraulic control could swing the turret through 360° in 12 seconds and was well balanced in elevation. The loading mechanism was not fully automatic; the vehicle commander had to crank a handle with his right arm to bring the next round into line with the loading tray. There were two six-round drum magazines in the bustle, so each could be loaded with a different nature, either HE or AP, and the commander could select the correct type of round for his next target. The disadvantage was that when both the magazines were empty, the crew had to dismount and reload through roof hatches over the rear of the turret, having first passed the rounds up from the internal stowage. The process took about 20 minutes, during which time the vehicle was virtually defenceless. One officer said it was 'like taking out your teeth'.

Being only 15 tonnes in weight the armour protection is not of a very high order; it is immune to small arms and splinters all round and to .50in (12.7mm) over the frontal arc. The turret will keep out 20mm, but the hull is not guaranteed to do so. However the layout of the tank contributes to crew safety in that the engine and transmission are at the front and the fuel tanks at the rear, while only 12 rounds of gun ammunition are carried above turret ring level. There are five roadwheels each side mounted on torsion bar suspension and it has a max road speed of 60kph and a good cross-country performance. The engine is a SOFAM eight-cylinder horizontally opposed gasoline engine giving 270bhp at 3,200rpm. In the 1950s 18bhp/tonne was not a bad effort. The transmission was a simple and robust synchromesh gearbox fitted with a Cleveland controlled differential steering. The engine was fitted very tightly into the front compartment under the glacis and was difficult to maintain. The gear change was a push-pull lever in front of the driver, mounted very close to the armour, which led to many cases of trapped fingers. One reason that the AMX13 has such a low silhouette is that it was designed for crew members not taller than 1.727m in height (cf the T-62).

The gear change was a minor hazard. More serious was the possibility that the driver's hatch, which was swung out to the left when the driver was head out, might swing in

Left: The AMX32 was developed from the earlier AMX30 mainly to interest foreign customers with a more powerful engine and improvements to the FCS. The coaxial MG has been replaced with a 20mm cannon in a mounting which can elevate to 45° separately from the main gun, for use in the anti-helicopter role. *ECP Armées*

Right: AMX13 armed with four SS12 missiles. The missile control and aiming equipment is in the box on the top of the turret. *ECP Armées*

again. A Dutch driver was decapitated in this way; the traversing gun hit the safety template on the hatch cover, overrode the lock and closed the hatch on the driver, cutting off his head. The driver's position was also very cramped and he was unable to lower himself quickly in his seat. An accident occurred when an AMX13, on entering a frozen canal, broke the ice. A sheet of ice rode up the glacis, decapitating the unfortunate driver, who was unable to duck.

The engine air intake was through the fighting compartment. In summer this was fine, providing a constant air-conditioning that was very much appreciated in Africa and the Middle East. Not so in Europe, in winter, when it was like living in a constant ice-storm.

Despite these criticisms the AMX13 was a well-liked vehicle with a fair reputation for realiability and a versatility that led it to be upgunned twice and used in a dozen variations. The first change of main armament was to the 105mm gun as used in the AMX30, of medium velocity, firing the Obus G shaped charge round as the anti-tank round and an HE round. This was not an unqualified success. The heavier load and greater recoil forces caused the upper front part of the turret to develop cracks. The main users of this model, outside France, were the Dutch, and there was a major international scandal which went on for a year until the customers were satisfied with the repairs.

More successful was the replacement of the 75mm by a version bored out to 90mm and fitted with a thermal sleeve. It carried 34 rounds of 90mm HEAT with a m/v of 950m/sec. One change was almost a down-gunning, when a short 75mm was fitted in a smaller turret, the FL-11, such as was used on the Panhard EBR armoured car; this was a special version for colonial wars which did not require an anti-tank capability.

The AMX13 has been mounted with 155mm and 105mm howitzers, various kinds of ATGW (the latest being the HOT), twin 30mm anti-aircraft guns in a special turret and a single 40mm AA gun. It has also been adapted for the usual role of APC, bridgelayer, ARV and engineer vehicle.

There are still over 700 AMX13s in service in the French army, as well as those overseas, though in Europe it is definitely relegated to reserve units in the anti-tank role. A final claim to fame is that the FL-12 turret with the 105mm gun has been adopted by Austria to arm their Kurassier SP anti-tank vehicle.

Germany, Federal Republic of

West Germany joined NATO on 8 May 1955. This left the way clear for the rebuilding of the army, but the German weapons industry had been destroyed or dismantled so supplies had to come from outside. The choice of tanks was limited: the British Centurion would provide good protection but delivery would be slow; the American M47 was quickly available and the Americans could also supply a wide variety of other equipments. Availability won and the Bundeswehr was equipped with M47s and, later, the M48.

The M47 was designed to American ideas. It would have been useful in 1945 but by 1956 it was regarded by the Germans, who had strong ideas of their own about how tanks should be designed and operated, as under-gunned, under-protected and slow, with a road range that was just dangerous. They did not like gasoline engines and the turret was too high. They knew they could do better and it would give them the chance to reconstruct their armaments industry.

In the 1950s there was much talk of standardisation and

interoperability. It was the era of multi-fuel engines to enhance strategic mobility and common components and munitions. It was also the age of the missile, when it was thought that the ATGW would see the tank off the battlefield. Any ATGW could over-match the armour of even a heavy tank, so there was no point in armouring against anything more than the cannon of light AFVs. Agility would give better protection than slabs of steel.

Neither France nor Italy were building their own tanks, though both had the industrial capability, so Germany combined with the other two with the object of designing and building a tank that would become standard among the European partners in NATO. The concept was formalised in November 1956 and the priorities were to be in the order firepower, mobility and protection.

Among the criteria in the German MOD document published in July 1957 were: weight 30,000kg; height 2.20m; width 3.15m; ground pressure 0.85kg/sq cm. The armament was to be capable of defeating 105mm of homogeneous steel armour at 30°, at ranges up to 2,500m. Power was to be provided by an air-cooled multi-fuel engine of around 900hp (din). Production of this 'Europanzer' would be shared among the participants.

Germany fielded two teams to design a tank to the criteria called for, and France one. In January 1961 both German teams produced two prototypes each, which tested at the German proving ground at Trier in February. All four vehicles had the same turret, which had been developed independently by Rheinstall, and mounted a 90mm Rhein-metall gun and used the same Daimler Benz engine, but the models from the 'A' team (Porsche/Mak) had torsion bar suspension and seven roadwheels, while the 'B' team (Hanomag/Henschel) offered six road wheels with air-hydraulic suspension. The 'B' vehicles were within the pre-scribed weight, but the 'A' tanks were up to 35 tonnes. Nevertheless, at Trier the 'A' team vehicles were the winners. They were less innovative, easier to produce and promised to be cheaper. At this stage it was recognised that the 90mm gun had reached the limits of its development and a Rheinmetall 105mm gun was fitted. This was later replaced by the British L7 105mm.

The next step was a comparative trial with the French tank, designed and produced at AMX (Ateliers de Construc-tion d'Issy-les-Moulineaux). The trials showed that, despite the original agreement on the characteristics of the Europanzer, it was national characteristics that counted for more. Political and technical differences were apparent and the French still headed in their own direction. The Germans went ahead with their trials and awarded a contract to Team A for 26 prototypes of their A-2 model. (The B team got a contract for six of the B-2 model, but only two were built and this line of development was stopped at the end of 1962.)

The A-2, now known as 'Standardpanzer', was modified and improved in building the prototypes. The original 600hp eight-cylinder engine was replaced by a 830hp 10-cylinder version. The Rheinmetall 105mm gun was dropped in favour of the British L7, already acknowledged as the best tank gun in the world at that time and carried in Centurion and M60. At first the RMG was also tried, but it was no use beyond 1,800m, and a cross-turret optical rangefinder was developed.

Trials continued throughout 1962, including a comparative trial with the French AMX30, in which the Standardpanzer showed up better. The French would not accept these results and further comparative trials were carried out in September 1963, in which the Italian

Lifting the MTU MB838 Ca.M500 powerpack. It takes three men only about twenty minutes to replace the complete powerpack, in the field, using the ARV. *BdV*

adjudicators tactfully found the two tanks of equal value in most phases. By this time, however, 50 pre-production Standardpanzer had been authorised, and the tank officially named Leopard. The French had no funds for tanks until 1963 and officially opted out of the project. Germany went ahead and ordered the full production of 1,500 Leopards in the 1964 budget.

The next two years were occupied in setting up the production and assembly facilities. Krauss-Maffei, of Munich, were selected as main contractors, with MTU (Motoren and Turbinen Union) and ZF (Zahnradfabriken Friedrichshafen) supplying the engine and transmission. The turret came from Wegmann, of Kassel, and the hull from Blohm und Voss, with a total of 2,700 firms, large and small, participating in the project.

Leopard 1

The first Leopard rolled out on 9 September 1965 and production continued at 50-60 tanks per month. Since then Leopard has become one of the most widely used tanks in the West. The following countries have adopted Leopard, in the face of some fierce competition, technical, commercial and political: Australia 90; Belgium 334; Canada 114; Denmark 120; Greece 110; Italy 800 (600 made under licence by OTO-Melara); Netherlands 468; Norway 78; Turkey 150. Many of these have local modifications but the original Leopard also went through many changes. Now designated Leopard 1, to distinguish it from its successor, the early production models had the following basic specification:
Weight: 39.6 tonnes
Length: 6.94m (hull
Height: 2.62m
Width: 3.25m
Engine: MTU MB838 giving 830hp at 2,200rpm
Transmission: 4 forward, 2 reverse ZF4 HP-250
Armament: 105mm L7A3 — 60 rounds stowed,
2+7.62mm MG3 — 30,000 rounds stowed

Leopard 1 is of conventional layout: driver at the right front, turret amidships, engine compartment and drive at the rear. The other three crew members (commander, gunner,

loader) are in the turret. The seven roadwheels each side have torsion bar suspension and five shock absorbers, which gives a comfortable and quiet ride. The roadwheels are interchangeable with the idlers, saving in the spare parts schedule.

The engine is a water-cooled V10 of 37.4 litres' capacity. This gives a top road speed of 64kph and a road range of 600km. The engine and transmission are assembled in a powerpack which can be removed as a unit and can be replaced, in the field, in 20 minutes by three trained men with an ARV.

The transmission and steering unit has four forward and two reverse ratios, with torque converter and a by-pass clutch. The torque converter is used cross-country, for maintaining drive at all times and smooth operation between the lower three ratios. On the road the torque converter is linked only in first gear, the clutch being used for the other ratios, reducing hydraulic slip and thereby saving fuel. Gear selection is electro-hydraulic. The driver steers with a 'figure of eight' steering wheel. Small movements produce large radius turns but if turned beyond a certain point the system brings in lower, fixed radii turns linked to the gear ratio.

The tracks are double-pin, rubber-bushed made by Diehl KG. The links are of steel and can be fitted with rubber pads for normal work, with steel combat shoes or even a special spiked shoe for snow work. This flexibility has helped enormously with sales outside Germany.

Leopard 1 has no pretensions to high levels of ballistic protection, relying on well-angled armour and agility, with a low silhouette. It is reckoned that 30mm APDS from the Rarden gun can penetrate the side armour. An efficient NBC sytem is incorporated, creating an over-pressure in the turret and driving compartments.

The designers of Leopard recognised that they would have to cope with a tactical problem that also faced their enemies; that of water crossings, in advance or retreat. The hull can be sealed hydraulically to allow deep wade — to a depth of 2.2m, that is to almost turret roof level, while addition of a schnorkel tube, mounted on the commander's cupola, permits river crossings to a depth of 4m, during which the tank is steered by a remote control in the turret.

During water crossings the cooling system compartment is flooded and there are two bilge pumps to deal with an ingress of water to the hull. The preparation for crossing takes about 10-15 minutes with a trained crew and the tank is ready for action almost immediately on reaching the other side.

Armament is the British-designed 105mm L7A3 and fires the same range of ammunition. It was this flexibility in armour killing that helped to decide the Germans in favour of the L7 against the French 105mm, which has only a HEAT round against tanks. The coaxial and loader's MGs are the MG3, a postwar version of the well known MG42, with its high rate of fire up to 1,500rpm and the characteristic noise, like tearing calico. The commander is not asked to act as his own anti-aircraft gunner in the Leopard, as the externally mounted machine gun is normally on the loader's hatch. Sixty rounds are carried for the main armament, 5,500 for the machine guns and two reloads for the two sets of smoke grenade launchers, one each side of the turret bustle.

Early Leopards had no stabilisation, but one of the first improvements was to install a Cadillac-Gage designed system which integrated with the existing electro-hydraulic gun control equipment. Where Leopard users are fortunate is in the fire control systems available, first at the design stage and later, in options and retrofits. The commander has eight periscopes in his cupola, one being mounted in the turret roof in front of the commander's hatch. It has a ×6 and ×20 magnification and affords excellent observation as it rotates independently of the turret, allowing a target to be tracked while the turret traverses. The sight can be replaced by an IR night sight working with an IR/white light searchlight mounted above the gun.

The gunner has a binocular, 170cm base, cross-turret rangefinder/sight which can be used in both stereoscopic and coincidence modes, avoiding the difficulties experienced by the Americans. The gunner's other sight is a coaxial telescope, articulated to allow the user easy following of the gun movement. All three sights are fitted with anti-flash shutters which close automatically for a quarter of a second when the gun is fired so that muzzle flash does not blind the crew.

When Leopard entered service in 1965 it was regarded by most of the world as the forerunner of a new age of medium weight, agile, hard-hitting battle tanks. Only the

Above : This view shows the additional spaced armour retro-fitted to the turret of the Leopard 1A1 to make it a Leopard 1A1A1. *Krauss Maffei*

Below left: Leopard 1A3 of the Australian Army. The curved ribs on the glacis are intended to carry special snow grousers for the tracks. *Australian Directorate of Armour, Department of Defence (ADA)*

Right: Leopard commander with his hand on the turret traverse override control. *ADA*

A Leopard ARV uses its crane to lift the rear of a Leopard 1A1 MBT. The dozer blade is used to stabilise the front of the ARV. *BdV*

British, with the 50tonne Chieftain just about to appear, still muttered about protection and thick armour. Leopard certainly looked good; sleek and low and fast. But there was no spaced armour and no skirting plates.

Like all its predecessors, Leopard was built in production batches, and each had changes in detail. From the early models of the first batch to the fourth batch there were changes to the engine exhaust louvres, the IR light projector was moved slightly to the left from its central position over the gun and the loader was provided with a vision device. The most easily visible changes were the thermal sleeve on the gun barrel, the addition of a fourth track support roller above the two front roadwheels and skirting plates with a distinctive scalloped lower edge.

By 1968 the number of changes since the original production model was formidable. All new build tanks incorporating the improvements were designated Leopard A2, while the tanks already built were A1. Then it was decided to modify all the Leopard A1s in the German Army up to the standard of the A2, the modified tanks being called Leopard 1A1.

The fifth production batch incorporated improved NBC and night vision equipment and vehicles were designated Leopard 1A2. Later vehicles of the same batch had a fabricated steel plate turret with spaced armour, which

makes them easier to identify as Leopard 1A3. It was from this batch that Denmark and Australia received their tanks.

The sixth and final batch of Leopard 1 production had a revised fire control system with ballistic computer and a new commander's sight. By now protection had been improved from the original concept and the weight had risen by nearly three tonnes. Many of the earlier batches have been retrofitted with late series modifications and Leopards in foreign service have adopted a number of optional extras offered by Krauss-Maffei.

The Belgian, Dutch and Australian Leopards are equipped with the Cobelda fire control system, developed by SABCA in Belgium in collaboration with Hughes Aircraft Co of California. This system was originally developed for the M47s of the Belgian Army, but it was so successful that a version was developed for Leopard. It was found that the Cobelda FCS took up less room than the optical system which it replaced and increased by 50% the chance of a first-round hit. This effectively extended the range of engagement to 3,000m. The Cobelda system also takes into account the meteorological data of the area around the tank (wind strength and direction, ambient temperature and pressure), propellant charge temperature, gun barrel wear, as well as the more usual range, trunnion cant and tracking rate.

Modern Leopards can be fitted with a dozer blade, as on the Australian tanks, and the IR/white light night fighting system can be replaced by passive image intensification or thermal sights. The Leopard family of support vehicles was part of the original plan for a MBT and includes the Bergepanzer (ARV), Pionierpanzer (AEV), Bruckenlegerpanzer (AVLB) and Flakpanzer (armoured AA vehicle), named Gepard. A private venture 155mm SP gun has also been built and tested, using the French GIAT 155mm GCT turret on a Leopard 1 hull, but is not yet adopted by any army.

With great forethought, the Germans also brought out very early in the production a special model for driver training, without a turret and with a weatherproof cab over the turret well. The one used by the German army even has a dummy gun sticking out over the front of the hull so that drivers may get used to the overall length of the vehicle. As well as the training vehicle there are a set of training simulators, for drivers and turret crew, which allow training

21

to continue indoors in bad weather, giving the crew the correct 'feel' of Leopard, even down to injected sounds of battle and movement.

While Leopard 1 has been very successful in the military market place, it has not yet seen battle, so its good and bad points are unconfirmed.

Leopard 2

The Germans never ceased to look ahead to what would be needed to combat the new Soviet MBTs. Although their experience of international collaboration (with the French) had not been very happy, they got involved with the Americans in the MBT70 project. Although this attempt at standardisation in NATO foundered on the rocks of national interest (see MBTs USA), the work done on MBT70 probably helped a geat deal in the design of the much needed replacement for the remaining 1,036 M48s in the Bundeswehr. Krauss-Maffei, in collaboration with Porsche and Wegmann had started on 'Kampfpanzer 2' even before they withdrew from the MBT70.

The design team had two objects: one was to improve upon the firepower and protection of Leopard 1 without degradation of mobility, the other was to design the components of the new vehicle so that they could be retrofitted into Leopard 1, thus extending the front line life of that tank. The Kampfpanzer 2 (also named Keiler, or Wild Boar) was very much in the conventional lines of Leopard 1A4. The turret was built of welded steel and mounted a 120mm smoothbore gun.

The Bundeswehr authorised 17 prototypes of the new Leopard 2 design in 1972. By 1974 they were under severe testing in Germany, Canada and the USA. Cold weather trials took place at Camp Shilo, Manitoba, where the temperature drops to $-50°C$; the same four vehicles then went to the Arizona desert, for hot weather trials at $+50°C$. The excellent results of these trials caused the Americans to think about a joint project and prompted the Memorandum of Understanding (MoU) in December 1974, in which the two countries declared their intention to 'harmonise' their MBTs. The Americans agreed to evaluate a Leopard 2, but asked for modifications in the existing design to match their own parameters.

The American criticisms were that the FCS was too complicated, the level of protection insufficient and the cost too high. The MoU called for comparative evaluation of Leopard 2 and the XM1 prototype which would be selected in July 1976. If the Leopard 2 proved superior then the US Army would recommend production in the USA. However, the choice between the GM and Chrysler versions of XM1 was not made in July and the 'comparative' trials began in September against an M60A1, used as a 'baseline' for data evaluation. There was no likelihood of the USA accepting the Leopard 2AV (American or Austere Version) for political reasons, so the trials boiled down to tests of components which might possibly be standardised. This reflected the wording of the addendum to the MoU which was issued in August (before the trials had begun) and said '...in the event that a common tank for the two countries is not achieved, maximum feasible standardisation of major components is obtained'. This seemed to mean German acceptance of the AVCO 1500 gas turbine powerplant and Texas Instruments thermal imaging sight, while the Americans would consider the Rheinmetall 120mm smoothbore gun and the Leitz auxiliary sight.

The Leopard 2AV looked different from the Kampfpanzer 2 prototypes. The turret had vertical sides enclosing a German version of the British Chobham armour. The 120mm gun had a thermal sleeve and the mantlet was also squared off. The long bustle accommodated about 20 complete rounds of 120mm ammunition. The engine deck had two circular vents for cooling air, and sloped upwards noticeably to the rear of the tank. The lower half of the tank was almost unchanged from the later production Leopard 1. The Leopard 2AV failed to meet all the requirements of the American Army and again Germany went ahead on their own lines.

The Leopard 2 which rolled out at the Krauss-Maffei works on 25 October 1979 was the first of 1,800 to be made by 1986. Production is split; 990 by Krauss-Maffei and 810 by Mak of Kiel. It was announced that the cost of a Leopard 2 (at that time) was DM7.2million (about £1.8million or $3.40million). This made it a very costly proposition but nevertheless, in March 1979, the Netherlands placed an order for 445 Leopard 2s, to replace their ageing Centurions and AMX13s. The Dutch negotiated a good 'offset' deal by which 60% of the vehicle would be manufactured in Holland and 40% in Germany, and that the Germans would also buy military equipment and ammunition from Holland to cover that 40%.

The production Leopard 2 looks more like the 2AV than the original 17 prototypes. It has the vertical-sided turret, the almost flat glacis plate with Chobham armoured nose and the thermal sleeve on the gun tube. Most of the improvements over Leopard 1 are not visible on the outside.

In order to keep the high standard of mobility associated with the Leopard, the Leopard 2 has a larger V12-cylinder

version of the MTU diesel. The MB873-Ka501 engine is supercharged and produces 1,100kW (1,450hp) at 2,600rpm. Transmission is a Renk HSWL354 automatic box with four forward and two reverse ratios. All the driver has to do is select forward or reverse and to steer with the flattened hemispherical wheel. This controls an infinitely variable hydrodynamic steering unit which permits turns depending on the gear ratio in use, down to a pivot turn. The seven roadwheels each side are mounted on steel torsion bars, with rotary shock absorbers at stations 1, 2, 3, 6 and 7. The roadwheels themselves are of light aluminium and have a hard-wearing metal surface sprayed on the outer edges to avoid excessive wear caused by contact with the track horns. The Diehl track has end connectors and rubber-bushed pins, while the rubber track pads are removable and can be replaced easily when worn.

German traffic laws require that drivers of all vehicles are provided with seat belts (and use them). They apply this also to MBTs, though the imagination boggles at the thought of a road patrol policeman climbing up on to a Leopard in order to see whether its driver is breaking the law. The cross-country ride is good and the Leopard 2 is very agile for a 55tonne tank, thanks to its 26hp/tonne power/weight ratio. (That apart, Leopard 2 comes very close to the firepower, protection and weight of Chieftain.)

To what extent the adoption by Germany of the 120mm calibre tank gun was influenced by the appearance of the Soviet 125mm gun is not apparent. They did, however, follow the smoothbore concept rather than go along with the rifled barrel. This limits the ammunition variety, but their line is that hollow charge and very high energy KE rounds are effective against modern MBTs. Their case was proven to their satisfaction during NATO firing trials in 1975 when the NATO triple target was penetrated at 2,200m by the Rheinmetall gun, compared with 1,800m by the 105mm.

A hollow charge round gets penetration in direct ratio with the diameter of the cone, so the larger the calibre the better. Also the hollow charge works best if it is not spun, so a large calibre, fin-stabilised round is the objective. With KE rounds the penetration achieved is related to the mass applied to an area of the target and the velocity at which it strikes. Since a spin-stabilised KE projectile cannot be much greater in length than five times its calibre it is limited in the mass that can be applied. A fin-stabilised projectile can be 12 to 14 times its calibre, and can have a greater mass. Both these arguments led to the smoothbore gun, which is easier to manufacture.

The Leopard 2, therefore, carries two natures of 120mm.

An APFSDS round, the projectile of which is 12 times as long as its diameter, and a HEAT round, which doubles as a HE round. The APFSDS weighs 19.8kg and is 889mm in length. Thus it is not easy to handle in the confines of a turret. It is fired at about 1,800m/sec and, Rheinmetall say, has an effective combat range of 3,500m. The HEAT round weighs 24.5kg and is 981mm long. Both rounds have combustible cartridge cases and stub cartridges. This saves weight and reduces the problems of disposal of empty cases and of fumes in the turret. The cases are treated with additives, to reduce the burning temperature of the propellant at the gun barrel wall, and with surface material, to prevent moisture getting into the charges. A total of 42 rounds of 120mm ammunition can be stowed in the tank. To the left of the driver, behind the protection of the glacis plate is space for 27, but the remaining 15 are carried in the turret bustle, behind safety doors. This places them in a very vulnerable part of the tank, and though there are blow-out panels in the turret roof (as in M1) it does not seem to be a good idea and is mainly necessary because of the size of the fixed ammunition and use of the semi-automatic loader. The Chieftain, by comparison, carries 64 rounds of separated ammunition.

The 120mm gun itself is made of cold drawn steel and weighs, complete with breech, cradle and recoil mechanism, 3.13 tonnes. The fume extractor is unusual, being made of glassfibre reinforced plastic, as is the thermal sleeve. The chrome-lined barrel is good for 500 EFC after which accuracy beings to fall off.

Owing to the size and weight of the rounds it was necessary to assist the loader by a semi-automatic loading device. This is a tray which accepts the round from the magazine and presents it to the breech for the loader to ram manually. The device was dispensed with in the 2AV as, with the stabilised sight, it was possible to bring the breech to the loading position each time and return to the aiming point.

The gun control system is an improved version of the Cadillac Gage electro-hydraulic system used in Leopard 1. Originally the gunner was provided with ×8 articulated telescope and a Zeiss EMEX-12 stereoscopic, cross-turret rangefinder incorporating a LRF. This has been replaced by a Hughes stabilised rangefinder made under licence in Germany by Krupp Atlas Elektronic. Doing away with the cross-turret rangefinder enabled the designers to build spaced armour on to the front of the turret, giving it the square look it now has.

The commander's panoramic sight can be used for target

Left: Leopard 2 on the range, wired up for test instrumentation. *BdV*

Right: Prototype Leopard 2 with experimental 20mm cannon mounting on the loader's hatch. *BdV*

acquisition, laying the turret in azimuth and handing over to the gunner for the rest of the engagement, or the commander can lay the gun himself using the gunner's sight picture seen in the panoramic sight. When using the integral thermal imager the commander can also use the LRF.

Secondary armament is as for Leopard 1: coaxial MG3 and another MG3 on the loader's hatch. Wegmann smoke grenade dischargers are mounted eight each side of the bustle.

Leopard 2 will probably develop at least the ARV and AEV variants once production of the MBT is completed, and there will certainly be add-on kits to improve versatility. The Germans claim that there is useful development potential in the 120mm gun, which will be necessary to keep Leopard 2 in the front line of MBTs into the 1990s as envisaged. At that point they will need a replacement tank for at least half their fleet (some 1,500 vehicles). This could be the result of co-operation with France on a mutually acceptable compromise, or Germany may again go it alone. So far the concept study has led to agreement on a two-man, low profile turret with a 120mm gun and auto-loader, but the Germans would probably prefer to keep the programme down to the level of improving the Leopard 2 chassis and FCS.

Israel

The Israeli Army is one of the most experienced in the world and has used the widest range of tanks since its birth in 1948. To start with it had 12 French Hotchkiss H35/39 light tanks, two Shermans and two Cromwells stolen from the British Army, together with an assortment of Shermans rescued from the scrapheaps of WW2 and sold as 'agricultural machinery'. Since then the Israelis have used British Centurion, French AMX13, American M4, M48 and M60, and Soviet T-54/55 and T-6S tanks, as well as a large selection of light vehicles, APCs and SP guns.

The Israelis fought three major campaigns in both attack and defence and have noted the advantages and shortcomings of all the AFVs with which they have had contact. They have developed their own tactics and evolved their own ideas of what they require of a MBT. On their formidable industrial base they have the capability to produce all the components necessary to meet their special requirements. In all their wars the Israelis suffered from embargoes on

supplies and they determined to reduce their reliance on foreign material as much as possible. In the late 1960s, with the successes of the 1967 war behind them, they started development of their own MBT, built to suit the peculiar circumstances of their beleaguered country.

Merkava
Word of this soon spread and soon the name 'Sabra' was being mentioned, but despite a lot of guesswork and supposition built around the components available, nothing was confirmed and no pictures appeared. Possibly ideas changed as a result of the 1973 war, in which the Israelis learned some lessons new to them, for it was not until 1977 that the new MBT was shown to the world.

It was called 'Merkava', Hebrew for Chariot, and revealed an interesting blend of the unconventional and the pragmatic use of existing components. Its unusual layout caused much speculation and comment, but it was the logical answer to many of the problems the Israelis had encountered. Only in Israel is protection given a higher priority than firepower and mobility. Israel is a small country with a small population. It cannot afford losses that would be tolerable even in a western army and therefore crew survival is a very high priority indeed. They did not go as far as

Below: The Israeli Merkava has a central access tunnel in the rear hull, the doors of which appear to be formed as water tanks. There are access hatches either side of the central doors, the left hand are shown open in this picture giving on to a generously sized battery compartment. *IDF Spokesman*

Top right: The Merkava's low profile turret and shallow boat-shaped belly plate to deflect mine blast are evident in this photograph. *IDF Spokesman*

Centre right: The IDF designation M-51 is given to this Sherman, modified with a French 105mm gun and a Cummins 460hp diesel engine, also known as the Super Sherman. *IDF Spokesman*

Bottom right: Both turret and hull front of this Israeli M60 are hung with steel boxes of spaced armour for added protection. The effect would be to detonate shaped charges outside their optimum stand-off distance and possibly to deny solid shot a firm strike. The boxes are easily replaceable. *IDF Spokesman*

reducing the numbers in a crew and retained the usual four men. This may be partly because they lacked an effective automatic loader, but mainly because the Israelis have a great experience of the 24-hour battle day extended over the seven-day week and of the necessity to spread the work load as far as possible.

The driver sits to the left front of the hull and the three-man turret has commander and gunner on the right and loader on the left. Protection is achieved by using very well angled armour, by using spaced armour where possible, by putting the engine and transmission in the front of the tank and by careful stowage of the ammunition, low down and at the rear.

The main hull is a single casting, with welded plate forming the sponsons, engine compartment and rear. The engine and transmission are in the front section under a very acutely angled glacis plate, the left half of which is flat and the right a very distinctive, shallow curve. It is not thought that the Israelis had the technology of composite armour at the time Merkava was designed and therefore spaced armour is probable. But a Mk 2 or Mk 3 version would most likely incorporate composite or laminated armour. Probably some of the hollow spaces are used for diesel fuel stowage.

At the rear of the hull are two doors, which led to all sorts of speculation about the ability to carry infantry or to evacuate casualties but in fact these doors are for access to the ammunition stowage. The Israelis tend to fight from prepared defensive positions and to reload in those positions, sometimes under fire. Passing rounds, one by one, up on to the hull and then down into the turret is always time-consuming and tiring. In action it is also dangerous. The Israelis have made 'bombing up' the Merkava both safer and easier by loading their ammunition through the two rear doors.

A distinctive feature of the Merkava is the skirt armour, which has a cut-out at each wheel station, probably for access to the wheel hubs for maintenance. Each plate is hinged, horizontally, at about the level of the return run of the track. This is to allow the skirts to pivot outwards while the lower sections remain vertical. The purpose of this arrangement is to allow mud to fall away, which would otherwise pack and jam in the space above the tracks. It is an ingenious idea which indicates that the Israelis suffered from this defect in other tanks in their service. Their only tank which normally uses skirting plates is Centurion, but it is not recorded that it suffers much from such defects in Israeli, or other, service.

The Merkava turret is also formed of castings, with welded plates on roof and front, where it tapers to a narrow nose, enclosing the gun barrel. Fighting from the prepared ramps which are the normal battle positions for Israeli armour, the turret is the most vulnerable part and attracts most hits. The Merkava design uses the whole width of the hull for the turret ring, but presents only a narrow profile, front and rear, rather like a refined version of the M60A2, though without the hatches in the side segments or the ugly, high cupola. In fact, the commander has no cupola as such, but a low hatch, with all-round vision blocks and a panoramic observation sight. Curiously, the turret has large overhangs both front and rear, which would appear to offer dangerous shot traps.

Israel has standardised on the British 105mm gun, now made under licence in Israel, for all its MBTs, even to the extent of rearming captured T-54/55s, so it was the natural logistic choice for the new tank. In fact it also matches up to their estimated requirements for coping with enemy armour for the next decade. They claim that the 105mm gun on Merkava is a new design of almost 100% Israeli design and manufacture. They have also designed for their new gun a new APFSDS round with slipping driving band, which is fired at 1,455m/sec and can defeat all current armour. Between 62 and 70 rounds can be stowed in the magazines, low down at the rear, out of harms way. Secondary armament consists of a 7.62mm coaxial and a similar one pintle-mounted by the commander's hatch. But although the 105mm is standardised now, the design of the turret would allow for quite an easy conversion to accept a 120mm weapon if necessary in the future.

The gunner's sight is located in a 'cut-out' to the right of the gun and, in front of it, the armour is ribbed in order to stop or deflect small arms fire or splinters that would otherwise have damaged the sight. This is another innovation following battle experience.

The fire control system includes a ballistic computer and a laser range-finder. After some bad experiences during the 1973 war, with high pressure hydraulic systems in the turrets of their American tanks, it seems probable that the gun control system of Merkava is all electric. Stabilisation is not a firm Israeli requirement, as their doctrine is to fight from prepared static positions, but the ability to remain on a target while moving is valuable, since it reduces engagement times. It is therefore likely that a stabiliser will be fitted.

Another innovation from experience gained the hard way, in battle, is a method of giving orders to the tank driver. The commander has a pistol grip control with which he can transmit simple commands to a visual display in the view of the driver. He can order left, right, and ahead, fast or slow and OK. At the same time the driver receives an audible command on his headset. This cuts down the necessity for real voice communication, and reduces the chance of mistakes and distracting the commander much less from his normal duties.

For the power train of Merkava, the Israelis chose the Teledyne Continental AVDS1790-5A diesel engine, coupled to the Allison CD850-6B transmission. These are about 95% identical to the units in their M60s and reworked M48s, so training, maintenance and the logistic loads are much less of a problem than if they had selected a completely new engine. But the suspension does not follow the same trend. It has been found that torsion bars, as on the American tanks, can be very difficult to withdraw from their housings if they are damaged and, at the same time, torsion bars take up about several inches of space in the bottom of the tank hull. The Horstmann type suspension of Centurion is, by contrast, completely external to the hull, taking up no valuable volume inside the armour, is easily removed and comparatively easy to repair. The Merkava suspension uses independent coil springs, and the housings are attached to hull by only four bolts, making them easy to change.

Apart from the possibility of upgunning to 120mm, it is probable that there is plenty of leeway in the Merkava design for uprating other components. Putting in the latest Teledyne AVCD1790-1A, with its adjustable compression ratio would give a lift of about 25% to the power output.

The Merkava first saw action in 1982, during the Israeli invasion of Lebanon. Although, at first, it was used mainly as a heavy sniper, to knock down buildings in Beirut and to give fire support, in the later stages the Merkava saw combat against the T-72 of the Syrian Third Division in the Beka'a Valley.

In this fighting the Syrians lost a dozen T-72 to 105mm gunfire, but all the casualties were removed from the battlefield before the Israelis had a chance to examine the kills. On the Israeli side the Merkava has established a good reputation for survivability.

The very flat angle of the front armour appears to have been effective and the rear exit made bailing out a safer operation than leaving via the turret hatches. Hits by RPG-7 were largely ineffective. The rear compartment of the Merkava was used, on one occasion, to carry an infantry section across open ground to attack an enemy position which had held up their APCs by RPG-7 fire.

The mobility of Merkava, and its ability to cross very rough going, was conclusively proved and the FCS was so effective that ammunition consumption per kill was halved, compared to other AFVs with the same 105mm gun. A Mk 2 Merkava will have improved agility and a Mk 3 is under development.

Japan

Type 61

Japan has not been known for any great achievements in the fields of tank design and production. Since 1945 Japan has had no army, but with the outbreak of the Korean war in 1950, a 'police reserve' of 75,000 men was created, which evolved into the Japanese Defence Agency in 1954. At first it was equipped with American arms, the armour including 120 M4 Shermans and 130 M41s. It also had a few M47s for trials and when, in 1954, design started on the first postwar indigenous tank, it obviously drew much inspiration from the American machine. The basic layout is conventional; rear engine, six roadwheels, three return rollers

and the turret amidships. The main difference is that the drive is at the front, which was very unusual at this period. The engine in the ST-A series of trial vehicles was a Mitsubishi V-12 air-cooled diesel developing 600hp. The track is single pin with central guide horn and straight steel grousers. The overall dimensions of the production version, the Type 61, are slightly less than the M47, which can be accounted for by the smaller stature of the average Japanese soldier. Production started in 1962 at Misubishi Heavy Industries and by 1977 the JSDF (Japan Self Defence Force) had 560 of the Type 61 in service. Type 61 has a turret that is very like that of the M47, slightly lower and more rounded, but when fitted with the 90mm gun with bore evacuator at the muzzle and T-shaped blast deflector, and a long bustle, the resemblance is more than a passing one. The commander's cupola carries a pintle-mounted .50cal MG, not one mounted in the cupola itself, but the cupola does have the American look. The tank is, however, 10 tonnes lighter than the M47. The JSDF is not, by law, permitted to go outside Japan, and in the islands it is essential to be able to cross most classes of road and rail bridges.

Type 74

Even though they had a reasonably modern tank in service, the Japanese felt that they had to go ahead with the design

The general configuration of the Type 61 MBT and the T-shaped blast deflector on the gun are very reminiscent of the M47, scaled down by about 10% in size and 24% in weight. *Japanese MoD*

The Type 74 MBT is a new and modern design with a well-shaped turret mounting a 105mm gun and an IR/white light searchlight (top). The suspension can be adjusted to alter the attitude of the hull. The side view (middle) shows the low profile of the turret and the .50cal Browning MG which is mounted behind the commander's hatch and is remote controlled. This MBT can wade to 3m depth with a schnorkel kit, or to 1m without special preparation (as at bottom), though exhaust extensions have been added. *Japanese MoD*

for its replacement. In 1962 work started on the ST-B, and this time it was a wholly Japanese effort, though undoubtedly the design team drew on the experiences of their allies and incorporated many of the most modern features, and a low silhouette reminiscent of the Russian T-55. Two prototypes, known as ST-B1, were completed in 1969 and put through exhaustive trials at the Fuji proving ground. They carried the British 105mm L7A3 with, initially, a form of automatic loader, though this was dropped in future vehicles. Another idea tried and forgotten was the remote control mounting for a .50cal MG behind the loader's hatch. In the Type 74 — as it was designated when it went into production in 1975 — the main and coaxial weapons are fully stabilised and the gunner is provided with a LRF and ballistic computer. The gunner has a periscope main sight and a back-up telescope sight and the commander has a periscope sight similar to the gunner's and six vision blocks. He has override controls allowing him to acquire a target and to fire the gun. Despite the small size of the tank it is said to carry about 50 rounds for the 105mm gun, probably stowed right of the driver. There is no reason to suppose that the Japanese are likely to court trouble by keeping ammunition in the bustle.

The glacis plate appears to be at about 40° and, given the modest overall weight of the tank, is unlikely to be very thick. The hull sides, above the sponson, slope inwards and meet the turret sides at about 45°, avoiding shot traps. The turret itself is cast and has a very good, low profile, ellipsoid shape, reminiscent of the Russian T-55. Agility is obviously a major part of the overall protection.

The 750bhp output of the Mitsubishi 10ZF air-cooled two-stroke diesel engine allows for the 120hp absorbed by the cooling fans, and gives a respectable power/weight ratio of 19.7:1. The tank does not have a remarkably high road speed: it can do 53kph, but it is light enough to be able to cross bridges found on secondary roads, while its hydro-pneumatic suspension helps, by giving an excellent cross-country ride to reduce crew fatigue and to confer good strategic mobility. Like modern MBTs, the Type 74 is able to ford unprepared to a depth of one metre and deep wade to over 3m, using schnorkels on the commander's cupola and the main air vents on the engine deck.

The suspension can also be used to adjust the height of the hull, giving a minimum ground clearance of 20cm and a maximum of 65cm.

The Type 74 is not intended to advance against the Soviets, more to make invasion of Japanese territory too costly an adventure. With this in mind, mobility took a priority almost as high as firepower. The overall result is a good looking tank, light at 38 tonnes, but strategically mobile within Japan and capable of getting a high percentage first round hits with its gun.

There appear to have been no variants of the Type 74, though a trial did take place with hull-mounted dozer blade. The needs of the small armoured force within the JSDF are still adequately catered for by the ARV (Type 70), AEV (Type 67) and AVLB (Type 67) variants of the Type 61, which are still in service.

In 1976 Japan started work on a successor to the Type 74, known as STC. It will have the same conventional layout and low silhouette but will be updated in all departments. An eight-cylinder diesel engine developing 900hp will improve agility while the design calls for multi-layer ceramic armour to afford better protection. The main armament could be the current 105mm gun but the Japan Steel Works Co Ltd has under test a new smoothbore 120mm gun for which HEAT and APFSDS rounds have been made by Komatsu and

The Type 70 ARV is derived from the Type 61 MBT. The superstructure is fixed; an A-frame can be erected over the front for lifting purposes and an hydraulically operated dozer blade is mounted on the bow plate. *Japanese MoD*

Daikin Industry respectively. In either case a new and fully modernised FCS is ready from Mitsubishi. The main worry is that the gun and ammunition will prove too large to fit, and be used, comfortably in the turret. The first prototype should be ready in 1983 and trials will start in the following year. The production could reach 600-800 tanks by the 1990s.

Sweden

S-Tank

In the mid-1950s the Swedish Army was studying its future tank requirements: two contenders were the AMX13 and Centurion. At the same time the tank design section of the Swedish Ordnance submitted a revolutionary proposal for an indigenous design. This was to mount the gun in the hull and lay it in both azimuth and elevation by moving the entire vehicle. Azimuth laying had been done before, by the French in the Char B, with technically good results. However, tactically it was not found to be satisfactory and was modified in later models to allow 10° of traverse for the final lay. The advantages of the fixed gun were that it could be mounted close under the roof, so exposing less of the vehicle when firing over cover, and could be fed by an automatic loader, enabling the armour envelope to be reduced in size.

In 1958 AB Bofors were awarded a contract for the development of the new tank, followed by a contract for two prototypes in 1959. Bofors had already done some work on both automatic loading systems and adjustable suspensions and they brought in Volvo, on the automotive side, and Landsverk on the running gear. Two mobile test rigs for the main components were made from prototypes of the Strv KRV tank, constructed by Landsverk, but cancelled by the Army, who preferred the prospect of the Bofors design. One test rig mounted a 20pdr as then fitted to Centurion, complete with mantlet.

Even before the prototypes were completed the Army placed a pre-production order for 10 units. Production of the Strv-103 started in 1966, going on until 1971 by which time some 300 had been built, fulfilling the Swedish requirement. None were sold abroad.

Left: The distinctive lines of the Swedish S-Tank. *MoD via G. Forty*

Right: The IKV-91 tank destroyer. *via G. Forty*

The S-Tank, as it became known, was very interesting technically. The low hull (only 1.9m to the roof) had the power unit and transmission at the front under a very well sloped glacis plate, the effectiveness of which is enhanced by ribs welded on the glacis to deflect AP shot. The rear of the hull is thus available to house the magazines and auto-matic loader. The S-Tank has two engines, a Rolls-Royce K60 diesel for normal running, when power requirements are low, and a Boeing 502-10 MA gas turbine which can be switched on for occasions when high power is required. (The two prototypes were fitted with Rolls-Royce B81 petrol engines.) Both are coupled to a common automatic transmission with Volvo hydro-kinetic torque converter, so that in the event of either engine failing the other can still drive the tank. The turbine is more easily started in very cold weather conditions and can be used as a 'starter' for the diesel. The K60, which has the same six-cylinder opposed piston layout as the larger L60 in Chieftain, is the more economical on fuel. Both the K60 and the turbine are able to run on diesel fuel.

The suspension of the S-tank has hydro-pneumatic control of the attitude of each of the four road wheels each side, by a complicated system of cylinders attached to the roadwheel arms. By means of transferring fluid from front to rear, or vice versa, the gun can be elevated to +12° or depressed to −10°. (Most Western MBTs can elevate to 20° and depress to −10°. Soviet MBTs +17° to −4°.) There is an automatic lock out on the suspension, operated by the gun firing button, which provides a stable base for firing successive rounds. The short (3.01m) length of track on the ground, necessary to achieve even the meagre 22° overall elevation, makes for an uncomfortable fore-and-aft pitching motion at speed, even on roads.

The integrated steering system is in two stages. First it is a double-differential regenerative system with an infinitely variable hydrostatic steering drive. This is very smooth and makes laying the gun in azimuth easy. The second stage is a clutch and brake arrangement which allows sharp and rapid turns. This makes slewing of the gun faster than con-ventional turrets over big arcs.

Although the hydraulic and control systems for steering and laying are, in themselves, complicated, from the user's point of view they could hardly be simpler. Both driver and commander have identical control boxes with handle bars. Conventional turning action steers the tank to left or right, while twisting the grips alters the pitch of the hull. There are

loading and firing buttons for both main and secondary armaments. Both driver and commander have accelerator and brake pedals, and the third crew member (radio-operator) who sits facing rearwards behind the commander, has a simplified set of controls for driving in reverse.

The commander sits to the left of the main armament and the driver/gunner to the right. The gun is a longer version (62 calibres instead of 51) of the British L7 105mm gun as used in Centurion and other MBTs. This extra length significantly increases the muzzle velocity of the APDS round, giving greater penetration at the same range as the shorter gun, or the same penetration at some 500m greater range. The barrel is supported by a bracket at the front of the tank, with the fume extractor just behind the bracket. The breech is located as far back as possible, over the rear roadwheel, leaving enough space behind it for the hydraulic rams which take the rounds from the magazines and load them. There are two magazines, one each side of the centre line of the vehicle. Each takes 25 rounds of 105mm ammunition, usually APDS in one magazine and HE in the other. Either can be selected as required. The magazines can be reloaded through two hatches in the rear plate, and it is claimed that two men can accomplish this in 10 minutes with less fatigue than a conventional tank crew stowing through the turret. Empty cartridge cases are ejected through a trap in the rear plate.

Both commander and driver/gunner are provided with periscopes with a wide 102° field ofview and including binocular sights with magnification of ×6, ×10 or ×18, selected by a lever on the periscope. The driver/gunner's sight is fixed but the commander's is gyro-stabilised in elevation and azimuth, which gives him very good observa-tion facilities on the move. Having acquired a target he can override the driver/gunner to aim and fire himself or to bring the target within the gunner's field of view while he con-tinues to search and observe. The S-Tank was originally built without either LRF or ballistic computer. The Swedes reckoned that, at the 500-800m battle range which they anticipated, a rangefinder was unnecessary. However Bofors developed a system including LRF and a computer which has been installed in many of the later vehicles. The S-Tank has a number of advantages compared with the con-ventional turreted vehicle. It is smaller and lighter and needs only a three-man crew, while only one man is needed to aim and fire the gun and manoeuvre the vehicle in emergencies. The low silhouette and well-sloped glacis give it a good

chance of survival. R. M. Ogorkiewicz, an authority on AFVs and a strong advocate of the S-Tank, estimates (in Profile Publications' *AFVs No 28*) that the chance of an S-Tank being hit is only 60% that of a conventional tank, by reason of its configuration. Against this, the armour is relatively thin and is thus more vulnerable to chemical energy attack, and the fuel tanks are carried high, in the sponsons above the tracks.

R. M. Ogorkiewicz also states that trials confirmed that the S-Tank can carry out all but one of the roles expected of MBTs, this being that it cannot move in one direction and fire its main armament in another. One must go further and state that it cannot effectively fire on the move at all, neither can it properly track a target while on the move, although the commander can do so with his periscope. The difference in engagement time between a gun which is stabilised to within one mil of a target when the tank halts to fire and one which has to be traversed and fine layed must be significant, even with the fast slew of the S-Tank steering system. In close country or near buildings, the necessity to slew the whole hull can be a grave disadvantage and, while although a tank pit does not need to be as deep as for a conventional tank, the S-Tank needs a greater area, if it is to have the same arc of fire, in which to turn the hull. The British carried out a series of troop trials in Germany from 1968-74, using Simfire battle simulation equipment. The trials did not impress either tank men or staffs with the fixed gun idea. When on the move the STrv-103 is a turretless tank, when at rest a tankless turret. In the two decades since the S-Tank appeared no other country has bought it and no other country has produced anything remotely like it. The S-Tank is an interesting vehicle technically, but it does not properly belong in the ranks of MBTs, being more a tank destroyer than a tank.

IKv-91

It is interesting to remark that, when the Swedes did design a tank destroyer, they reverted to the conventional turreted vehicle. The original requirements were drawn up in the mid-1960s, for a vehicle to replace the Strv-74 light tank and the IKv-102 and 103 SPGs. In 1968 Hagglunds and Soner won the contract and prototypes were built in 1969 and 1970, with production starting in 1974.

The IKv-91 designation gives the clue to the main role of vehicle. It is intended as an infantry support weapon with a good anti-tank capability and high mobility. To achieve this

the weight has been kept down to 15.5 tonnes, though the bulk of the hull gives sufficient displacement for it to be inherently buoyant. This means a low immunity and the glacis is protected only against 20mm projectiles. Though the sponsons, containing fuel and other components, give some protection, the IKv-91 is very lightly armoured for a front line role.

Its armament consists of a low pressure, medium velocity 90mm Bofors-designed gun and a 7.62mm coaxial MG. Another MG can be pintle-mounted on the loader's cupola. The 90mm fires HEAT rounds at 825m/sec and HE at 600m/sec. The ammunition is fixed, and the projectiles finned for stability. The fire control equipment includes a laser rangefinder in the gunner's periscope sight and a ballistic computer. The gun and turret are moved by hydraulic power provided by an intermittently working electro-hydraulic pump and an accumulator.

Britain's S-Tank

Between 1968 and 1974 the British Army borrowed a number of Strv 103B from Sweden and carried out a series of trials, the results of which have not been released. Two troops of S-Tanks took part in tactical trials in Germany, but the British crews showed no enthusiasm for the fixed gun concept, nor have British designers tended that way.

But Britain did experiment, once, in the late 1950s and early 1960s, as part of a general study of possible configurations for future fighting vehicles. At that time it was envisaged that there could be a requirement for a small vehicle, armoured to 'medium tank' standard, with MBT type firepower and good mobility, with a weight of about 20 tonnes, at which it would be air-portable. The multi-fuel engine of about 400bhp would have given a speed of 55-60kph and a range of 800km.

The armament was the 105mm gun being developed for Centurion. It was mounted in a modified Comet hull, fixed in elevation, but with a limited$\pm$ 20° traverse. The two-man crew had the driver on the right and the commander/gunner on the left. The latter would have had an all-round viewing capability in the finished design. There was to have been an automatic loader, but it was not fitted to the concept study model.

Tests showed the feasibility of laying in azimuth by roughly aligning the vehicle and then making a controlled fine lay, and in elevation by altering the attitude of the hull by means of hydraulic rams. There were two of these

mounted externally on the suspension arms, to which fluid was metered via the aiming controls.

The experimental hull was open-topped and two small fuel tanks were carried on the track guards. There were four roadwheels each side and two return rollers. Since the concept was carried no further, the vehicle was used only for trials of a photoelectric gun control apparatus, which was also dropped. The vehicle is now an interesting exhibit in the Royal Armoured Corps Tank Museum at Bovington, named, very appropriately, *Contentious*.

Switzerland

At first the terrain of Switzerland seems a most unlikely breeding ground for MBTs, an area where every metre of track or road is overlooked and which would be a prime example of non-tank country. In fact the only use made by the Swiss Army, of AFVs, up to the end of WW2, was in the infantry support role and as tank destroyers. But in 1951 they decided to acquire proper modern gun tanks, and not just in small numbers. They envisaged a total of 550.

The first step was, however, an equivocal one. They ordered 200 of the light tank or tank destroyer AMX13. From this base they could either use them as tanks or return to the previous strategy and use them as SP anti-tank guns. They called the AMX13 the Leichter Panzer 51, which gave away no sign of their intentions, and allotted them to reconnaissance units. It was perhaps reports from the Korean War that decided them to buy 100 Centurions Mk III which were ordered in 1955 and delivered in 1956-57. This became known as the Panzer 55 and was followed by the Panzer 57, being the Centurion Mk 7 in Swiss guise, of which another 100 were bought. Later, in 1960, the Swiss were offered another 100 Centurions, this time Mk 5, when South Africa decided that they were surplus to requirements. (They must have regretted this sale later on, when in 1977 they paid about $32,000 each for Centurion Mk 5 sold by India as scrap.)

Pz61

While the Swiss were building up their equipment and experience, they were also considering the advantages of building their own tanks. This would free them from the problems of foreign sources of supply. The Federal Construction Works, at Thun, had never built a tank before but was

Contentious with the suspension at full elevation. The controlling hydraulic rams and actuating arms are visible below the top run of track. The vehicle was fitted with the experimental photo-electric gun laying equipment in this picture. *RAC Tank Museum*

very experienced in overhauls of guns and other items. It was to their great credit, then, that they built, in 1958, prototypes of a remarkably sophisticated vehicle (the Panzer 58, naturally).

The first two prototypes were armed with a 90mm and a British 20pdr, with a 20mm Oerlikon cannon in a coaxial mounting and a 7.5mm MG on the loader's hatch. By the time that production was due to start in 1961, the Swiss had seen the performance of the new British 105mm gun and decided to adopt it. Thus the first Swiss MBT to be produced was the Pz61, with 105mm gun.

The Pz61 was built with the requirements of the Swiss Army in mind. It was one of the lightest MBTs of its time, only 30 tonnes fully loaded. Only 3.10m wide, it could manoeuvre more easily through narrow streets, cross lower class bridges and be easily transported by rail. The design of the Pz61 was a tribute to the application of the available technology and it did not follow slavishly the ideas of other tank builders. The first difficulty was that rolled steel plate of the required thickness and specifications was not available in Switzerland. So both hull and turret of Pz61 were formed of one-piece castings, which required some very special skills and quality control. Using this technique gave the glacis a smoothly curved line and the turret a very good ballistic shape, rather like a T-55, except for the front. The engine compartment is accessible over the whole deck, through 14 easily handled hatches. The driver sits in the middle of the hull, with a one piece access hatch and three periscopes for closed down vision.

The engine of Pz61 is a V8 diesel made by Daimler-Benz, developing 630hp. The transmission is a Swiss-designed gearbox with six forward and two reverse ratios and a double differential steering system and an infinitely variable hydrostatic steering drive. The suspension is unusual being externally mounted trailing arms with stacked Belleville washers instead of coil springs.

The armament of Pz61 is the British 105mm L7A1, modified with a Swiss-made horizontal breech block and recoil system. It fires the same range of ammunition, plus a Swiss-

Above: The G-13 tank destroyer is a development of the German JdPz38 Hetzer, based on the Czech Pz38 tank hull. The Swiss version had a 160hp petrol engine or a 150hp diesel, and was armed with a 75mm gun. This picture shows an AA mounting for a MG. *Swiss Army*

Right: The French AMX13 was designated Leichter Panzer 51 in the Swiss Army. A spare roadwheel was carried on the glacis, with a neat cover to keep out dirt. *Swiss Army*

designed HE round. Fifty-two rounds of 105mm are carried of which the majority are stowed in racks either side of the driver. A very novel feature is that these racks are set into the fuel tanks so that each round is surrounded by diesel fuel. Although it might not appear so, this is a safe method of stowage, akin to the pressurised water jackets of Chieftain, and is a protection against hollow charge attack.

Secondary armament is the 20mm Oerlikon cannon mounted alongside the 105mm gun. It is useful against soft targets but does not have any extra elevation to give an anti-aircraft capability. The 7.5mm MG is fired by the loader, whose hatch is split to give some flank protection when head and shoulders out.

Fire control is simple and basic. The commander operates a coincidence type cross-turret rangefinder with a base of 1.55m. The gunner has a periscopic sight and gun control is electro-hydraulic.

When the whole production run of Pz61 had been completed the Swiss army decided to buy 170 more tanks. Rather than design a new one, it was decided to modernise the design of Pz61 and have them made under the designation Pz68.

Left: The Centurion Mk 7 in Swiss guise as the Panzer 57. The commander has an MG51 mounted on his cupola and the smoke dischargers are the Swiss type neb 8 cm51. Main armament is the 105mm L7, retro-fitted to replace the 20pdr. This gave the tank the designation Pz57/60. *Swiss Army*

Below: The smooth lines of the cast hull and turret of the Pz61 are evident in this picture. Other unusual features are the cupola for the loader, with AAMG mounting, and the 20mm Oerlikon cannon mounted coaxially with the main armament. *Swiss Army*

Pz68

There were few changes visible from outside the tank. The track was altered from an all-steel single dry pin type to a rubber-padded one with rubber-bushed pins. The engine was uprated to 660bhp, which pushed the maximum road speed up by 5kph to 60kph. The gun was now stabilised by an electro-hydraulic system and an improved sight fitted.

One visible change was the replacement of the 20mm cannon, which had proved a disappointment, by a second 7.5mm MG. This took up less space in the turret, gave the sustained burst capability necessary for harassing or pro-phylactic fire and allowed for greatly increased numbers of rounds available. In order for the loader to be able to clear the turret of empty cartridge cases, the Pz68 has a small

port in the left wall of the turret. This opening would possibly be of help when 'bombing up' as well. The Pz61 has been developed into two variants, an ARV and a bridgelayer. The former (Entpannungpanzer Ent Pz65) is the basic Pz61 hull with a box-like superstructure for a five-man crew and their equipment. It has a main winch of 25 tonnes capacity and a secondary winch for running out the 120m of heavy main winch cable. It has no actual ground anchor but a bulldozer blade which is used as an anchor and to steady the hull when lifting with the jib.

Most bridgelayer tanks use the scissors type bridge or a simple up-and-over single span bridge. Laying either of these entails hoisting the bridge up high over the hull, which is very conspicuous and gives away the bridging operation

Above: The Pz68 shows little difference from its predecessor. The 20mm cannon is replaced by a 7.5mm coaxial MG and a pistol port is visible in the left side of the turret. *Swiss Army*

Right: The Entspannungspanzer (Entp Pz)65 is armed only with a MG and four smoke dischargers. It is equipped with dozer blade, lifting A-frame and two winches. *Swiss Army*

Below: The Bru Pz68 bridgelaying tank is based on the Pz68 hull and carries a single piece bridge 18.2m long, made of aluminium, capable of a 50tonne load. *Swiss Army*

immediately. The Swiss Bruckenpanzer (BruPz68) carries a one-piece bridge which is slid into position along a telescopic beam, so that it is at no time any higher than its position on the tank hull.

NKPz

There has been no new tank put into service in Switzerland since 1968. A programme to re-engine and update the Centurion was studied in the early 1970s, and in 1978 Contraves AG of Zurich, were given a contract to carry out design studies for a possible new tank (Neuer Kampfpanzer, or NKPz) for the 1990s.

The NKPz would have the Rheinmetall 120mm smoothbore gun with an automatic loader and the most modern FCS, including primary stabilised sight with the gun slaved to the sight, LRF and passive thermal imager and a built in test capability. The layout would provide for a three-man crew, engine and transmission in front and hydropneumatic suspension. The main armament ammunition would be stowed in the rear of the hull (cf Merkava), low down and out of harm's way and in two revolving band magazines. From here the auto-loader would select rounds as required and put them into a ready magazine in the turret.

The hull is designed with a very acutely angled glacis and is compartmentalised so that there are fireproof bulkheads separating the crew from the fuel and ammunition. Special armour would be used only on the front and sides of the low profile turret and as skirting plates. But this proposal has already been shelved and the Swiss GRD (Gruppe für Rüstungsdienst) has been evaluating offers from three countries with a view to replacing the 300 Centurions and 150 Pz61 still in service. The tanks under consideration are the Leopard 2, the British FV4030 and Valiant and the American M1.

Two Leopard 2 are under trials in Switzerland, having been altered to meet Swiss requirements. Local assembly in Switzerland would be an attractive part of any German offer. The most interesting parts of the British tanks would be the Chobham armour and the fact that Valiant, being designed for the export market, is able to take a variety of engines, transmissions, armament and FCS so it could be tailored to fit the Swiss requirement.

Although the M1 Abrams is under consideration as a whole, it is more likely that the Swiss are evaluating the components which could be of interest: fire control, gun control and sighting and the Rheinmetall 120mm smoothbore gun and ammunition. The Swiss are unlikely to adopt a gas turbine main engine, on logistic grounds. The American tank is likely to be the cheapest option, even at $1 million each, as the US production run will be several times that of the European tanks.

United Kingdom

At the end of WW2 the Allies still had both cruiser and infantry (or medium and heavy) tanks in front line formations. The British Cromwell, Comet and Churchill, American Sherman and M26 Pershing and the Russian T-34 and IS-3 remained in service for many years after the war. But the shortcomings of these types and the disadvantages of having to manoeuvre and maintain two categories of tank had been noted for three years or more; only the pressing need to keep production going and deliveries to the troops flowing, prevented earlier introduction of new designs.

Britain had already designed the FV201 (A45) and decided that it was to be the basis for a truly universal tank,

to combine all the functions of gun tank, ARV, bridgelayer, AVRE, mine clearer, etc. As a gun tank FV201 was armed with the existing 17pdr until the projected 20pdr became available, so it had no greater firepower than the A41, which was just coming into service as a cruiser. FV201 had started on the drawing board as an infantry tank and was built in that style, with very thick frontal and roof armour. At 55 tons it was too heavy for any of the ancillary roles, it would not go in the new tank landing craft and in any case it did not match up to the threat from the Soviet heavy tanks.

Work on the A41 Centurion showed that it was not only capable of being up-gunned but was also suitable for all the ancilliary roles. Army and Treasury agreed to save time and money and shelved work on FV201, putting more effort into the development of Centurion, which was now to be designated the Universal tank. However, even the up-gunned Centurion, mounting the 20pdr, which came into service in 1947, was not regarded as being capable of dealing with the Soviet heavy IS-3 at long ranges. The immediate need was to get more guns into the field quickly, and as the 20pdr was coming off the production lines quicker than Centurions, it was mounted on the most available hull. There were hundreds of out-dated Cromwells in the tank parks. It was cheap and quick to put the 20pdr in a new two-man turret, replace the hull gunner by ammunition racks and put into service a lightly armoured, but swift and powerful tank killer. This was named Charioteer and it plugged the gap in the anti-tank defences until the late 1950s, remaining in service with other armies well into the 1970s.

But an even bigger gun than the 83.4mm 20pdr was needed to counter the threat. A 32pdr, adapted from the 3.7in anti-aircraft gun, had been carried in the heavy A39 Tortoise, in a limited traverse mounting, but that vehicle was essentially a self-propelled gun with such limited mobility that it was never taken beyond prototype stage. The 32pdr was dropped in favour of an Anglo-American 120mm gun which had been tried, experimentally, in a version of the M6 heavy assault tank and again, in 1951, in the T43. The 120mm was mounted in a well shaped cast turret and carried on the revived FV201 hull. It had an advanced fire control system with contra-rotating cupola which enabled the tank commander to locate and lay on a new target while the gunner engaged the earlier one, bringing the gun to bear by pressing a button and overriding the gunners controls.

Top right: The low, lean lines of the Cromwell are apparent in this picture of a Charioteer. The turret, of welded plate, gave protection against small arms fire and splinters only. Charioteer was a stop-gap vehicle and lacked refinements of fire control, yet it remained a very effective counter to massed tank attacks. It was the first effective vehicle of the Jordanian armoured corps. *RAC Tank Museum*

Middle: Tortoise in hibernation. The only remaining example of this type before it was housed in the Tank Museum at Bovington. This vehicle had been used on the troop trials in Germany and is fitted with multiple smoke grenade dischargers on both sides of the hull and on the commander's turret. *Author*

Bottom: With an all up weight of 65tons Conqueror was the heaviest tank to serve in the British Army. The huge, cast turret carried the commander in a contra-rotating cupola in the bustle. He could lay the 120mm gun on one target and then search for another while the gunner took over the engagement. *RAC Tank Museum*

But it carried only 35 rounds of 120mm ammunition, and at 65 tons it lacked the mobility required. The Conqueror FV214, at it was called, was a powerful addition to the tank-killing strength of the British Army, but it was only another stop-gap expedient. Only 180 were built and so Conqueror never achieved the status of Universal Tank, serving its time as a tank destroyer until 1968.

In parallel with the British development of light and heavy tank destroyers to support their tanks both the USA and France (now back into AFV production) built 120mm-armed vehicles. The AMX50, which was produced in small numbers from 1950, carried its 120mm in an oscillating turret. The M103 was the only American heavy tank to be standardised after WW2. There were a series of experimental designs, leading to what was really an extended M48 with an extra suspension station and wider tracks to reduce the ground pressure. In the huge, cast homogeneous armour, turret the commander sat in the bustle, directly behind the gun which was served by a gunner and two loaders. Fire control was aided by a cross-turret rangefinder. It main role was to 'overwatch' the 90mm-armed M47 and M48 tanks which formed the main force in Europe — an exact parallel to that of Conqueror. Only 200 were built and, after troop trials in Europe had shown that the M103 was not up to the required tactical mobility, they were eventually allocated to the US Marine Corps. Quite how they would have been used in assault landings was not made clear, and the Marines could not have been very happy at being handed down the Army's cast-offs. The M103 was withdrawn from service and joined the other mastodons in retirement.

The Soviets continued to develop the IS-3, which had initiated the super-heavy league. The IS-4, with a 12.7mm coaxial MG and an improved engine was built in small numbers, but its successors, IS-5 to IS-9, existed only as prototypes. The last of the series, the IS-10, eventually entered service in 1957 as the T-10, losing its name as a result of de-Stalinisation following the death of the dictator.

The T-10 served in the heavy tank battalions of the Soviet Army into the late 1960s. The hull was basically a long version of the IS-3, with an extra wheel station. It was

Above: The hull of Centurion changed comparatively little during its life, but the Mk 1 turret shown here carries the early main armament of a 17pdr gun and a 20mm Polsten cannon. The latter was in a ball mounting, separately controlled by the gunner, though it could be linked to the main armament sight. The turret of this prototype is of mild steel, bearing the warning triangle on the left side. *RAC Tank Museum*

Right: Centurion Mk 3 ready for a test run at the Leyland Motors Tank Factory. *Leyland Motors*

powered by an improved engine, which later powered the T-54. Its 122mm gun remained the largest tank gun in service until overtaken in the late 1970s, but the crude fire control system never made it the super killer that the western tank men had feared.

While armies deployed multiple categories of tanks it was not proper to describe any one as a main battle tank. The withdrawal of the heavy tank and the decision to standardise on one basic category created the MBT, at last fulfilling the requirement for a tank for all roles.

In length of service the laurels must go to Centurion. It is still a major force in many armies, nearly 40 years after its first appearance. It might have been one of the shortest lived: in the same month that Centurion entered service (December 1946) the General staff decided to supersede it by FV201, because it was felt that Centurion would not be suitable for the various ancillary roles required. Their crystal ball must have been unserviceable. Centurion ran to 24 marks and six major ancillary roles, some of which were also made in several marks. It has served in as many armies as the M48 or M60 and proved itself in battle against tanks from Russia, China and the USA, acquiring an enviable reputation for its ability to absorb punishment and still keep on fighting. There have been many criticisms of Centurion but it has consistently been in the van of the evolution of the MBT as we know it, and it has had a great influence on AFV development worldwide.

Centurion

Centurion was powered by the best available engine from the beginning, the Rolls-Royce Meteor, and apart from minor modifications, was unchanged in design throughout the life of the tank in British service, although the power output was improved by about 50bhp in later models. The Merritt-Brown Z51R combined gearbox and steering unit (the R indicated two reverse speeds) and the Horstmann suspension remained standard for the same period, until 1970.

The original armament of a 17pdr was dictated by availability: it was a powerful and accurate weapon, having proved itself in the Sherman Firefly. At first the secondary armament was either a 7.92mm Besa MG in a ball mounting to the left of the gun, or a Polsten 20mm cannon similarly mounted. Both could be fired independently by the loader, or by the gunner when the mounting was mechanically linked to the main armament.

The Polsten was not popular. It was too big for anti-infantry work and only 950 rounds of 20mm could be carried. It took up a lot of room in the turret and disposal of empty cases was a problem. The 3,375 rounds carried for the Besa MG gave greater scope for prophylactic fire, and gun and ammunition took up less space. Three prototypes had a ball-mounted Besa fixed in the turret bustle, instead of the circular hatch, and there was another proposal to carry a Besa in an armoured box on the front of the hull, controlled by the driver; both ideas were later dropped. Given the continual necessity to clear jams in the Besa the latter project would have been quite unworkable. All production vehicles of the Centurion Mks 1 and 2 carried the 17pdr and a coaxial Besa MG, and the original welded plate turret was replaced by a cast one incorporating an improved commander's cupola with a single hatch. From the start an electro-servo stabiliser was fitted to allow firing on the move. The additional power requirement was catered for by installing a 3kW auxiliary generator in the engine compartment, driven by a four-cylinder Morris engine. This, however, meant reduced space available for fuel and caused a low operational range of 90 miles on road or 50 cross-country.

By the time the 8th Hussars went to Korea in 1950 they were equipped with the Mk 3, armed with the 20pdr gun and coaxial Besa MG. The accuracy and lethality of the 20pdr became legendary in Korea, where Centurions were used as 'pill-boxes' or as 'snipers' more often than in their true tank role. Their ability to climb seemingly impossible hills enabled them to be sited where the enemy would be most surprised. The Mk 3 carried 65 rounds of 20pdr ammunition, of which the APDS round was fired with a muzzle velocity of 4,800ft/sec (1,477m/sec), a very respectable figure even 30 years later. It was aimed by means of a periscopic sight and could be controlled in elevation and traverse by the powered stabiliser. Target acquisition was improved by a linkage between the commander's sight in the cupola and the gunner's sight, which gave both the same sight picture. Engagement times were considerably reduced as the gunner only had to adjust for range and deflection.

With adequate mobility and excellent armament, the Centurion combined very good protection. The glacis plate was 3in (76mm) thick and well sloped for the first time on a British tank. The mantlet was 6in thick, the hull sides sloped inwards below hull roof level, to minimise mine blast effect, and skirting plates protected against hollow charge attack. Obviously many lessons had been learned from the war, to the greater comfort of the tank crews.

Another most important change was the stowage of all main armament ammunition below turret ring level: this reduced the risk of fire in the event of a hit when hull down. In fact, despite the use of gasoline fuelled main and auxiliary engines, Centurion was difficult to set on fire. It is recorded (Simon Dunstan, *Modern Combat Vehicles: 2 Centurion*, Ian Allan) that, in Korea, two Centurions had to be abandoned and, in order to prevent their falling into enemy hands, orders were given to destroy them by gunfire. Even close-range pounding with 20pdr AP shot failed to ignite them and they were eventually recovered.

There still remained the shortcomings of low operational range, and a number of expedients were tried to remedy this. Standard 40gal fuel drums were mounted in pairs behind the rear plate, and later purpose-built 180gal tanks in the same way, but both were fragile and vulnerable to accident

Above: Australian Centurion in bivouac in Vietnam. Note the spare roadwheels carried on the glacis. *AWM*

Left: Fine view of a Centurion Mk 3. The 20pdr gun is without the fume extractor fitted to later models and the loader's periscope mounting still incorporates the 2in bombthrower and is located on the turret roof, rather than on the front sloping plate. *MoD*

Right: South Africa has some 250 Centurions, modified with 105mm guns and renamed Olifant. Both coaxial and commander's MGs are Browning 7.62mm. *H-R Heitman*

and small arms fire. However unpopular this might have been it was nothing compared to the loathing of Centurion crews for the 200gal monowheel fuel trailer that was issued in 1953. These lightly armoured tanks were attached to the rear plate by two hooks and supported on a single trailing wheel. It extended the length of the tank, was frequently 'side-swiped' against obstacles when the tank turned while moving forward and was an unmanageable menace in reverse. It articulated in the vertical plane, and was known to ride up on to the engine deck or disappear below the hull when reversing over rough going. Always prone to fuel leakage, the mono trailer was blamed for many fires. It was supposed to be released, before going into action, by explosive bolts in the hooks, but any distortion of the trailer arms made it very difficult to uncouple. Sometimes one hook

would 'blow' and the other remain fast: the trailer then twisted and acted as a sort of ground anchor. This most unpopular device was succceded by a 100gal armoured box attached to the rear armour plate, which was far less of a hazard.

Not until the Mk 7 was fuel carried under armour raised from 120gal to 228gal, by means of an extra tank in the rear of the hull, which was lengthened by 6in. There were other changes too in the Mk 7, which raised the all up weight from 49.9 tons to 50 tons. The revised figures for operational range indicated a fuel consumption of 1.93gal/mile on the road, and a staggering 3.6gal/mile cross-country.

The Mk 7 was noted too, for the change to the .30-06in calibre Browning MG as coaxial secondary armament and flexibly mounted on the commander's cupola. This was a

change much desired after experience in Korea, where many Centurions had been so equipped, unofficially. Many officers had regarded this as a retrograde step, giving the commander yet another responsibility to distract his attention from the vital tasks of map-reading, communications, target acquisition, and, above all, commanding his tank — and troop. Though the cupola-mounted MG might seem to be a distraction, the extra weapon for prophylactic fire in close country and against hordes of bugle-blowing infantry was a comforting thought for those who had felt the lack of such a weapon in Korea. The Browning became the standard AFV MG throughout the Army and thousands of old 1919 models were brought out of store to fill the requirement. Although its introduction meant another calibre of ammunition to be carried, this was balanced by dropping the 7.92mm round which had been used only in the Besa.

With the gradual improvement and refinement of components in the gun control and fire control systems, and the addition of 2in of armour to the glacis plate, Centurion was 'keeping up with the Ivans' in performance and protection. But the back-room boffins were not resting on their laurels. The RARDE at Fort Halstead had looked to the future and designed a 105mm replacement for the 20pdr. It was literally a replacement, engineered to fit into the existing mantlet, and with a killing performance some 25% better than the 20pdr. With the stabilised 105mm L7A1 gun, Centurion crews astonished foreign visitors with their

accuracy and firepower and were envied by their NATO partners, winning the Canada Cup challenge trophy for tank gunnery many times.

One item of equipment lacking in British tanks was a rangefinder. Tank commanders had been trained to judge distance using the Mk 1 Eyeball and when effective ranges were no more than 1,000m, with a fairly flat trajectory round this was accurate enough. However, being able to engage and kill at ranges up to 2,000m was a different matter and to get even a 50% chance of a first-round hit at the longer distance necessitated a little help.

In Conqueror the commander had a 49in base optical rangefinder mounted across his cupola. Sighting on his target and bringing the two images together he could read off the range, which would be transferred to the gunner's sight. Using a coincidence rangefinder demands a critical degree of skill and training and it is often necessary to average two or three 'takes'. This is time-consuming and there was, in any case, no room in the Centurion cupola for a useful size of optical rangefinder. Putting one across the interior of the turret roof, in the American fashion, would have meant a great deal of redesign of what was regarded as a very satisfactory fighting arrangement.

The last major modification to Centurion was, therefore, the installation of the .50in RMG. Firing a special .50in round with a tracer and an incendiary tip which gave a flash when hitting the target, the RMG was a simple alternative to the optical rangefinders of the 1960s. It had the advantage over all optical systems that it took into account external ballistic factors such as crosswinds, ambient temperature, drift and trunnion tilt. The .50in ranging round was designed so that its ballistics matched those of the HESH round near enough, but it could be used in most conditions to find a target range which could then be used for any nature of round. The RMG did not give away the tank fire position and it was a quicker method of ranging than most. It remained the usual method of ranging until the laser took over, even in the next generation of MBT. Another aid to accuracy was the thermal sleeve, a jacket around the gun barrel which protected it from severe changes in ambient temperature such as a cold wind, which, striking one side of the hot barrel could cause it to bend sufficiently to cause the round to miss.

The night fighting capability of Centurion was enhanced, as the state of technology improved, from IR filters over headlights to special night periscopes enabling drivers and commanders to identify objects as far away as 500m, when bathed in IR light. However, if the enemy provided himself with IR viewing devices, tanks using IR head and search-lights might just as well have been moving under the glare of white light. Even the heat from engines and exhausts showed up clearly at night. The passive night sight takes the minute amount of light that exists, even on the darkest nights, and amplifies it, electronically, projecting the result as a picture on to a lens at the viewing end. Since it is a collecting device, not emitting a beam, it is undetectable, yet gives an adequate sight picture for engagements.

Centurion was superseded in British service by Chieftain before the final round of improvements. These were left to foreign users and commercial interests, namely Israel, South Africa, Vickers Ltd and Teledyne Continental Inc.

One of the major drawbacks had always been the gas-oline engine, high on fuel consumption and low on time between maintenance tasks (particularly the air filters, which had to be cleaned two or three times a day in dusty con-ditions). The Israeli solution was to design a new powerpack, with the Teledyne Continental AVDS1790-2AC diesel engine driving through a modified Allison CD-850-6A auto-matic transmission. Since the new engine was air-cooled it did away with the radiators, but the hull had to be con-siderably modified to allow the new power pack to fit. The results were gratifying in terms of performance and ease of logistic support, since the bulk of powerpack spares were already used in M48A3, M60 and converted M47S.

Vickers Ltd designed a similar retrofit using the GM12V-71T turbo-charged diesel engine with a gross output of 720bhp, coupled to the Self-Changing Gears Ltd TN12 'hot shift' transmission, as used in Chieftain, with modified final drives. This resulted in an increased top speed and a 50% improvement in fuel consumption. The package was intended for modernising the 300 Centurions in Swiss service and included additional armour and a completely modernised fire control system, but only two prototypes were completed.

Apart from the power train, improvements have been incorporated in armament and fire control. The 105mm is almost universally mounted, though a few 20pdrs remained in Indian service until 1978. South Africa will have replaced all their 20pdrs with 105mm by now. Ammunition stowage has been improved and augmented, in the Israeli retrofit, to 72 rounds. Laser rangefinders have replaced RMGs and ballistic computers are a feature of most new fire control systems.

Centurion is still a potent MBT in front line service, but it has been by-passed and superseded by technological advances and by many new designs in an increasing number of producing countries. It was the embodiment and proof of the British concept of firepower, protection and mobility and had a premier place in the battlefield for three decades, but its extraordinary longevity was not apparent in the early 1950s, when the 20pdr needed the long range power of the 120mm to complete the defence system. The original

This rear view shows the modified engine louvres of the South African Olifant and the array of French type smoke pot throwers. The crew are wearing overalls with lifting straps across the shoulders, to facilitate removal of casualties. *H-R Heitman*

planned production of Centurion was due to stop in 1954, so there was every reason to plan for its successor.

Chieftain

The programme which eventually led to the Chieftain started at FVRDE at Chobham which carried out a study in 1951 which established certain criteria. A more powerful gun was obviously a priority, and 60 or more main armament rounds were to be carried. The weapon would be stabilised and have a 1,000yd night firing capability. A power/weight ratio of 20bhp/ton was desirable though the available engines could not provide this at the envisaged weight of 45 tons, or more. Protection was to be at least as good as Centurion, with special attention paid to attack by hollow charge weapons and mines.

As usual the requirements were all very much at odds and a number of unconventional ideas were studied to see if they could be of use. The 1950s saw the start of the 'all missile' theory, and it was proposed to replace the high velocity gun by guided weapons, but the bulk of the missile, compared with a gun round, and its long flight time, outweighed its long-range accuracy. A guided missile was far too expensive to use in the HE role against troops and soft targets. Nevertheless, even the American tube-launched Shillelagh was considered.

Mounting the gun externally would save volume under armour, as would the cleft turret,* while the fixed gun, as in the Swedish S-tank, was even more attractive an idea from that point of view. In fact such a layout was very seriously considered, as was the oscillating turret used by the French. Both concepts lend themselves to automatic loading, but neither found much favour.

In the end it was decided to adopt a 120mm gun, to give the versatility needed to fire a variety of rounds and a good

*See Fig 9 on p139.

The 40ton Centurion was a stage in the development of the Chieftain. Shortened by one roadwheel and provided with a sharpened turret profile, the 40ton vehicle provided much valuable data. *Author*

tank-killing capability at 3,000m range, which would probably be outside the range of the enemy tank. However a 120mm round of fixed ammunition would be a problem to store and to handle in the confines of a turret. The size of cartridge case to hold the propellant for a high velocity APDS round would be half empty when used for a medium velocity HE round, and would be very difficult to dispose of. Liquid propellant seemed an attractive proposition, but could not be made into a practical solution.

Semi-fixed ammunition was easier to handle than fully fixed, but took longer to load and still left the problem of disposal of cartridge cases. Combustible cartridge cases seemed to offer an answer, but they still needed a stub cartridge which had to be disposed of. The designers turned to the old naval system of bagged charges, which are no larger than the necessary bulk of propellant and have no useless weight penalty. However, the lack of cartridge case in itself produces the problem of obturation of the breech, while there was considerable fear that the bagged charge might be more vulnerable to attack and a serious fire hazard.

The problem of obturation was solved by using a metal ring on the sliding breechblock, which was expanded by the gas pressure in the chamber to seal the breech. The fire hazard was reduced by stowing the bagged charges in racks surrounded by a jacket holding water under pressure. Experiments showed that, on penetration, cooling water followed the projectile so closely that the incipient fire was quenched even before it began.

In order to reduce the height of the hull it was proposed that the driver should be in a reclining position when closed down. In order to prove the concept in 1956 Leyland Motors modified a Mk 7 Centurion by shortening the hull, dispensing with one set of roadwheels. The idler was mounted on the front of the leading Horstmann suspension casing. The normal driver's hatch was welded shut and new, centrally placed hatch provided, under which the driver sat in a semi-reclining attitude. Fully reclining was not necessary, since the depth of the hull remained the same, but it gave enough information for the reclining seat to be adopted.

The turret of the test rig, known as FV4202, or the '40ton

The Leyland L60 engine acquired a reputation for unreliability in the early years. The powerpacks included radiators which could be raised for access to the engine compartment, but there was always too much heat in the middle of the engine which could not be dissipated. Vibration was another major problem, which necessitated the use of adhesives on the inaccessible nuts and bolts at the bottom of the engine. *Leyland Motors*

Centurion', was given a well-angled and pointed nose and the 105mm gun mounted without a mantlet. This not only saved weight and reduced the out-of-balance of the turret, but improved protection and did away with the hazard of a mantlet jammed by a shot.

The hull itself was given a well-sloped cast glacis and roof, with slightly sloped side plates and a shallow V-shaped belly, this to reduce the effect of mine blast and also to give more vertical height in the engine compartment.

In 1957 it became NATO policy that all military vehicles should be capable of running on a wide range of fuels, making battlefield replenishment easier. Originally the tried and proven Meteor V-12 gasoline engine that had powered Cromwell, Comet and Centurion was considered for FV4201; then a new V-8 gasoline engine was proposed. But multi-fuel meant compression ignition (CI) and Leyland Motors were given a contract, in conjunction with FVRDE, to develop a multiple-fuel six-cylinder, 12-piston vertically opposed two-stroke engine. Similar to the German Junkers aircraft engine, the L60, as it was called, was a disaster from the start. It was rated at 760hp but early models only produced 585bhp and Leyland designers and engineers told FVRDE that they were lucky to get that. FVRDE insisted that the concept was the right one and anyway L60 was the only engine that would fit the hull. Even before it was installed in a prototype, cylinder liners cracked and the seals between liners and block failed. Most of these problems had their origins in poor dissipation of heat from the centre of the block. Unlike a conventional engine, in which the heat is produced at the end of a cylinder block, the opposed piston produces maximum heat in the middle of the block. This may have been acceptable in the low ambient temperatures of an aircraft engine, but in the conditions of a tank engine com-

partment it caused problems. Many remedies were applied and new materials tried, but the problems only seemed to get worse when installed in a tank. Vibrations caused massive oil leaks and air cleaners needed servicing two or three times a day. The vibration problem was ameliorated by fitting dampers to the two crankshafts, but the air cleaners were not modified until 1970.

Before that, a regiment on its first major exercise with Chieftain in Germany, suffered 90% casualties on the first day, due to engine faults. Leyland Motors sent a 'trouble shooter' out to visit the unit in the field and reported that lack of attention to the air cleaners was a major cause of the failures.

The L60 ran most easily on diesel fuel, but if it was fed kerosene or gasoline its output dropped noticeably. It was also noted for its ability to produce a thick, though unintentional, smokescreen which added to the problems of concealment in the field. Leyland engineers believed that the low MBTF (mean time between failures) of the L60 was due to attempts to get too much out of the engine. Certainly it seemed that the failure rate of the L60, when installed in the lighter (40tonne) Vickers MBT and operating at between 600-650bhp, was lower. Subsequently the L60 was run reliably in Chieftain at a regular 720bhp, though this power output proved too much for the characteristics of the suspension and too much for the TN12 transmission. All major modifications were completed by 1979 and most Chieftains in British service had been brought up to date.

The auxiliary generating set, which was powered by a Coventry Climax H30 engine of similar layout, with three cylinders and six opposed pistons, operated reasonably well. It was seldom overloaded, ran at constant speeds and did not suffer the same problems as the L60.

The transmission of the FV4201 Chieftain is the TN12, a development of Self-Changing Gears Ltd of the Merritt-Brown regenerative steering and transmission which had proved so successful in Centurion. In order to make life easier for the driver the new box was fully epicyclic, provided with a centrifugal clutch and operated by an electric gear shift. The almost instantaneous 'hot shift' change of ratio was a great advantage when going cross-country, since it eliminated the period of slowing down between gears, when a tank could lose so much of its momentum. But until the problems of selection were sorted out it was not uncommon to engage two gears at the same time, an expensive and irritating fault.

One of Chieftain's great advantages was the comfortable ride given by the improved Horstmann-type suspension. Although other ideas, such as torsion bars and hydro-pneumatic systems, had been suggested, none appeared to have any advantage over the Horstmann. Its workings are external and take up no valuable floor space in the hull. It is simple and, being completely outside the hull, even though it is open to mine blast, damage can be more easily repaired. During early troop trials in Germany it was found that Chieftain crews fared much better in cross-country going than their counterparts in Leopard. The latter had a great advantage in its power/weight ratio but could not use the extra agility without shaking the crew about violently. The same thing was noticed in competition against the American M60 during trials in Israel, when Chieftains arrived at firing points with, or even in front of, the M60s, and their crews in good condition.

The intention was to carry 60 rounds of main armament ammunition. Chieftain Mk 2 carried only 53, but subsequent improvements allow the Mk 5 to carry 64 rounds, of which 10 APDS projectiles are stowed externally. All the propellant

Top: Early Chieftain showing its paces at Chobham with the crew closed down; note the lack of skirting plates so that the spectators could see the extent of wheel movement. *AEC*

Above: The normal camouflage scheme for British tanks is the black disruptive pattern over a dark green overall finish. Fine for open country, but it stands out like a foreigner in the urban areas of West Berlin, where the British Army keep a squadron of MBTs. Major

Daukes of the 4th/7th Royal Dragoon Guards discovered this during his period of command of the Berlin Squadron, and studied the alternatives. After three months' experiments with vehicles and models, he found the rectangular pattern, in white, light grey and black, to give the best effect in built up areas. Of course, should the tanks have to go out of town, they would be easily identified. *4th/7th Royal Dragoon Guards*

charges are stowed in the hull, below the turret ring. The bulk of the ammunition load is made up of APDS and HESH, though other natures are available, including smoke, canister and illuminating. The APDS is fired at a m/v of 1,370m/sec and can penetrate all tanks with homogeneous armour at 3,000m and more. The other armour-defeating round, HESH, also doubles as HE. It is fired at 670m/sec and causes less than half the amount of barrel wear of APDS. The smoke round is of the bursting white phosphorous type, and is also a medium velocity round. Canister, which was 're-invented' after the mass attacks experienced in Korea, has a murderous effect at close ranges, like a sawn-off shotgun.

With separate ammunition it is necessary to ensure that the projectile is rammed firmly into the chamber, far enough to engage the rifling, so that the gas does not escape past the round. The first Chieftains had been provided with an electromechanical rammer, but on trials this suffered many defects and was eventually discarded. Despite the scepticism (and horror) of designers, gunnery experts and sundry other boffins, it was proved possible to ram the projectile with the propellant bagged charge without splitting it, though this practice is still frowned upon. The propellant is ignited by a small cartridge, called a vent tube, which is inserted into the rear of the breech and fired electrically. The vent tubes are kept in 10-round magazines and these have not been trouble-free, causing many stoppages and misfires, and many crews find it simpler to load the vent tubes by hand, though this can add a second or two to the loading time.

To utilise the lethal power of the 120mm L11 gun to full effect, Chieftain has superb gun control and fire control systems. The gun is stabilised in azimuth and elevation, with electronic power and servos. The tank commander and the gunner both have controls in traverse and elevation, with the commander having override control. The gunner also has manual controls, which are normally used only during maintenance or in extreme emergency.

The stabiliser has been a feature of British tanks since the Centurion came into service 35 years ago. Its main use is to enable the gunner to keep the gun pointing at, or very near, the target while on the move. A pair of rate gyros produce electrical signals proportional to the movement of the gun in traverse and elevation and these signals put power into the servos which move the gun and the turret relative to the hull. Since there has to be an error before there can be a correction, the major refinement of the system is in speeding the reaction of the servos in starting and stopping these movements. The latest stabiliser can hold the gun to within .5mil of the target when Chieftain is moving cross-country, so that there is the least possible delay in engaging the target when the tank comes to a halt. Firing on the move is possible, but not used often on point targets.

Chieftain is well provided with observation and target acquisition devices. The tank commander, in his cupola, a ring of nine static periscopes giving all round vision, each periscope being furnished with twin wipers. In front he has ×15 periscopic binocular sight for observation and target acquisition. Having sought and identified a target, the commander can lay his own sight then select 'contra-rotate' on the Cupola power control and, on pressing a button, bring the main armament to bear precisely on the target, whereupon he can hand over to the gunner and search for a new target.

In early Chieftains the gunner had a day-only periscopic sight with simple ballistic graticules for the APDS and HESH rounds and for the coaxial machine gun and RMG. This system, modified from Centurion, uses a .50in machine gun

similar to the .50 calibre Browning, mounted to the left of the main armament. The .50 calibre spotting round has a close ballistic match with the HESH round up to 2,500m (1,800m in the Mk 2), and shows a trace in flight and a flash on strike. The gunner fires a series of three-round bursts (there is a burst limiter built into the system) going from minus to plus of the target. The range at which the tracer hits or goes over the target is transferred to the main graticule and an armour defeating round fired. Although this seems to be a lengthy and chancy process, it has proved to be as quick as optical range-taking and, since the flight of the .50 round is affected by the same down-range conditions of wind as the main gun, gives an excellent chance of a first-round hit.

The availability of the laser range finder in the late 1960s and its incorporation into the gunner's sight gave a new dimension to fire control. Now, with both commander and gunner able to take ranges accurate to ±10m at all distances, and sensors able to provide information on wind strength and direction, temperature, humidity, charge temperature and trunnion cant, tank gunnery became more lethal than ever. This information could be put into a computer which would, by itself, make the necessary corrections to the aiming mark in the sight and monitor expenditure of ammunition. The only task left for the human eyeball was to align the aiming mark with the desired target and for the finger to fire as required. This comprehensive system, installed in later marks of Chieftain is known as the IFCS (integrated fire control system).

With the addition of night vision devices and thermal pointers, enabling targets to be engaged in darkness and through smoke, there seemed little more could be done with fire control. The gun had already been provided with a thermal jacket, to prevent wind or rain cooling one side of the tube more than another, so inducing a bend. The L11A5 model of the 120mm gun incorporates a muzzle reference system (MRS) — a small mirror attached to the muzzle to help the gunner calibrate his sight. He can align the sight with the axis of the bore without having to dismount from the turret and insert the muzzle boresight, so that even at night he can check the accuracy of the sights.

The latest guns are made from ESR (electro-slag refined) steel, a method of production which eliminates most of the impurities from the metal and enhances its tensile strength. This means more powerful propellants can be used to obtain a higher muzzle velocity.

Chieftain was the best MBT in service in the world in the 1970s and is still in the top class. Both Libya and Israel asked the British Government to sell them Chieftain, but both were turned down 'in the interests of peace', if not in the interest of thousands of workers in British defence industries. An order for Kuwait was accepted and 160 Mk 5/2 (K) were delivered: these differed from the ordinary

Top right: Chieftain's rifled 120mm L11 gun makes it still one of the most potent MBTs in the world. *MoD*

Middle right: The very good angles of the turret armour of Chieftain are shown to good advantage. In close country the commander and gunner must take great care to avoid damaging the 5.68m long barrel of the 120mm gun. *MoD*

Right: Chieftain on training in Germany, with Schloss Marienberg in the background. A Simfire gunfire simulator is mounted over the mantlet and the skirting plates have been left at home. The traffic lamp on the rear of the turret is to comply with German traffic regulations. *MoD*

Mk 5/2 in that the large searchlight on the left of the turret was deleted.

The major sale of Chieftain was to the Imperial Iranian Ground Forces. By the end of 1976 a total of 707 Chieftain Mk 5(P) (excluding the ARV and AVLB which had also been ordered) had been delivered and British-run training school and workshops set up in Shiraz. Iranian crews were trained and had attained a reasonable state of efficiency at the time of the Shah's downfall, whereat the Army went into a decline.

Before that, in 1974, the Shah had asked Britain to supply a further 1,200 tanks. But not standard Chieftains. There had been considerable acrimony between His Imperial Majesty and Sir Lester Suffield, Head of Defence Sales, on the subject of the output and reliability of the L60 engine. Sir Lester had promised the Shah that the remainder of his order of Chieftains would indeed produce the 750bhp mentioned in the brochure. The Shah asked for a new, more powerful engine, better shock absorbers and better belly armour against mines, but the new Rolls-Royce CV12 engine and TN37 gearbox from David Brown were not yet ready for the FV4030, as the improved Chieftain was designated.

The first delivery of the new order consisted of 187 tanks with improved mine protection and shock absorbers, larger fuel tanks and electronic control of the TN12 gearbox. These were to be followed by a delivery of 125 tanks named Shir Iran 1 (Lion of Iran) with the Rolls-Royce CV12 engine, and the remainder of the requirement would be fulfilled by Shir 2, with the new Chobham Armour and other improvements, including the tank laser sight (TLS), the IFCS and the Air-screw Howden cooling system, which reduces power losses to the fans. Although prototypes of both FV4030/2 (Shir 1) and FV4030/3 (Shir 2) were built, none were delivered before the contract was abrogated in 1979.

The Chieftains in Iranian service have given a good account of themselves in the Gulf War with Iraq, against Soviet T-55, T-62 and T-72 tanks. Although the Iraqis captured at least 200 Chieftains, which they put on show in Baghdad (along with 34 M60, 11 M47 and 10 Scorpions) this was largely due to defects of the crews rather than the tanks. The Iraqis have learned a healthy respect for the 120mm gun when properly fought. Many of the captured Chieftains have been refurbished with the object of putting them into service on the Iraqi side.

When the fall of the Shah cut short the work in the Royal Ordnance Factories, the MoD Defence Sales Organisation went to work to find other customers. The Jordanian Army ordered 278 vehicles which they named Khalid. This is basically the FV4030/2, for which most of the material had already been ordered for the Iran contract, with TLS and ICFS. Khalid has a fire control system with more modern components than those in current British service. The Pilkington Condor commander's sight is mounted on a No 15 cupola and gives the commander the facility to fire the main armament as accurately as the gunner with his Barr and Stroud TLS with neodymium-YAG laser rangefinder. The laser can be used by either commander or gunner, with readouts in the TLS and at the commander's station. The IFCS, combined with a new solid-state gun control system, gives Khalid a very high probability of a first round hit and makes a significant improvement to the striking power of the Jordanian Army.

MBT80

In the meantime the British Army had started planning for the replacement of Chieftain in the 1990s, by which time, it was felt, it would no longer be viable in the face of the latest Soviet MBTs. This was to be a new tank called MBT80, all British, not a collaborative design such as MBT-70, although consideration has been given to use of the American AGT1500 gas turbine power plant. On 13 September 1978 it was announced that MBT80, the British replacement for Chieftain, had entered the 'project definition phase'. This is the time when the outline of the design is firmed up and the major components are nearing the end of their development. It is the period during which the time frame for building prototypes, production and service life is established.

'Project definition will be based on a tank of conventional design carrying a four-man crew, protected by Chobham armour and mounting a British rifled bore 120mm gun.' This simple statement pointed the way British tanks would go for the next 20 years or more.

The conventional turreted tank was preferred to any of the fancy designs which have appeared. No S-Tank; no externally mounted main armament and no missile main armament. The additional height of a turret is acceptable when the advantage of being able to train the gun without shifting the whole vehicle is considered. Though many countries have gone to the use of automatic loaders, with the advantages of smaller turret volume, lower weight and elimination of the loader, MBT80 would retain the fourth crew member. He may or may not handle the ammunition (though that is the probability) but he will be a welcome figure when it comes to maintenance, refuelling, bombing up, cooking, sentry duty, etc on the 24-hour battlefield.

Protection of MBT80 took into account the improved performance of its attackers, so Chobham armour over as much as possible of the hull and turret is desirable. Probably the shallow V-shaped hull, with sloped sides, would be retained and skirt armour against infantry launched hollow charge weapons. Almost certainly the ammunition would be stowed below turret ring level, in the water-jacketed bins which have been successful in Chieftain.

Despite the pressures of standardisation and the professed advantages of the smoothbore, MBT80 would stick to the rifled gun which the British believe is more versatile and capable of more development. The target barrel life will be about 500 EFCs. It will have separate ammunition, with combustible cartridge cases, and the range of projectiles will include APFSDS with slipping driving bands and a similar HEAT round.

In July 1980 the Secretary of State for Defence announced that a new tank, called Challenger, would be ordered to supplement Chieftains in 1 BR Corps in Germany.

Left: An early Chieftain ARV 1.

Below: Challenger crossing a Medium Girder Bridge. The slab-sided effect of using Chobham armour is evident. Its use on the glacis means that the driver's side vision is restricted, even when head-out. *MoD*

He did not state, then, that MBT 80 had been abandoned, or at least shelved for the time being, but it is probable that work done so far on the MBT 80 project will be utilised in development and improvement of Challenger.

Challenger

FV4030/4 Challenger is constructed with integral Chobham armour over the frontal arc and is considerably heavier than its predecessors. It retains the low silhouette of Chieftain and the hull is approximately the same size. The turret appears to be set slightly further forward, but the driver can still drive 'head out'. The new driver's seat gives a better position when closed down and also allows the driver to be evacuated into the turret if necessary.

The engine is the Rolls-Royce 12V 1200 diesel, which was developed to replace the L60 in Shir Iran. With 1,200bhp output at 2,300rpm, the Condor almost doubles the power of the L60 and achieves about 20bhp/tonne. This is the highest power/weight for a British tank since the Cromwell at 21.8bhp/tonne. The engine is combined with a TN37 transmission and steering unit made by David Brown and a cooling system developed by Airscrew Howden to form a powerpack which can be quickly and simply lifted in and out of the hull. There is a separate H30 auxiliary generator with a capacity of 350A, but the main engine also drives a 500A generator. The huge electrical power requirements of a Modern MBT are catered for by six large batteries giving an output of 100A/hr per pair at 24V. The auxiliary unit is also installed as a powerpack which can be changed in about an hour without disturbing the main engine. The main powerpack can also be changed in about an hour and great attention has been given, in its design, to the ease of

accessibility to all items which have to be regularly inspected or exchanged. The powerpack can be placed on a trolley, developed by MVEE, on which it can be test run before installation in the hull.

Although the Khalid has a bogie suspension similar to that of Chieftain, Challenger is fitted with a completely new hydrogas suspension. Each wheel station has a completely separate suspension unit bolted to the hull and requiring no access to or space within the hull and an overall weight saving has been achieved. There are three top rollers, also separately bolted to the hull. The hydrogas type suspension allows greatly improved wheel travel, gives a better ride and allows faster acceleration, but it does require the unit to hold reserve supplies of nitrogen gas for topping up.

Challenger's main armament is an improved version (L11A5) of the 120mm guns in Chieftain. It incorporates a muzzle reference system, to help calibrate the IFCS, and fires the same range of ammunition. In addition it can fire the new types of APFSDS and HESH that have been developed by RARDE. There are conventional 7.62mm coaxial and commander's machine guns and the usual smoke grenade dischargers, with five barrels each side of the turret.

Challenger will be in service from the mid-1980s, probably into the next century. Although it came into existence almost by mistake, as a by-product of foreign sales, it continues the evolutionary development of the British MBT and will provide much useful data for the next stage.

USA

M26 Pershing

The USA ended WW2 with a new tank just entering service. During the war they, like the British, had concentrated on maintaining production of their existing tanks at the levels needed to win the battle. Like the British they had also learned many lessons in combat and had designed what they hoped would be the answer. The T26E3 first went into action in February 1945, before being standardised, in March, as the Heavy Tank M25 (this designation was changed to Medium Tank M26 in May 1946). It was named the General Pershing, after the WW1 general who had been responsible for the first American tank units.

Instead of the puny 75mm and 76mm guns of the M4 series, the M26 carried a 90mm which had been developed from an AA gun. It had thicker armour, a more powerful 500hp SAE engine and torsion bar suspension with six independent roadwheels and five return rollers each side. Naturally it was heavier, weighing 41 tons, and slower than the Sherman, but it had rear drive and a better ride.

M26 was a new design owing nothing to the M4, but derived via a series of experimental models, each of which contributed a step in the development programme. M26 retained the five-man crew, including the hull gunner, which had seemed necessary during the war.

The 90mm M3 gun, although it was a great improvement over the 76mm, had a disappointing performance, inferior to the German 88mm and even to the British 17pdr of 76.2mm calibre. Improvements were tried, using a longer barrel and more propellant, and there was also an alternative version with separate ammunition, but neither was ready before the end of the war. The M26A1 version had a gun tube with bore evacuator and a smaller muzzle brake with single baffle; some of these were fitted with stabilisation in elevation.

The Pershing became the main gun tank of American armoured units in the postwar period and served in the early

stages of the Korean War. It was not widely developed, one of the few variants standardised being the M45, which was the M26 with a 105mm howitzer mounted in the mantlet and used as a support weapon within armoured units. There were various SP artillery mounts and experimental vehicles using M26 chassis and components that appeared as a result of the common component concept. This was part of the US Army approach to improving standardisation and reliability. A series of engines, from single-cylinder charging sets to 16-cylinder tank powerplants, was to be built using only two sizes of cylinder and a majority of common parts. At the same time it was recommended that the mechanical and hydro-kinetic drives that had been developed to date should be replaced by a form of cross drive. A new Allison design combined regenerative steering and torque converter drive in a single unit controlled by a single 'wobble stick'. This made driver training easier and decreased fatigue in the field.

As part of this programme the M26 was fitted with the new Continental AV1790-3 petrol engine and the DC850 transmission and designated T40. In 1949 a programme was authorised to rebuild 800 Pershings to the new specification and at the end of the year, when 16 vehicles had been completed, the T40 was standardised as the M46 and named after General George Patton.

M46/M47 Patton

The M46 hull had few differences from its predecessor. There were minor modifications to the engine compartment louvres and the exhaust outlets were re-routed from the centre of the back plate to silencers on the track guards. The Track design was improved to give better traction and a small jockey roller was added to provide tension to the track on the short run between the rear roadwheel and the sprocket, with the object of preventing the track being thrown on tight turns. The turret of the M46 was also largely unchanged from the Pershing.

Despite the improved reliability of the new engine and transmission in the M46, it was obvious that many more improvements were necessary if American tanks were to match the performance of the British Centurion and the Russian T-54. A new medium tank requirement was agreed, to be in the 36ton weight bracket and with improved mobility and protection. The armament would be the same 90mm calibre, but a new high velocity design coupled to a cross-turret rangefinder. The T42 turret was long and narrow, with sloped cast sides leading to an overhanging bustle. The 60in base optical rangefinder was mounted above the gun and protruded each side in two small armoured 'ears' overlooking the 'pig's snout' mantlet. The length of the turret bustle was increased by the addition of an armoured box of similar cross section.

Below the long, lean turret was a long, lean hull with five roadwheels and three top rollers. The hull front was a well-shaped casting and the bow MG was eliminated, leaving room for more ammunition stowage. Production was authorised in 1950 and six pilot models approved. But in June 1950 the North Koreans attacked the South, and the USA was embroiled in the first United Nations war.

All available armour was sent out, including Shermans, Pershings and M46 Pattons. It was not good tank country and there were few chances for conventional tank action, but tanks were an important part of the forces engaged on the UN side, performing mainly as armoured outposts and pillboxes. In the early stages American losses were low, but in 1951 over 400 tanks were knocked out — mainly Shermans. There appeared to be two choices; they could revive

Right: The M26 Pershing was the main US gun tank in the postwar period and formed the basis for future American AFVs. *IWM*

Below: M47 of the Italian Army on training, bearing exercise markings. *Stato Maggiore dell'Esercito*

the M46, or they could accelerate work on the new T42. In fact they compromised and mounted the new turret of T42 on the old, reliable hull of the M46 an called it M47 putting it into production in July 1950.

They also took the opportunity to make numerous improvements. The glacis was given a better angle and the blower housing between the driver and hull gunner removed. It would have been possible to have eliminated the bow MG at this stage, as on the T42 but it remained, possibly as a reaction to the phenomenon of mass infantry in Korea. The number of return rollers was reduced to three each side, but the track-tensioning roller stayed.

By the time M47 went into production the AV1790 engine had been improved and the 5B model was installed. Being air-cooled, two large fans were mounted on top of the engine, which was coupled to the CD850-4 transmission to form a powerpack that could be removed as a single unit for maintenance or replacement. Control of the cross drive was by a single lever which had four positions; neutral, low, high and reverse. By moving the same lever to one side or the other, the appropriate steering took place. The lever (known sometimes as the 'wobble stick') was between driver and co-driver and available to each. The cross drive provided steering radii proportional to tank speed; the lower the speed the tighter the turn. The driver's other controls were foot and hand throttles and a brake. The change from the muscle power needed to steer and change gear on a Sherman must have been greatly appreciated. The torque converter drive also gave a smooth transfer of power and eliminated the clutch pedal.

The cast turret of the M47 is very distinctive. The long bustle tapers sharply from the centreline, where there are slight bulges in the otherwise smooth outline to accommodate the commander's cupola and the loader's hatch. The gun is carried low in the turret, so that a large silhouette side view is apparent when firing hull down, but this is partly compensated for by the narrow front aspect. The length of the bustle is augmented by the stowage box and there is a prominent blower housing on top of the bustle.

Traverse and elevation are either manual or hydraulic, giving very positive control and a full 360° traverse in only 10 seconds. The M47 was one of the first tanks to have a rangefinder and ballistic computer, which automatically put on the required super-elevation for the range taken. The commander's periscope was also connected to the rangefinder and the gun, and he has override controls so that he can aim and fire the gun. The gun is carried in a concentric recoil system, in place of the external cylinders of the earlier 90mm, and though there were several different types of blast deflectors (T-shaped, cylindrical or flared) all had the bore evacuator at the end of the barrel.

The M47 was produced too late to be of use in Korea, so the first units to be equipped with it were those of the US Army in Germany. Later, when the US Army began to get M48, the M47s were given to Germany and reserve units of the Bundeswehr were equipped with M47s until the late 1960s. In fact, since France, Italy, Belgium, Greece and Turkey also used M47 it could be considered almost a NATO standard tank. It was widely used, some 20 countries having it in service.

Apart from its use as a gun tank, the M47 put in a lot of time in many variants. It served as ARV, bridgelayer, CEV and flamethrower, and carried a number of devices and weapons for experimental purposes. The Germans, when they got M48 as their front line tank, used the M47 to test concepts and components for the Leopard. One such was to move the driver to the right side of the hull and to add extra

ammunition stowage in the space vacated, bringing the total up to 105 rounds of 90mm ammunition. The Italian firm of OTO-Melara modified the M47 to carry the British 105mm gun and many users tried to substitute their own engines for the Continental, sometimes having to rebuild the engine compartment and decks. In Germany many of the 90mm guns were eventually taken out of their turrets and mounted in the Jagdpanzer Kanone.

Although the M47 missed the battle in Korea, it served in three other important theatres, on both winning and losing sides. Pakistan deployed about 300 M47s against India in 1965, but they did not show up very well against the Centurions Mk 5 and Mk 7, armed with the 20pdr. In South Vietnam hardly any tanks were used properly and there was little chance for the M47 (or any other AFV) to have an influence on the outcome. But in the Middle East both Jordan and Israel used the M47. A large number of the Jordanian ones were trapped in the Nablus area in the campaign of 1967, when they changed owners.

The M47 is perhaps most remarkable for its longevity, although it was superseded in front line service within a few years of its debut. There are still some 300 M47s in the Spanish Army, which, having served long, arduous years in Spain's African territories, have been modified to bring the up to date. Chrysler Espana started this work in 1975. It involves stripping the hull down to its basic parts, moving the drive line to match the new Allison transmission, which is driven by a Teledyne Continental AVDS1790-2A diesel engine. The fuel tanks can now take 1,500 litres — nearly double the original capacity of an M47. The suspension is improved with M60 type shock absorbers and new tracks. Range has been increased to 600km and the reliability of the new M47 is said to be 1,000% better than the gasoline-engined model. In the turret the 90mm gun has been replaced by the British 105mm L7 gun and a Cadillac Gage gun control system, incorporating stabilisation, has been fitted. With the addition of laser rangefinding and passive night fighting equipment, the M47E is capable of taking on most modern MBTs. However, the level of armour protection has not been improved, so the modernised vehicle cannot be described as a first rate tank in modern terms.

In fact, although the M47 has lasted a long time, it was being criticised even before it went into production. The US Army was not happy at the small amount of fuel carried under armour, nor with the armour round it. The turret, designed for the lighter T42, was also suspect. Even at that early stage, doubts were being expressed about the ability of the average soldier with good eyesight to use the steroscopic rangefinder.

In 1951 the USA had attended a Tripartite Conference on Armour, together with Britain and Canada, at which the basic characteristics of future tanks were agreed: weight 40 tonnes; height 2.945m; ground clearance 0.432m; speed 45kph. With these ideas in mind the Detroit Arsenal design team began to look at what could be done to improve M47. They wanted better protection, more punch in the gun and fire control systems and longer operational range, combined with the overall reliability that had been characteristic of the M46 and M47.

Their labours were rewarded when, in December 1950, the Chrysler Corp, which ran the Detroit Arsenal on behalf of the US Government, was given a contract to build the tank, 90mm gun, T48. They created a new plant at Newark, Delaware and rushed through the construction of the first six prototypes by the end of 1951, as per contract. Tests of these showed many defects and a lack of reliability that should have given a clear warning that all was not well.

OTO-Melara modified an M47 with the AVDS-1790-2A diesel engine and the British 105mm gun for overseas sales. In this tank the cross-turret optical rangefinder was retained. *OTO-Melara*

However, military and political pressures connected with the Korean war prevailed and orders were placed for production, even while the first vehicles were under trial.

Chrysler Corp, the Fisher Body Division of General Motors and the Ford Motor Company all received contracts for a total order of 1,348 tanks. These deliveries started in April 1952 and were completed in 1956 but it was to prove a costly mistake. The M48 was standardised in May 1953, just about the time that the war for which they were intended ground to a halt.

M48 Patton

The M48 was named Patton, by the widow of the late General, in July 1952, when the tank was first shown in public. This was to cause much confusion later, when both M47 Pattons and M48 Pattons were involved in the same actions, and possibly was the reason why the Americans have preferred to use the standard designations rather than the name of a tank. (This seems to apply to the latest MBT as well. No-one calls it the 'Abrams', just M1.)

The new design had several significant improvements over the M47. It weighed some five tonnes less and stood 11cm lower, but was 20cm wider owing to the greater width of the tracks. This gave a 29% reduction in ground pressure. The engine, transmission and suspension were the same as in the M47, but the power-weight ratio went up to 13% and the maximum speed rose by 3kph. The M48 had a one-piece cast hull of ellipsoid shape which promised good ballistic protection. For some reason the fuel capacity was reduced by 69 litres in the M48, despite the already low range of the M47. Fuel under armour gave the M48 the very poor range of only 112km, less even than the early marks of Centurion, and only half of the range agreed at the Tripartite Conference.

Apart from a longer based optical rangefinder and a quicker method of changing the gun barrel, there was no important change in the armament. It is interesting to

remember that the T-54, with its 100mm gun, had been seen in 1949. However, one important feature of the design which had no immediate significance, but which permitted upgunning later on, was the increase in size of the turret ring. Only 1.75m in diameter on the M47, the 2.16m ring of M48 allowed the easy installation of the British 105mm gun in the M48A5.

The cast turret was curved in all planes and presented a good ballistic profile. The long bustle of the M47 turret was merged into a smoothly curved shaped with a slight undercut to clear the engine deck louvres. In front the 90mm gun protruded through an almost square mantlet, 4.5in thick with the .30cal coaxial MG on the left and nearly all M48s have the T-shaped blast deflector.

The T46 rangefinder was of 2m base, instead of the 1.52m of the M47, and was set further back, neatly in front of the commander's cupola and easy for him to use, the two 'ears' showing almost at the roof line. These 'ears' had to be kept clear at all times, and this inhibited the use of camouflage and prevented the crew hanging their kit above a certain level. In fact, two sets of rails were welded on the turret sides for kit and stowage basket fixed round the rear of the bustle.

The decision to install a stereoscopic rangefinder caused many problems and much controversy. They are clumsy pieces of equipment when compared with a LRF, but in the early 1950s there was little choice. It took up a lot of room in the turret, and if it was jarred it could give false readings without the crew knowing. But the main problem was that not everyone has stereoscopic vision. This alone caused great difficulty in training and eventually many crews disconnected the device, preferring to rely on the trained eye of the commander. The original 'stereo' rangefinder was later replaced by a coincidence type, which was easier to use. The optical rangefinder becomes less accurate as the range increases, so while it gave greatest accuracy at the distances which are easiest for the naked eye to judge, it is less useful at the longer ranges when the shell trajectory is highest and needs the most accuracy. An advantage of the system as installed in M48 was that the range information was fed mechanically into a simple mechanical ballistic computer

Above and right: German M48s: note training device on barrel, German style searchlight and smoke dischargers.
Both: Ranier Karras

and combined with data on ammunition and other ballistic corrections put in manually by the gunner. The result was transmitted to the sight and automatically put on the required super-elevation angle. The position of the rangefinder in the M47 had been convenient for the gunner to operate, but its new station on M48 brought the responsibility for ranging back to the commander. This meant that he had his eye glued to the rangefinder instead of observing the strike of the round.

Although in the early models of M48 the commander's cupola was a simple device similar to that on the later Shermans, it was replaced by a sub-turret, mounting a .50cal Browning MG with 200 rounds of ammunition. The cupola was of clamshell shape with a hinged (later models pivoted) door at the rear. The commander had a periscopic gun sight and five periscopes giving a limited all round view. It also meant that if the commander wanted to observe head out he had to be even higher than with the earlier type of cupola. The vision from the M1 cupola was so poor that, in the M48A3, after experience in Vietnam, a 'vision riser' was inserted between turret roof and cupola. This consisted of an armoured ring containing eight vision blocks, and added about 25cm to the height of the tank. Most foreign users of M48 have dispensed with the M1 cupola and prefer a simpler device with an externally mounted MG for the commander.

As originally designed, the M48 could stow 60 rounds for the 90mm gun. This was 11 rounds less than the M47, and did not endear the M48 to its crew. 90mm ammunition is long and heavy, and not easy to handle in the confines of a turret, so the more ample lines of the M48 turret improved matters slightly. Six natures of ammunition were available, with improved performance and all were stowed below the turret ring.

The driver of the M48 sits in the centre of the hull, behind a glacis of 110mm armour. The driving controls have been modified from the 'wobble stick' to a sort of oblong steering wheel, with the range selector control on the righthand side of the wheel. The shift is controlled by a lever, with a spring-loaded gate for reverse. The space either side of the driver is occupied by ammunition stowage.

The torsion bar suspension is virtually the same as on M47, but the number of return rollers went back to five. The

track tensioning idler between the rear roadwheel and the sprocket was retained until 1959 when it was dropped on M48A2s. Track was the usual American type of double pin with end connectors; there were both rubber-padded and steel blocks available.

Right from the start M48 was ripe for modification. The designation M48A1 was given to one of the initial versions of the M48, with the larger driver's hatch and M1 commander's cupola, and the M48A1 became the first standard production model of which 1,800 were issued to the US Army. All told some 11,000 M48 tanks were produced, plus several hundred variants.

The M48A2 incorporated five major changes. The engine compartment was redesigned to allow a 50% increase in fuel capacity under armour, which brought the range up to a more useful 256km. At the same time the exhaust system was changed to run under the engine decks and vent through the louvred doors at the rear of the hull, with the cooling air. This helped reduce the excessive IR signature which was a disturbing characteristic of the M48A1. The Honeywell hydraulic gun control system was replaced by the Cadillac Gage type which has been in all subsequent American tanks. Ammunition stowage was increased to 64 rounds and the number of return rollers was cut to three.

There is much argument between the proponents of the electro-hydraulic and the electric systems of gun control. The hydraulic system has the advantage of slightly quicker and more positive action, but it requires the use of oil at over 2,000lb/sq in. The system must, therefore, be strong enough to withstand such pressures and incorporate filtration to a very fine degree to avoid damage to the valves. Any leak, whether accidental or caused by enemy action, is likely to result in a jet or spray of highly volatile oil at very high temperature, 90°C. The spray alone can injure, but it is a very serious fire hazard and was the cause of a number of casualties (both tank and crew) in the 1973 Yom Kippur War. The electrical system is inherently safer and easier to install, since wires are simpler to run than high-pressure pipes.

There was no lack of realisation that the M47 and M48 were outclassed in many respects by the Russian T-54/55. A series of experiments and developments had taken place; the M103 heavy tank with a 120mm gun was developed in parallel with the M48. Many variations of armament and fire control components were tried out in the T54 (not to be confused with the Russian tank) and the T95 programmes. In the former a 105mm gun was mounted in an oscillating turret with automatic loader while in the T54E2 the same gun was put into a conventional turret of very good shape, presaging the needle-nose effect of Chieftain and Merkava. These experiments were put on to M48 hulls, with little or no modification to the power train and running gear. A follow-up programme on the T77 was similarly carried on M48 hulls but mounted a 120mm gun. None of these experiments went further than a few pilot vehicles.

The T95 never reached production either, but provided invaluable information on a very wide range of components and techniques which were tried out in the course of the T95 programme. 90mm, 105mm, 120mm and even the 152mm Shillelagh gun/missile system were mounted. The running gear went back to the large roadwheel, and looked rather like that of the Cromwell, using torsion bars. One hull was fitted with a hydraulic suspension, allowing control of the hull attitude.

Despite all the very useful data acquired during these programmes, there was no new tank anywhere near ready for production. The army was still far from pleased with the M47 and M48. It was decided to incorporate as many improvements as possible in the M48 basic hull and turret, both as straight development of the series and as a potential successor to M48. The new tank was called XM60, and it would mount the 105mm gun on a hull powered by a diesel engine.

Meanwhile the M48 itself was improved. A diesel version of the AVDS1790 engine had already been tried in an M48 and a further series of six hulls were modified to take the Continental ADVS1790-2, for which the engine compartment had to be modified. The standardisation of this conversion as M48A3 took place only in 1963, and the vehicles were all converted from older models. At the same time other improvements were added to the fire control system, using items developed for the XM60, including IR

night sights. A NBC filter system was introduced, not to clean the whole of the air inside the hull, but piping filtered air to an individual mask for each crew member. The main advantage of the M48A3 was the increased range of nearly 500km with fuel under armour.

The M48A3 was the main tank used in Vietnam, and as such was subject to a great deal of local modification. Apart from the vision riser previously mentioned, many were fitted with improvised shields and machine gun mountings, and a large number were modified to carry a full width dozer blade on the front of the hull for 'jungle busting'.

The latest (and presumably the last) models of the M48 came about as a side effect of the failures and delays in the development programmes of its successors. The M48A4 was to carry the 105mm gun and fire control equipment of the M60 on a hull modified to take the AVDS1790-2 engine. It fact, there would be a quantity of surplus M60 turrets complete with gun and fire control system available, which had been removed from M60s modified to take the Shillelagh, and these were to be merely exchanged for the existing turret. But events overtook the M48A4 and it never went into production.

The lack of tanks was so acute that it was decided to bring as many M48 as possible up to the standard of the M60. Instead of the piecemeal improvement by stages, one or two components at a time, a major programme was initiated covering all parts of the vehicle to make the M48A5, with 105mm gun, diesel engine, the latest gun control and fire control systems. Apart from the shape of the hull front, it is difficult to differentiate at a glance between the M60 and M48A5.

M48 has been the basis for the usual variants. The AVLB could span a 19m gap with a scissors type bridge. A flamethrower version, the M67A2, was used in Vietnam and is still in service with the USMC. Although its hull had different dimensions from the M48, the major components of M88 recovery vehicle are derived from the M48. Dozer blade attachments and various mine-clearing roller devices have been used with M48 and outdated chassis never seem to die in the US Army, but turn up again in new roles. The most recent use is as the basis for the mobile AA defence system for armoured units, with twin Bofors 40mm guns.

Nor have the US Army been the only one to modify M48.

Above: Sergeant York, the twin 40mm Bofors AA tank to fill the Divisional Air Defence role. Both search and tracking radar arrays are erected. British type smoke grenade dischargers are fitted. The hull is a modified M48. *Ford Aerospace*

Right: M60 crosses a floating bridge. *US Army*

Some 6,000 served in other forces, many of which have carried out their own improvements, while commercial modifications are even more numerous. The two most common improvements are replacement of the gasoline engine and up-gunning with the British 105mm gun. The German company Rheinmetall have designed installations for both the 105mm and 120mm versions of their smoothbore gun, but it is not known whether any of this modification have been built. Oerlikon proposed an AA defence version using the Gepard twin 35mm turret on M48, but none were made.

Another lucrative commercial field is the up-rating of fire and gun control systems. France, Germany, Italy and Britain have all offered modern equipments with LRFs, ballistic computers, passive and thermal imaging night sights and numerous sensors. The cost of such an exercise can vary according to the sophistication required, between £50,000 and £100,000, while engine changes and new gun can double the cost. It is, however, still well below the cost of a new MBT, and the latest M48 brought up to the standard of M48A5 or M60 is still a useful front line tank.

M60

As we have seen it is hard to distinguish between the later M48s and the M60 which followed it, so blurred is the dividing line in their development. M60 is very much an evolutionary design, descending in a direct line from the M26; engine — turret — hull — engine — gun, it went one or two components at a time. This meant that there was a useful continuity of training and parts, particularly when the retrofit programmes and up-rating took place. But the reason for this small advantage was a serious breakdown in the development of new tanks, and the battlefield capability of the US Army remained almost static when compared to that of its allies, and more seriously, to its enemies. A great deal of money was expended on seeking the answers. The experimental T42, T54, T95 and MBT70 all were believed at the

time of their inception to be the correct thing for the next generation of tanks. The cost of these programmes probably runs to £100,000,000, but they did produce a tremendous amount of useful information and stimulated ideas.

Looked at in this way, the M60 was a comparatively cheap development. In 1960 the first 180 tanks were ordered and sent for unit trials. When these proved successful another order was placed for 720. The M60, with the 105mm gun and AVDS1790 diesel engine, was about the equal of the Leopard 1 and AMX30, though it lacked the punch and range of the British Chieftain. When compared with its opponents, however, it towered almost one metre higher than the Russian T-54, weighed 14 tonnes more and has nearly 10% less power per tonne.

M60 was much more comfortable for the crew; the loader could use his right arm; the driver had a form of handlebar steering and a simple four-position shift lever to control his fully automatic transmission. However, the early M60 still had the simple mechanical ballistic computer, which was not changed for the electronic type until the M60A1. In this version the gunner had built in night vision devices and LRF. Finally, in 1968, money was found and AOS (Add-on-Stabilisation) was allowed. This was followed in 1972-75 by a programme to modernise existing M60A1s. A wider, rubber-padded track was fitted, with tube-over bar torsion bars and rotary shock absorbers. The AVDS1790 engine had been put through a reliability programme and came out with a nominal 900hp. In the turret a new solid state computer and LRF became standard. This model became the M60A3.

In 1982 the M60A3 was the most advanced American tank in front line service. Fire control was improved by the addition of a ruby LRF and the ballistic computer was modernised to solid state electronic. The coincidence rangefinder was removed and the LRF is fitted in place of the right-hand optic. From 1979 all new M60A3s were fitted with a thermal imaging sight in place of the passive image intensifier, and retrofit programme will bring all FCs up to the same standard. The cupola is still the M19, fitted with the usual .50cal machine gun.

The 105mm gun has been given a thermal sleeve, and M60A3s are fitted with the British type smoke grenade dischargers, made under licence in the USA as the M239. At the same time, there is a new round in the 105mm armoury, which enhances the overall performance of the system. This is the M735A1 round which uses a penetrator of depleted uranium (DU), the densest material available. This, together with the improved FCS is believed to give the M60A3 a significant advantage in kill probability over previous American tanks and certainly over the Soviet T-62.

Long before the M60A3 programme, another saga had started to unfold. With the realisation that the 90mm gun was no match for the T-54/55 and its successor, much thought was given to what was the most effective system to kill enemy armour at the long ranges that were desirable for the survival of American tanks and crews. It was the age of the missile and everyone was developing their own ideas for anti-tank guide weapons (ATGW). The Americans looked at the other attempts and decided that they would have a larger warhead fired at longer ranges and that a wireless command link was preferable to trailing wires. In 1958 the Aeroneutronics Division of Philco-Ford Corporation started development of Shillelagh.

Shillelagh was designated for use in a reconnaissance tank, but the tank also had to carry a weapon to deal with soft targets and meant that only a few missiles could be carried in the vehicle.

The Shillelagh missile weighs 27kg and is over a metre (1,140mm) long, which makes it very difficult to handle in the turret. It has a hollow charge warhead and a single stage solid fuel rocket motor and flies at medium velocity to a maximum range of 3,000m, guided by an IR command link. It is powerful enough to kill most MBT targets that are not protected by special armour, but it has the disadvantage that the IR command link is easily picked up and the firing point identified, while spurious IR sources, of which there are many on a battlefield, can seriously affect the guidance system. The gunner has to guide the Shillelagh all the way to the target (14sec to 3,000m) and the turret is exposed all this time.

The conventional round is the same size as the missile and is as heavy. In order to obviate the problem of disposal of the huge cartridge cases, the round was designed with caseless combustible propellant charges. These were the source of much trouble. The material proved to be hygroscopic (absorbed water) and they were fragile. When fired they left smouldering residue in the chamber which could ignite the next round. The gun was, therefore, fitted with a scavenging device which blew jets of air down the tube from the open breech. It was almost as dangerous, as the burning material sometimes got blown back into the turret, where the loader was ready with the next round in his arms and a closed breech scavenger was more acceptable. The problem of moisture was solved by keeping the rounds in nylon bags, but stripping these off caused a reduction in the rate of fire. The breech is closed by means of a crank, and only four to five rounds a minute are feasible.

Work started on the M60A2, mounting the Shillelagh as main armament, in 1964, but owing to the deficiencies in the weapon system, did not become operational until 1974 after a great deal of acrimony at Government level and the expenditure of much money in attempts to rectify faults. A new turret was designed specially for the system.

At each side there was a low profile segment in which

was placed an entry hatch for the crew-gunner on the right, loader to the left of the gun. Down the middle of the turret ran a 'spine' of square section, in which the gun was mounted, quite far forward. This, by itself, produced a fairly low silhouette, with a narrow front view. The gunner's periscope was necessarily low down on the right-hand segment, so there has to be a complicated aiming system containing eight prisms, 10 mirrors and 16 lenses to connect him to the main armament. But on top of the turret has been mounted the commander's cupola, centrally, at the rear, giving him a superb view of the surrounding countryside and raising him like a target on a range. The M60A2, is 3.3m high, and was described by an American tanker as 'towering like Godzilla over the battlefield'.

The cupola is stabilised so that the commander can take full advantage of the target acquisition facility which enabled him to line up on a second target while the gunner is still engaging the first. The commander can also carry on his own engagement with the 12.7mm machine gun mounted in the cupola, though, at the ranges at which the machine gun would be effective, he might be better employed keeping his head down and commanding his tank.

The M60A2 turret is stabilised in both axes by an electro-hydraulic system connected to the ballistic computer. The first batch of 300 turrets ordered in 1967 were kept in store for three years — as were the 243 turrets ordered to modernise existing M60A1s — because they did not match up to the reliability required. The problem lay with the stabilisation system, mainly with the hydraulics. The slightest bit of dirt in the fluid could jam a valve open or shut, so there had to be a very fine (down to four microns) filtration and the high pressure, of over 3,000lb/sq in, found every possible leak. Eventually it was decided that the system had been sufficiently improved to bring the tank into service and it was standardised as M60A2; the first battalion was worked up at Fort Hood in 1973 and went operational in the following year.

It really did not matter whether the M60A2 had stabilisation or not. By reason of its type of main armament, it was destined to be a static firing weapon system. The large conventional round was fired at a low muzzle velocity which required a high accuracy in range-taking to obtain a hit on a point target, so it was best suited to large area targets, unlikely to be engaged on the move. For missile firing the tank must remain halted during the time of flight so that the gunner can guide the Shillelagh all the way.

The Americans claimed that the power of the heavy warhead and the range of the missile gave the Shillelagh system in the M60A2 a significant advantage in the long range battle of attrition which, it was hoped, would take out a large proportion of the attacking enemy forces on the NATO front. While the M60A2 was being brought up to an acceptable level of reliability, the 120mm gun of Chieftain was showing that it did not require a large and expensive missile to hit tanks at around 3,000m range. By this time, however, so much time and money had been spent on the gun/missile system that it could not easily be abandoned. Back in 1963, when the faults of the system were still largely unknown, it was agreed between Germany and America that there would be a joint development programme to produce the Main Battle Tank for the 70s (MBT70), which would incorporate all the most advanced technology so as to make it a viable weapon well in to the 1990s. Germany was unhappy about the gun/missile concept and continued with the development of the 120mm gun which was their answer to the problem.

MBT70

The Americans acknowledged that there were faults in the Shillelagh and made a number of improvements. The new XM150 gun/launcher had a longer barrel which enabled it to fire high velocity armour piercing shot. An APFSDS round was developed for the MBT70, but this meant strengthening the recoil system. The size and weight of the conventional rounds was far greater than necessary for the performance required to attain the tank-killing capability, and few could be carried. The disadvantages of the missile remained; it could not satisfactorily be fired on the move, it took a long time to reach its target, reducing the effective rate of fire and it needed to be flown all the way, in contrast to the 'fire and forget' normal round.

The MBT70 was unconventional in more than its armament. It looked normal, with good, clean lines, but it had all three of its crew members in the turret, so that they could be more easily protected against nuclear explosions. The commander and gunner had more or less conventional environments, and the loader was replaced by an automatic loader. But having the driver in the turret produced problems. So that he would always be facing the direction of travel the driver sat in a contra-rotating capsule. All the controls had to be taken from this rotating unit through another rotating unit (the turret) to the stationary power pack. Although the driver remained facing the same direction while the turret traversed, he travelled on an arc relative to the hull and could never get the 'feel' of the vehicle.

Among the other advanced component, MBT70 had an adjustable, hydraulically controlled suspension which could alter the attitude of the hull and raise or lower it over a 610mm range. The powerplant produced more than any other tank engine to date; the American prototypes had a Teledyne Continental AVCR-1100 with variable compression ratio pistons which developed 1,475bhp; the German vehicles had a Daimler-Benz MB-873 diesel giving 1,500bhp. Since the driver could face front or rear as required the fully automatic transmission permitted the same 70kph in both directions. It was a very agile tank, but its cross-country ride was not up to expectations and crews suffered on the trials.

MBT70 must rate as one of the most expensive tanks on record. It had been estimated that a total of some $80million would pay for the development programme and the 12 prototypes, six from each country.

By the time the prototypes were built the development cost had reached more than $300million and there was much more work to be done. Estimates for the cost of production vehicles had risen from $600,000 in 1967 to over a million by 1970. The Germans could not face such costs and had, in any case, lost interest in the American dominated project. They pulled out and returned to their own line of development.

By 1968 the American Congress had become very alarmed at the rate of cost escalation and demanded that the Army reduce the specification so that production tanks would cost little more than half a million ($585,000) dollars. The Army cancelled MBT70 in all its glory and started work on the 'austere' version called XM803. Troubles with the engine and the weapon system continued and the estimated price of even the emasculated XM803 could not be brought within the limits set by Congress, which refused to fund further work in 1971. The project was killed off and used as a study for a new future MBT.

M1

The Americans now had two options. They could by a foreign tank (or make one under licence in the USA) or they could spend another, even larger, sum of money on a new design. They chose the latter course. It would, thanks to the knowledge gained on the MBT70 and XM803, not be back to the drawing board at square one. And national pride, not to mention the power of the arms industry lobby, would never let them buy overseas.

That is not to say that they were not prepared to take ideas from their allies. Details of Britain's Chobham Armour had been handed over under an old agreement, and there were numerous American officers in Germany who had the highest opinions of the engine and gun of Leopard 2.

The story of the M1 is full of hopes fulfilled and unrealised, errors of judgement, accusations and double crosses, all to the background murmur of accountants and their adding machines. XM1 is a tank designed to be designed to a strict cost schedule. It may help to have a chronology to refer to along the way.

1970 Jan Department of Defense announces cancellation of joint US/German development of MBT-70. The US goes ahead with an austerity version, the XM-803.

1971 Dec Congress stops the project on grounds of cost, then reaching $635,000 each, and rising.

1972 Feb US Army sets up MBTTF (Main Battle Tank Task Force) at the Armor School, Fort Knox, Kentucky.

Aug MBTTF publishes Material Need document stating the users' requirements for the new tank.

Sept XM1 Project Managers office set up in Warren, Michigan, with a brief to set up a refining and cost reduction programme.

1973 Jan Final programme approved by Army and Dept of Defense. Within eight years a new MBT is to be in service at a cost of not more than $570,790 each for 3,312 tanks. This odd figure is accounted for by the supply from Government sources of equipment worth $570,790.

June Validation contracts awarded to Chrysler and General Motors.

Oct The Arab-Israeli war causes a rethink on some aspects and a Tank Special Study Group is set up. They recommend design changes in range of engagement, ammunition stowage, improved bustle protection and changing the coaxial secondary armament from the 25mm Bushmaster cannon, with which many problems had been experienced in development, to a simple 7.62mm MG.

1974 Dec Memorandum of Understanding on Tank Development is signed by the USA and Germany. The USA agrees to evaluate a modified 'austere' version of the German Leopard 2 against the winning prototype of the XM-1 competition.

1975 A series of trials of various NATO tank guns was held. Guns tested were the German 120mm smoothbore, the British 110mm (a new design under development but showing great potential), and the British 105mm as made under licence in the USA and fitted on M60.

1976 Feb Prototypes delivered to the Army for trials.

July Full Scale Engineering Development phase postponed; the two contractors are told to try to get more commonality with the Leopard 2.

But, also in July, a Letter of Understanding was signed by the USA and the UK, confirming the selection of the 105mm gun as main armament for the first production XM1, but also stating that a 120mm gun was the long term aim and that collaborative tests would continue.

Aug An Addendum to the US/FRG Memorandum gives priority to the standardisation of components. Congress are alarmed at the delays, fearing increased costs and reduced combat effectiveness.

Sept Congress Armed Services Committee states '. . . XM1 program must take precedence over secondary objectives such as standardisation or interoperability of components'. A comparative evaluation of Leopard 2 with XM1, using the M60A1 as base standard for both, completed in December, but the results of the trials are kept secret. (They still are.)

Nov The Chrysler version of XM1 is selected for production. A total of 3,312 tanks is authorised, with the first full production vehicle to be delivered by 1 May 1981.

1977 Jan It is announced that the competition between the XM1 and Leopard is over, but that evaluation of Leopard components would continue.

1978 Jan The US Army recommends development and testing of the German 120mm gun as the future main armament of XM1.

1979 April GAO (General Accounting Office) recommends that procurement should be limited until problems with the gas turbine engine are ironed out, and, significantly, that a back-up programme should be started at once to continue development of the diesel engine which powered the unsuccessful General Motors version.

May The Secretary for Defence gives qualified approval for the first production batch of 110 tanks, despite shortcomings in the pilot batch.

A total of 7,058 tanks is called for, at a cost of at least $10,900,000,000.

1980 Jan GAO reports to Congress 'XM1' making steady progress but 'doubts still remain about its turbine engine in view of the alarming number of losses in power . . .'

Feb The first production tank comes off the line at the US Army facility at Lima, Ohio.

The M1 is a tank of conventional layout, with advanced armour and fire control systems, novel in only one respect — powerplant. It is in this area, and that of main armament, that most of the controversy has taken place. A major objective of the design was to make significant improvement in RAM-D (Reliability, Availability, Maintainability-Durability) and under the financial constraints which they had laid upon them by a Treasury wary of another MBT70 disaster, the Army sought economies in LCC (life cycle cost).

Chrysler's approach to this problem was to use new technology where such use would result in longer time between overhauls (TBO), less time spent on maintenance and longer overall life of components. It was a bold decision

Above: The General Motors contender for the XM1 contract, powered by a 1,500hp Teledyne Continental Diesel engine. *General Motors Detroit Diesel*

Right: M1 Abrams seen during a Reforger exercise in Germany. Note the two turret-mounted MGs and training gunfire simulator on the barrel. *US Army*

Below: M1 Abrams during the 1983 Canadian Army Trophy. In its first attempt at the competition, the Abrams performed effectively and finished second to a German Leopard 1 battalion. *Martin Horseman*

to choose the AVCO AGT-1500 gas turbine, particularly as the use and TBO data on which they based their calculations was derived from turbines in helicopter service. The TBO of the turbine was predicted to be three times that of a diesel of comparable output. It has 30% fewer parts than the AVCR variable compression piston diesel, and runs on a wide range of fuels without much power loss, thus improving flexibility. A turbine takes little power for fan cooling; the AVCR-1360-2 diesel requires some 160hp to drive the cooling fans, leaving the turbine over 100hp advantage, used to drive the tank.

A gas turbine starts more easily in cold temperatures and does not suffer the power losses of a diesel. It is generally quieter, once it has wound up, and produces less exhaust smoke. The turbine itself is smaller than a comparable diesel, and nearly a tonne lighter. In the event of a breakdown the modular engine concept means that only the unserviceable module need be changed, reducing the need for spare engines to be held in units. A division having 324 tanks would, it is claimed, need to hold only six spare engines as opposed to 15 diesels. The LCC saving for a fleet of 3,300 tanks over a 20-year period has been calculated at over $72million (*IDR* 3/77). The powerpack of M1 can be removed and replaced in one hour, compared with four hours for the M60.

All these advantages have to be paid for, and the first major problem is that the turbine uses roughly double the fuel of a comparable diesel engine over a normal battle day of mixed running. The volume saved by having a turbine is therefore used up by the extra fuel tankage. The extra cost of the turbine, over that of a diesel, is said to be saved on RAM-D and LCC costs. These claims were not fully borne out in trials, and it was hinted (by GM) that the Chrysler figures for economy and down time were extrapolated from data of helicopter service, and that things were different in the enclosed hull of a tank, in a dusty atmosphere and under varying load conditions (cf the opposed piston configuration of L60 in Chieftain). GM had been a supplier of aircraft gas turbines for years 'so we know a lot about gas turbines', but for the M1 'we had to consider their state of development'. Chrysler, on the other hand, said 'We feel that the diesel is nearing the end of its life cycle development'.

Engine performance caused great concern during trials and development testing. The air filtration system revealed excessive ingestion of dirt, leading to erosion of turbine blades. ('We told you so', said GM). Fort Knox mobility trials had shown only 129.5 MMBF (mean miles between failures) which caused the turbine school to reassess the trials to give 145MMBF. Neither figure approached the 272MMBF which the Secretary of Defense had made a condition of production. A special panel of independent experts convened in 1979 reported that the turbines' level of durability and reliability were so low that, even if they were doubled they would still be short of the requirements.

However, the same panel, reconvened in December 1979, reported that reliability of the XM1 now exceeded both threshold and requirement, with 306MMBF. They still recommended a number of modifications and improvements, and also that the engine be regarded as a government furnished equipment 'to ensure that adequate resources be applied to the engine maturation'. In other words, Chrysler wanted government money to continue development. This caused General Motors to press again for a diesel option, and also gave Rolls-Royce encouragement to offer their CV12 diesel. An $11.6million development contract awarded at this time to Teledyne Continental for its AVCR1360 was said to be entirely unconnected with the problems with the AVCO turbine.

However, the Army, which had made a firm commitment to the Chrysler XM1 and wanted something in service within the scheduled programme, to show that it knew what it was doing, decried the diesel option. They said it would cost over $100million and take over three years to develop and test the diesel. 'The Army', they said 'has never considered this a prudent venture and, at this point, correction of problems that might arise with the turbine are expected to be much less expensive, time-consuming and risky than creating the potential for a powerpack change'. This was a remarkable stand from the Army, who, in other projects, had shown great willingness to take all the time they wanted, spend any amount of money without result and to return to the drawing board. The Army may have been stung by the comment of Representative Samuel Stratton, who called an Army press release of July 1976 'a triumph of obfuscation which does not even address the length of delay in getting a new tank for the US Army or the increase in cost that will result'.

The Army must have blessed their talent for 'obfuscation', for it was not until 1980, after production had started, that fuller details of their fiddling of the figures came out. They carried out trials at both Fort Knox and Fort Bliss and whichever results came out best were incorporated into the report. At Fort Knox extraordinary maintenance precautions were taken, outside the schedules, to keep vehicles on the road and the tests were not as stringently applied as at Fort Bliss. But the most extraordinary procedure was the panel of four officers who decided whether a failure should or should not be recorded in the trials. Of 615 'incidents' during the tests they decided that 521 (85%) should be disregarded. Of the 94 remaining they decided that 64 were serious faults, but this still gave a record of MMBF below the requirement. So they dropped a further 37 'incidents' and achieved a very satisfactory 495MMBF. Realising that this looked too good to be true against the background of known failures, they revised the report to give a final result of 299MMBF, good enough to get the green light for production. They glossed over the tests that showed the M1 needed 1.34 hours of maintenance for every hour of operation, against the requirement of 1.0 to 1.25 hours.

They had not been very fair to the Germans either. In 1972 the US Army has purchased a Leopard 2 chassis for automotive trials. These showed that it fell short of US Army requirements. Krauss-Maffei then produced a modified version which included Chobham armour and a simpler and cheaper fire control system. The prototype of this 'American version' or 'austere version' (AV) would not be ready until 1976, when the Germans wanted side-by-side trials with the XM1. When the US went ahead with their own design before the trials the Germans protested. On 24 February 1976 the Secretary of Defense stated 'There is no commitment on the part of either Government to adopt the tank of either country based upon those tests and evaluations, though this is a possibility.' He added that, if the Leopard 2 proved to be a 'clearly superior design', the USA would consider adopting it 'for completion of development and production in the US'. Heads the US wins; tails, the FRG loses.

In order to curb the German feelings of anger and betrayal, the Memorandum of Understanding was amended in August 1976 to allow for efforts to standardise components. The Leopard 2AV prototype arrived at Aberdeen Proving Ground in November, just as the US Army announced the selection of the Chrysler version for production.

The evaluation report in May 1977 assessed the priorities in Leopard 2 in the order protection, firepower and mobility.

This is an interesting reversal of the 1950s philosophy, to which both Germany and France then subscribed, in which mobility was seen as a prime source of protection and allotted the higher priority. By 1976 both the USA and Germany had come round to the British way of thinking and give protection a higher status than mobility, though their understanding of the latter was way ahead of the British concept.

The report considered that the German application of Chobham armour technology was inferior to the US technique. The US Army generously gave the details of their analysis to the Germans for their edification. After firing 2,532 rounds of 120mm ammunition the Aberdeen trials concluded that, in firepower, both Leopard 2AV and XM1 were about equal. The Americans were still using their 105mm gun but provision for mounting a 120mm had been authorised in 1974.

Mobility was expressed in terms of a weight comparison in the 1977 report, and not strictly in terms of performance. The US Army had laid down a maximum of 58 tonnes and they achieved this with the 105mm gun. The Leopard 2, with its 120mm gun, was always just over the limits, but the Americans also realised that the XM1 with a 120mm gun would be just under 60 tonnes, so the weight difference was really insignificant.

The final conclusion was that the Leopard 2AV met nearly all the US Army requirements, though US armour protection was better. It was noted, too, that the XM1 failed to meet ALL the requirements. The Army were furious. Their previous assessment was that Leopard 2 failed to meet most of the specification, and now their own trials proved the contrary. However, Army procurement procedures called for a three-year development phase, and the Army decided that the delay was unacceptable. The Germans countered with their already acquired development experience, and said that three years was unnecessary, but as plans for XM1 production were so far advanced they had to be content with a promise that their 120mm would be considered for the future up-gunning of XM1, but if the Germans wanted to consider US components as an offset against the hypothetical gun purchase, the States would be only too happy.

It is still questioned, in some quarters, whether Leopard 2AV was ever seriously in the running. FMC, the American licencees for Leopard, believe that, no matter what the outcome of the trials, the US Army would never have adopted a major weapons system from a foreign source. German opinions were, at the time, muted, in the interests of the forthcoming gun trials.

While the engine controversy was internal to the USA the choice of main armament caused international complications. The initial competition had been based on the use of the current 105mm gun, though both contenders had been prescient enough to allow for the extension of the turret to take a 120mm, since it was obvious that something of this sort would be needed to combat the new Soviet tanks. The announcement of the winner was delayed when the USA agreed to evaluate the Leopard 2 and Representative Stratton said 'the eleventh hour change in plans is a shocking breach of sound competitive procurement practices'. He was probably unconsciously echoing the normal American practice of NIH (Not Invented Here), as well as expressing concern at the changing of the ground rules for XM1 along the way.

The Army had already told the Senate Armed Services Committee that redesign of the XM1 for a 120mm turret would cause a delay of one year and cost an extra $517.7 million, not including procurement of the 120mm ammunition, and that the resulting turret and vehicle would weigh more and have a higher silhouette with no resulting increase in firepower. It was obvious that a turret was needed that would take the 105mm gun at first and the 120mm at a later stage when a suitable one had been selected. That is what in fact has been decided, with very little modification of the original turret design.

But having agreed to evaluate the German 120mm smoothbore, Britain felt that the Americans should, in all fairness, try the new British guns too. They proposed trials of a new 110mm gun with a muzzle velocity of 1,800m/sec, which was still under development and an updated 120mm with new ammunition.

In 1975 a series of trials took place. The contenders were the British 110mm, for which at that stage only an APDS round was available, the German 120mm smoothbore, firing APFSDS and the US/British 105mm firing the M735 fin-stabilised round and the XM774 APDS with depleted uranium core. The trials presented a puzzle to the authorities, for the British gun and German ammunition appeared to have produced best results under each heading; so in the true spirit of compromise, the 105mm was chosen as the main armament for the first five years of service life of the XM1, with a decision to follow on which 120mm would be selected.

This necessitated further trials in 1976, between the three weapons. Although there was no official winner, unofficially the Chieftain 120mm firing APFSDS was first, the 105mm firing the depleted uranium core second, the Rhein-mentall third and the 105mm with the existing M735 a bad fourth. Understandably there was no official statement, and lack of this caused claims of unfairness and bias, which, though they may be unfounded, have left a bitter taste outside the USA. The Letter of Understanding between Britain and the USA stated that a 120mm gun would be required in the future and hinted that the British one would be considered. Three weeks later the Addendum to the US/FRG Memorandum gave priority to standardisation of components, hinting to the Germans that their 120mm smoothbore was a prime contender, in exchange for German acceptance of the AVCO gas turbine engine in place of the MTU diesel in Leopard 2. It also gave January 1977 as the date for decision on which 120mm would be considered, and as that date ruled out the new British 120mm, leaving only the Chieftain gun in the running, the British MoD protested that the Addendum was inconsistent with the US/UK Letter.

By 1978 it was fairly clear that the Americans would go ahead without further change to the Chrysler version of XM1, which was formally selected for production in November 1976. The pressures were manifold. Time was not on the side of the Army, who desperately needed to get a replacement for M60 into the field early in the 1980s. They were being leaned on by Congress to stay all-American and to keep the cost down. The spectre of the MBT70 at $1 million, hung over every conference and would not be exorcised until after production started in 1980, when it was estimated that current costs had arisen to $1.55 million per tank and to $2.6 million in June 1981.

The first XM1 rolled off the production line on 28 February 1980, and was named after the late General Creighton Abrams who had been Chief of Staff during most of its development. It was put into service at Fort Knox, with the 6th Armoured Cavalry, who proceeded to carry out user trials on the first vehicles. They liked it. It is easier and faster to train on than the M60, and cheaper, as less ammunition is expended to get results.

Once the turbine is wound up it is very much quieter than a diesel, and even at close quarters the loudest sound is track clatter. A silent watch capability, with large battery capacity and a small turbine auxiliary generator, is a welcome relief from having to start the main engine every 45 minutes, as on the M60.

Life in the turret is also a great improvement over the M60. Turret crews feel the bumps more than the driver, who, they are sure, lives in armchair comfort down front and deliberately seeks out bumps to shake them up. In the M1 each of the crew has a fairly comfortable position. The gunner's controls are adjustable to his size and position and the loader can operate sitting down. The commander's cupola has less instrumentation and fewer controls than most modern AFVs. His main sight is an extension of the gunner's sight, giving the same picture and magnification. The commander has a turret traverse controller which can override the gunner, but he cannot himself acquire a target and lay the main armament. This is doubtless the result of financial restrictions, and makes the M1 commander less well-equipped than any of his NATO colleagues. It is no compensation that he can control and fire his own .50cal MG.

The gunner has a ×1, ×3 and ×10 sight, incorporating LRF and thermal-imaging night sight, with the gun movement and firing controls built into a two-handed yoke. The main gunner's sight is stabilised in elevation and the main and secondary armaments are slaved to it. Financial restrictions precluded built-in azimuth stabilisation, but this was regarded as an acceptable trade-off for economy. The ballistic computer is supplied with range, lead angle, cant and wind corrections automatically, but other data such as muzzle reference and meteorological information, charge temperatures and ammunition are put in manually.

Loading the 105mm ammunition is manual. There is a total of 55 rounds on board. Eight are stowed in a compartment in the hull, and three in spall-proof containers in the turret floor, but there are 44 in the turret bustle. This makes them readily available to the loader. While stowage of inert armour piercing projectiles may be acceptable above the turret ring, such as in Chieftain, having the whole round, including propellant stowed so high seems to be risky. Even more so when not only AP rounds, but HEAT as well, are stowed in the bustle. However the M1 design obviates much of the risk to the crew from fire or explosion of the ammunition by putting 22 rounds in each of two separate compartments which are closed off to the turret by sliding access doors. Should an armour piercing round penetrate the bustle and set off an explosion in the magazine, the force of the explosion will be vented through blowout panels in the roof, and the sliding doors are reckoned to be strong enough to direct the explosion upwards . . . provided they are shut. The loader obtains access to the ammunition by a knee-operated switch which opens and closes the doors. The doors can be opened manually if there is a system failure, but if they jam open (or are left open to speed up loading) then the safety of the tank is jeopardised. Full manual operation of the doors for each round loaded would reduce the firing rate to four, or even three, rounds per minute. The blow-out panels in the turret roof are, however, a weakness against top attack.

Whatever the criticisms of the M1 Abrams, it is undoubtedly the best MBT the US Army has got. It has good survivability, due to Chobham armour, low noise signature, compartmentalisation of fuel and ammunition and a good (British) smoke discharger system. It packs a good punch and is agile and manoeuvrable. If it matches its targets of reliability and life costs it will have proved a good buy, but

this is still in question. In December 1981 the GAO again urged that production of M1 be slowed or stopped because of unsolved problems with the AVCO AGT1500 gas turbine powerplant. The Pentagon approved stepped up production in September 1981 when a group of experts predicted that performance and reliability would improve sufficiently to justify the increase. In fact, says the GAO, tests show that the probability of tanks being able to drive 6,400km before major repairs to the engine was only 37%, against the Army's stated requirement of 50% probability. The GAO again suggested that alternative designs be studied to replace the gas turbine. At the same time the Army is considering whether to look for a second source of production for the Abrams and the AVCO gas turbine. By October 1981 Chrysler had only delivered 205 tanks of a scheduled 363 and AVCO only 270 of a planned production of 497. The first M1 in Europe was handed over to A Company, 3rd Battalion, 64th Armour of the US Seventh Army, at Vilseck, in Germany, on 15 January 1982.

The M1 Abrams was conceived in the early 1970s to withstand attack from the then existing anti-armour weapons and to counter the Soviet T-72. Over 10 years have passed in which tanks and methods of attack of armour have developed much. Even before it is in full service thoughts are directed towards its successor. In October 1981 the US Army issued a request for proposals for a vehicle with better protection, within the weight of a current MBT. They called for a turretless vehicle with an externally mounted gun, using M1 components and advanced composite armour. Development contracts were expected to be issued in 1982.

USSR

T-54/55

Though the Soviet 122mm gun that had caused such a stir in 1945, and prompted the development of similar weapons in the west, continued in service with heavy tanks until the late 1960s, there was a similar surprise in the medium tank armoury. The 100mm D-10T appeared in 1949 mounted in a new turret of excellent shape on the T-54. The T-44 was developed from its predecessor, the T-54 and continued the evolutionary pattern of Soviet tank design. The Christie suspension gave way to torsion bars and the hull was enlarged to take a bigger turret ring. The obvious change was the turret. This was a flattened egg shape, with noticeable overhang all round and undercuts at front and rear, which formed excellent shot traps and detracted from the otherwise good ballistic shape. The commander and gunner were stationed on the left of the turret and the loader on the right, similar to British practice up to the Comet. The 100mm gun had an external mantlet up with sighting telescope and coaxial machine gun. The disadvantages of this arrangement were partially rectified over the two subsequent models. The overhang of the turret was eliminated, the mantlet narrowed down and the telescope and coaxial MG emerged through slits in the armour at either side. The distinctive smooth outline of the turret was broken by the grab handles for tank-riding infantry, on the sides and the 12.7mm AAMG mounted on the loader's hatch.

The gun fired APHE, AP and HEAT rounds. The APHE left the muzzle at 1,000m/sec and could penetrate 185mm of armour; while the HEAT, fired at 900m/sec, was claimed to penetrate 380mm. This could easily defeat all known enemy tanks, the thought of which accelerated the development of more powerful guns in the west.

T-54/55 fitted with Weston Simfire. *via C. Foss*

Things inside the turret were not so good, however. There was little room to spare above the turret ring, where the gun breech and ready use ammunition used most of the space. Below, there was no turret basket and the loader had to walk around on the floor as the turret traversed, bent over under the curve of the turret. He had seven rounds available in racks on the rear of the turret, but further replenishment depended on the position of the turret. There were 10 rounds on the bulkhead between fighting and engine compartments, four on the right wall of the fighting compartment and two on the left. The remainder of the total 42 rounds were stowed in a rack to the right front of the hull, next to the main fuel tanks. The 100mm round is fixed ammunition and not easy to handle in the cramped space of the T-54/55 turret. The AP round weighs 25.8kg and the loader has to ram the round into the breech left-handed. An American officer commented 'The Soviets are going to be in trouble (for tank crews) when they run out of strong left-handed midgets' — indeed it was remarked upon by western observers that even the crews of T-72s shown to military attaches in 1979 ranged in height from 1.55m to 1.60mm (5ft to 5ft 4in).

Fire control in the early T-54 was crude, relying on the eyeball and a stadiametric range scale in the sighting telescope. This gives a quick approximation of range for targets of 2.7m in height, if the whole vehicle is visible. If, as is usually the case in combat situations, the lower half of the tank is obscured, ranging comes down to training and judgement. With a high velocity, flat trajectory weapon this is adequate out to 1,000-2,000m, but beyond that distance other aids are needed. There is no room in the T-54 turret for an optical rangefinder so it was not until the 1970s, when LRFs were perfected, that a better system was provided. British and Yugoslavian companies offered laser devices to be mounted on the commander's cupola, which gave digital readouts for commander and gunner. More recently Vickers Instruments Ltd have designed a telescope sight (L50) with built-in LRF which can be mounted in place of the standard Soviet articulated telescope sight in T-54/T-55, T-62 and Chinese T-59. It has dual magnification of ×4 and ×8, while the laser gives ranges out to 10km with an accuracy of ±5m. It can be combined with a Ferranti micro-processor-based fire control system originally intended for the British MBT80, the new system being very compact and easy to install.

To start with, the gun in T-54 had only manual elevation, though it did have electrical power traverse. This was improved in 1955 when the gun was fitted with gyro-controlled stabilisation in elevation and provided with power elevation. The gun, now called D-10TG, had a small counterweight fitted to the muzzle. Traverse was still unstablised. On later models a fume extractor was fitted to the muzzle and various IR equipments mounted above and to the side of the mantlet.

The practice of carrying fuel externally continued and three 93-litre cells can be found on the track guards of T-54 and its successors. It is not a practice that commends itself to other nations. The main fuel tanks are placed under the glacis plate and next to the largest ammunition stowage. The T-54 went through six major models, with few visible differences, but multiple changes in detail, to improve the design. The T-54B was the first to carry the D-10T2S gun with two-axis stabilisation. This was carried over into the T-54X which was the last version before the introduction of its successor, T-55, in 1961.

This, again, showed little external difference, but included an uprated V-55 engine, and, for the first time, a turret basket with floor. T-55 went through a number of modifications and has been fitted with many varieties of extra equipments to improve fighting performance. Many T-54s were modified to T-55 standard, losing the hull machinegun in the process, and both tanks have been retro-fitted with IR and passive night fighting devices, externally mounted LRF, searchlights, etc. A number of T-55s captured by Israel in the 1973 war have been taken into service and modified to take the British type 105mm gun. In these it is probable that the fire control arrangements have also been improved, but little can be done to make loading easier. In fact, unless turret accommodation has been reversed things may even be worse. To manoeuvre a 105mm round into the breech, working left-handed, must be incredibly difficult.

T-54/T-55 qualifies as a most important MBT, not only in the quantities in which it was made and its service in 33 countries. It has been the basis for a large family of variants, including ARV, bridgelayer, flamethrower, dozer, mine clearer and engineer vehicle. But more significant is its parentage of the subsequent T-62, T-64 and T-72.

It was the numbers of T-54/T-55s that caused most anxiety in the west. Over 40,000 were built in the USSR and around 20,000 more in Czechoslovakia and Poland. The People's Republic of China (PRC) made its own copy of the tank, designated T-59, and sold some 1,200 to Pakistan, where they fared poorly in the 1971 war with India. In 1974, according to the International Institute of Strategic Studies, there were about 7,500 of the T-54/T-55 models in service

Above: A T-62 captured during fighting on the Golan Heights in 1973. An access hatch over the engine is open so engine failure is the likely cause of its being abandoned in otherwise good order.

Left: Ammunition stowage inside the hull of the T-62 includes APFSDS and HEAT rounds for the 115mm gun. The empty clips show where two more rounds had been stowed.

outside the Warsaw Pact. In 1981 the comparable figure was 14,000. The increase is partly from tanks released for sale as they are replaced by T-72 in Warsaw Pact stocks, but the T-55 remains in production for export and is quite good value at under £500,000 each.

T-62

In the west the 105mm gun was known about, well before its introduction into service in 1962. To counter this threat the Soviets mounted a new 115mm gun in a new, low, cast turret and carried it on a hull modified from the T-55. This vehicle, known as the T-62 and first shown in public at the 1965 Moscow May Day parade, has most of the same characteristics as its forebears: well-shaped armour, low silhouette, powerpack and running gear adapted to swift cross-country movement, ability to schnorkel across rivers and a powerful main armament. It is also very uncomfortable by western standards. The crew positions are the same as in T-54/T-55, the turret being very cramped. The loader has the problem of handling rounds weighing 22.5kg (APFSDS) or 26.2kg (HEAT), of which only two are ready rounds in the turret. Once those are expended he must replace from the 20 rounds stowed in the back of the fighting compartment, or the 16 in the front to the right of the driver. The turret must be in the correct position to allow access, which is never easy.

The designers of T-62 attempted to solve a problem which attends all but a few tanks; that of disposal of empty cartridge cases. After a short engagement the first thing to do is to clear the turret of debris and refill the ready use racks. Centurion crews used the pistol ports and in tanks

where these do not exist cases are thrown out of the loader's hatch. In the cramped space of a T-62 it was thought that even a few empty cases would be an embarrassment, so a system was devised by which the recoil of the gun activates a tray to carry the cartridge case to an ejection port in the rear of the turret. The ejection cycle takes some six seconds, during which time the gunner cannot track a target as the loader's safety device is made safe, cutting off electrical power to the traverse and elevation. The loader must wait until the cycle is complete before loading the next round, when he is able to make the safety switch so that the gunner can continue the engagement. Thus effective firing is reduced to four to five rounds per minute.

The main armament of the T-62 is a major step in Soviet gun design and the first modern smoothbore tank gun. It is the 115mm U5-TS, with a fume extractor a third of the distance from the muzzle. It fires HE fragmentation and HEAT rounds and a high velocity, fin-stabilised APDS projectile with excellent penetration characteristics. When it showed its capabilities in the 1967 Arab-Israeli war many people felt that they day of the rifled tank gun was over: that fin-stabilised APDS and HEAT were all that was necessary for tank main armament. But although the kill probability of APFSDS is high, its accuracy drops off beyond 1,200-1,500m, and the 105mm and 120mm guns of current NATO MBTs are accurate to 2,000m. This was proven in battle on the Golan Heights in 1973 when Israeli Centurions managed to hold off the Syrian assault. A contributory factor was the 4° maximum depression of the T-62 gun, which meant that the T-62 had to expose more of itself than western tanks, when firing from reverse slope positions. The electro-hydraulic traverse and elevation mechanisms can operate in stabilised or unstabilised modes, but the traverse rate is slightly slower than western tanks, taking 20 seconds to move through 360°, against 15 seconds for a Leopard 1 or M60A1.

The commander has a TKN-3 day/night binocular periscope sight which incorporates the stadiametric ranging graticule. This is unnecessary at night, for the effectiveness of the IR sight combined with the OU-3GK searchlight is limited to 400m. The commander has a turret traverse override but no elevation control.

The T-62 gunner has two separate sights. The standard articulated telescope day sight has five sets of graticules plus a stadiametric rangefinder. The central graticule, on the aiming mark, is for HE18 (one of two HE rounds available) with HEAT and APDS to the left and HE11 and coax MG to the right. If he is not given a range by his commander, the gunner must move his sight picture on to the stadiametric gauge, transfer the reading to HEAT or APDS graticules (assuming a tank target) by setting the range line to the correct mark then aim on the centre mark, a procedure which seems time-consuming compared with modern techniques but which a trained gunner can carry out quickly and instinctively. The gunner's night sight is the periscopic TPN1-41-11. It has a maximum range of 800m when working with the main IR searchlight mounted over the main armament. It has been reported that most T-62 are being retro-fitted with a laser rangefinder.

Although the T-62 is a comparatively modern tank the Soviets do not seem to have considered using modern components or techniques to make the lot of the driver easier. The transmission still uses a crash gearbox, necessitating double de-clutching when changing gear, and steering is by two tillers. Though hydro-pneumatic assistance to clutch operation is available it does not make gear-changing any easier, nor does the unusual design of the gear selector gate. Though 1st is used only as 'emergency low' and the change from 2nd to 3rd is straightforward, from 3rd to 4th is right across the gate, with a fair chance of hitting the reverse slot en passant. The tillers have three positions: fully forward, when normal power is transmitted to both sprockets: a second (or middle) position which changes the ratio of the output from the planetary steering gear and slows down the relevant track: fully back, when the track is braked and a tighter turn made.

Suspension is by torsion bars, with hydraulic shock absorbers at front and rear wheel stations. The tracks are all steel, without the facility to fix rubber pads, and the pins are pushed through from the inside, without any retaining device. When a pin eases out of its position it is knocked back into place by a wedge-shaped 'pin hammer' welded to the hull side just in front of the sprocket. The track is fully guided by horns on each plate which engage the road wheels on both top and bottom runs.

The T-62 has no smoke round for its 115mm gun nor smoke dischargers on the turret. It relies, as Soviet tanks have done before, on making smoke from its engine. Diesel fuel is injected, at the rate of 10litre/min, into the exhaust manifold, which produces a screen which lasts from two to four minutes, according to the wind. Recent research shows that a YAG laser (Yttrium, Aluminium, Garnet) cannot penetrate diesel smoke, but this is coincidence rather than the cause of changes to other types of laser.

Not all the fuel on T-62 is carried under armour. The tank capacity is 960 litres but this includes three external fuel cells on the right-hand guard (and a single external auxiliary oil cell on the left). The road range is quoted as 450km,

which is roughly the same as the American M1 (440km claimed) but less than Leopard 2 (550km). Fuel capacity can be increased by using two jettisonable auxiliary fuel tanks on the back of the vehicle. This increases the road range by about 40%.

The T-62 looks like, and in fact is, the result of an evolutionary line of development starting with the revolutionary T-34. It has enabled the Russians to maintain a continuity of training while improving or testing new components.

T-64/72

The next stage in Russian MBT development caused a great deal of confusion in the west. It became known that a new tank was on the way, in design, in prototype or even starting production. It was designated M-1970 and there was much speculation as to its capabilities. Photographs appeared in the defence press, showing a typically low, long hull carrying a huge gun in the usual low profile turret. The early pictures were of vehicles in the snow and the running gear was partially obscured, but, later, a departure from standard Soviet practice was noticed. Instead of the large road wheels of the T-62, the new vehicle had six smaller wheels and the track was supported on four rollers. The track itself was different too, with double-pin links, but the most sinister change was the main armament.

Guesswork soon gave way to the awful certainly that the Russians now had overtaken the west once more and had the biggest tank gun in the world. It was of 125mm calibre and another smoothbore, though details were obscured by the thermal sleeve. What could be seen and deduced sent shivers along the corridors in Bonn, London and Washington, and gave considerable impetus to the development programmes in each country. The Germans saw the big smoothbore gun and were pleased that they had picked the same philosophy, for German technology was sure to produce greater accuracy than the Soviet. The British said little but went ahead with crossed fingers and Chobham armour. The Americans screamed blue murder about delays in the XM1 programme and started to cut corners in trials.

The new Soviet tank soon became known in the west as the T-72, and gradually a little more emerged about it. The hull was even lower than previous models and it was thought that, instead of a conventional V-shaped diesel engine, the new tank was powered by a horizontally opposed piston engine. The clutter on the track guards of the T-55 and T-62 had been cleaned up and although there might well be external fuel cells, these were now integrated with other track guard stowage. However, the typical rear jettison tanks were also on the T-72, and the turret sported searchlights and AAMGs.

Then, in 1977, the devious Russians pulled another surprise — they paraded another new tank. It looked, at first, like a modification of the previous one, but the running gear was different: instead of six small road wheels and four top rollers the new tank had six larger wheels and three top rollers. The track reverted to single-pin. The engine was again a transversely-mounted V12, but up-rated to 580kW (780hp). Significantly, the main armament was the same 125mm smoothbore. It was soon learned that the new tank was in full production while the earlier one was seen only occasionally and in small numbers. The west redesignated the first with the 125mm gun as the T-64, and called the second model the T-72. It took some time to sort out the arguments and misunderstandings that ensued among observers and experts. It was believed that the new components of the T-64 had proved unreliable and that it had

been necessary swiftly to redesign the hull with conventional and typical Soviet components. T-72 became the major bogey of the west. It was, therefore, with some astonishment that the French Minister of Defence was shown the T-72 during a visit to Moscow in 1977. He was not allowed inside, but the ammunition was openly displayed on a table, and he and his staff got enough data to double the files on T-72 in western archives.

The most significant information was on the turret, in which the crew is reduced to two, commander on the right and gunner on the left. The loader is replaced by an automatic system, which leaves the commander the job of servicing the coaxial MG to the right of the main armament, and the 12.7mm AAMG on his cupola.

The T-72 can carry 40 rounds of 125mm ammunition, stowed in a circular magazine below the turret floor. There are three natures available, all fin-stabilised, comprising APFSDS, HEAT and HE. The location of each round is kept in the ballistic computer. The rounds are stowed horizontally and pointing towards the centre of the turret base, with the semi-combustible propellant charge clipped to the top of the projectile. To load, the tank commander selects the nature required, whereon the computer locates the nearest one in the magazine and brings it to the automatic loader. Simultaneously the gun is brought to the loading position at 4° elevation. The projectile is rammed, followed by the charge and the gun is free to return to the superelevation needed to attain the range. This all takes time and the movement of the gun to and from the loading position gives further opportunity for error to creep into the system. It cannot be an easy task to stow the ammunition in the magazine, and although there is surely a manual back-up system for loading, it would not be easy for the commander to operate. The great advantage of this design is that it has allowed a very low silhouette and excellently angled protection, while the ammunition is stowed as low as possible and is unlikely to receive a direct hit, reducing the fire risk considerably. The problem of disposal of empty cases has been avoided by using a semi-combustible propellant casing with a stub cartridge.

T-72 has been seen both with and without skirting plates. When fitted they can be spring-loaded to swing outwards to about 40° to increase the stand-off distance to the lower hull over the frontal arc. One source (IDR) gives the thickness of the glacis plate as 200mm, with an effective thickness of 600mm at horizontal angle of attack. (This is roughly twice the thickness of armour which 105mm HEAT is said to penetrate, but would succumb to a HESH round acting at 90° to the armour.)

The armour penetrating ability of the APFSDS 125mm round must be considerable. It is 545mm long and 48mm in diameter, a length/calibre ratio of 11.3. It is fired at a muzzle velocity of 1,615m/sec and would certainly penetrate all other MBTs, until the advent of Chobham armour, the protective ability of which against such a powerful attack is, as yet, undisclosed. It is probable that the Soviets themselves are developing their own composite armour, and such information as has filtered through to the west on the next Russian MBT indicate that composite armour is used on the glacis and around the front and sides of the turret.

In general all Soviet vehicles are designed for winter conditions and, though almost every type has found its way into the hands of users in hot dry and hot wet climates, no concessions have been made by the designers.

There have been many re-engine and rebuild projects, initiated by Middle Eastern wars, with western companies. Steve Zaloga, in his book *Modern Soviet Armour* quotes Romania as having had 'such serious problems with its T-54s that it approached several West German companies for bids to completely rework the existing vehicles, adding new suspension, track, wheels, engine and other components'. The author was involved in a project to rebuild a large number of BTR-152 on to a European chassis and a French company, SSCM (Societe Sidurgerienne de Constructions Mechaniques) retrofitted some 150 Egyptian BMP-1 with a Poyaud 520 6LCS-2 diesel engine. OTO-Melara was asked by Egypt to quote for the large number of T-54/55, but the complexity and cost of the operation was too great.

The necessity for such reworks is threefold. The original vehicle designs are intended for arctic and temperate climates; components and assemblies are often of unsuitable quality (particularly air cleaners and oil filters are not made for desert conditions) and users find great difficulty in

Left: With a 125mm automatically-loaded main gun, the T-72 is quoted as being a potent adversary to the Leopard 1 and Chieftain although not up to the Challenger/Leopard 2/Abrams standard. *via C. Foss*

Right: Tank production in the most modern AFV plant in Europe. The new Armstrong works in Newcastle builds Vickers MBTs and Valiants and the Valkyr wheeled APC. A Vickers Mk 3 MBT is in the welding jig in the foreground and an ARV hull on the ground line to the right. *Vickers Ltd*

obtaining spare parts. The Soviet policy with client countries appears to be to keep them short of spares but to offer new vehicles.

One curious fact is that, although the T-64 is reported to be in service in substantial numbers in the Soviet Army, it has not been issued elsewhere in the Warsaw Pact, let alone sold to Syria or Libya. One theory is that it suffers from problems with engine, tracks and gun, and that it is being kept out of sight for these reasons. But there are those who think that the T-64 is the basis for the next Soviet MBT and security is the main reason for not allowing it to be seen abroad.

If so, then the pattern of steady evolution is, to some extent, broken. New hull, new major components and the Russian version of Chobham armour are all prognosticated for whatever appears as the T-80 or T-82, or whatever is the designation. Artists' impressions have been published which indicate a sort of Soviet M1 in looks, though with the 125mm smoothbore gun. The drawing shows that the low silhouette is retained and the running gear consists of six small roadwheels, with an unknown number of return rollers concealed by skirt armour, giving credence to the theory of development from the T-64. The appearance of smoke grenade dischargers not unlike those made by Peak Engineering in the UK, shows that the Soviets are taking seriously the need for instantaneous cover in front of the tank and not relying on engine-produced smoke, as in the past. It may be that the engine of the new tank is not suited to smoke production in the usual fashion of injecting fuel into the exhaust system. Since some T-64s have also been seen with turret-mounted smoke dischargers it may be that the same engine is used for both.

Whatever does come into service it seems certain that it will be a conventional turreted vehicle with a large calibre gun. It will certainly have composite armour of some description and will be a difficult problem for the west.

Private Ventures

Given the cost of a modern MBT as being around £10,000 ($20,000) per tonne, and that development programmes usually take about eight years, it is not surprising that few companies are prepared to take the risk of designing and building their own type of tank. Few PV tanks are completely new and most rely to some extent on components and technology used in 'official' designs or evolved as by-products of the government-funded development.

Vickers MBT/Vijayanra

Britain has, except for a short period before and during WW2, been in the van of AFV design, so it is not surprising that there have been three private venture MBTs since 1945, despite the economic conditions. Nor is it surprising that Vickers should be responsible for two of them. In the 1950s the company designed a light/medium tank which was armed with the then current 20pdr (83mm) gun and carried a secondary armament of Vigilant wire-guided ATGW. It never went beyond the design stage, but the company went ahead with another project. This was a 37ton MBT armed with the 105mm gun and powered by a lower-rated version of the L60 engine which powered Chieftain. In 1961 Vickers signed a contract with India to assist the establishment of a factory in Avadi, near Madras, to build a new MBT.

The first prototype was built in 1963 and the first production unit in 1965. The first tank was built at Avadi in January 1969, and named Vijayanta. For the next five years the number of components made in India was increased until engines and gun barrels were the only major items imported. The Vijayanta served in the 1971 war with Pakistan, but despite much propaganda, the Indian Armoured Corps were reluctant to give up their Centurions in favour of the new design. Over 1,000 have now been built.

The Vickers MBT is of simple welded construction, with no large, expensive castings. The height has been kept down to only 2.71m to the top of the cupola. With the comparatively low weight of 38,600kg the armour protection is not great, with a maximum of 80mm thickness on nose and turret front. The L60 engine, working more within its true capacity, gave less trouble than in Chieftain, but in the later Vickers MBT Mk3 it was replaced by a GM V12 diesel powerpack developing 800bhp, which raised the power/weight ratio to a very respectable 20.7bhp/ton. The turret is

mounted well forward, which allows plenty of space for the engine compartment in which there is also a Coventry Climax H30 auxiliary generating set and the TN12 transmission, both adopted straight from Chieftain. Suspension is by torsion bars and trailing arms and there are three track return rollers, though these are usually obscured by the distinctive ribbed skirting plates.

Main armament is the well-tried 105mm gun, supported by a 7.62×51mm coaxial MG, .50cal RMG and twin multi-barrelled smoke dischargers. Gun and fire control systems have been modernised to customers' requirements and LRF

has been added to the original, simple stabilised system. Although the overseas sales of the MBT have largely been to areas where water crossings are unlikely (Kuwait 70, Kenya 72) the original design included a flotation screen which gave the Vickers MBT an inland water crossing capability.

With the cost of a MBT closely related to its weight, the lighter Vickers MBT was an attractive potential purchase for many of the less affluent nations. Its lighter weight also made it a better proposition for road and rail transport and bridge crossing. However, the AFV market is very competitive and Vickers did not have the success for which they

Above left: Heavily camouflaged Vickers MBT Mk 3. *Vickers Ltd*

Left: The Vickers Valiant is the latest in the line of private venture developments from one of the oldest firms in the British defence industry. *Vickers Ltd*

Above: The Vickers Valiant MBT has several important features well illustrated here. The flat glacis and the slab-sided look of the turret indicate that it is protected by Chobham armour, and the hull sides are covered by spaced skirting plates. On the cupola is the commander's day/night sight, while below is the aperture for the gunner's laser rangefinder sight. The 105mm gun has a muzzle reference sight. *Vickers Ltd*

had hoped. This did not deter the company from bringing out a new design in 1981. Vickers had years of experience in building Centurion and Chieftain and had been design parent to the latter. They saw that the German Leopard 1 and its Italian-made version, the French AMX30 and 32 and the Krauss Maffei private venture TAM were having sales success and produced their own competitor.

Vickers Valiant

The Vickers Valiant is a medium weight MBT, using Chobham armour for its protection and capable of mounting either a 105mm or 120mm gun. Its Rolls-Royce CV12 TCA diesel engine develops 746kW which gives it a top speed of 61kph and road range of over 600km, driving through an automatic transmission derived from the TN12. The suspension and running gear are similar to the earlier 37ton MBT, but the overall weight is up to 43.6 tonnes.

The driver is positioned to the right of the tank, with ammunition stowage to his left. He sits in the normal upright position and looks out through a single periscope, which does not give a very wide view. Control is by a handlebar incorporating throttle control, steering and transmission control functions. The left-hand switch allows the driver to hold a gear, to allow the automatic box to change normally, or to change gears down by throttling back so as to reach the correct ratio for an obstacle before reaching it.

The hull of Valiant is of aluminium armour, with Chobham

armour at the front and thick skirts. The turret is of welded steel, with Chobham type armour applied to front and sides. Bins and an NBC pack protect the bustle, and make entry and exit via the driver's hatch very difficult when the gun is traversed rear.

The Valiant is entirely for the export market and in order to appeal to the widest range of customers can be offered with 105mm L7 rifled gun, the 120mm L11 rifled gun as in Chieftain, or the 120mm smoothbore from Rheinmetall. The larger the calibre the less ammunition can be stowed: 60 for the 105mm or 42 for either of the 120m. There are options, too, for the secondary armament. Either 7.62mm or 12.7mm (.50cal) MGs can be fitted coaxially and on the commander's cupola, while the 120mm version of Valiant can mount the 7.62mm Hughes Chain Gun as its coaxial MG.

Observation and sighting devices are very much at client's request. Naturally all the most modern equipments are available: gyro-stabilised commander's sights, night and day vision, LRF, thermal pointers and thermal imagers with TV monitors for commander and gunner can be fitted. Fire control is the Marconi Radar SFCS 600, and includes a sensor on the turret to measure wind and other meteorological data for putting into the ballastic computer.

Chieftain 900

The Vickers Valiant is a private venture design using information and experience gathered during decades of government contracts. Another MBT offered from Britain relies even more on such sources and, since it is designed by the Royal Ordnance Factory at Leeds using public money, should perhaps not be described as a private venture. It is designed exclusively for the export market and is very unlikely ever to serve with the British Army.

There have been several derivatives of Chieftain, tailored to the requirements of overseas users, and one of these — Challenger — has been further modified to fill the gap between Chieftain and a future MBT in British service. The ROF decided in 1981 that there was sufficient market potential for it to be worth while bringing out yet another derivative, using all the new techniques and components available. It is called Chieftain 900 but it is more than just a modified Chieftain. The hull is protected by Chobham armour and the

well-sloped glacis and nose have a shape reminiscent of the IS-3 (and the possible T-80) Russian tank. The belly plate also seems well angled against mine blast. Even in the 'head out' position the driver has little side vision. The sides and running gear are protected by skirt armour and are very similar to Chieftain.

The turret is also constructed of well sloped Chobham armour and maintains a low profile and overall height. Main armament is the same as Chieftain, with stowage for 46 rounds for the 120mm gun and 4,000MG rounds. Since the tank is designed for the 'third world' market, it can be offered with a wide variety of fire control systems, all including LRF and passive night vision, thermal images and pointers etc. The commander's cupola carries a day sight and has good all round vision capability.

Chieftain 900 has the same Rolls-Royce Condor series engine as Chieftain and Challenger, but rated at 900bhp as against the 1,200bhp of the others. However, at a battle weight of 56 tonnes this gives the excellent 16bhp/tonne power/weight ratio and a maximum (load) speed of 52kph.

Chieftain 900's main assets are in the tradition of British tanks, the firepower of its 120mm gun, the protection of its well-angled Chobham armour and the mobility of its sturdy power train. All are proven and reliable components which should have considerable appeal on the world market, though many possible clients will put higher speed before the weighty level of protection.

Chrysler Project K

Although there have been many experimental models on the American scene only the Chrysler Company and Teledyne Continental have actually offered private venture MBTs. The Chrysler Project K was not a new design but a modification of the M60A2. It used the long barrelled Shillelagh gun/launcher in a stabilised mounting, with a coaxial M73 MG. The turret of this hybrid was low and well angled welded armour plate. Ammunition handling was improved by a three-round 'loader's assist device', and 57 rounds of 152mm ammunition could be stowed. The low silhouette was achieved by using a new design of commander's cupola with a remote-controlled .50cal MG. The ride was improved by using a double torsion bar suspension and hydraulic

shock absorbers, and an aluminium track with detachable rubber pads.

Teledyne Super M60

The Chrysler Project K never got off the ground commercially since there was widespread suspicion about the gun/missile weapon system and it was too complicated and costly an option. In any case the US Government seemed prepared to supply tanks, old and new, to anybody who aligned themselves with the USA, at very favourable prices — or even free. Teledyne Continental, well known for tank engines have designed a much improved and modernised version of the M60 which, it is thought, could be an attractive proposition for users of M60 who want to keep up with the times without changing models completely. Their version is said to cost 17% more than the standard M60A3, if purchased new, but a a conversion cost would cost substantially less than buying a new tank.

The 'Super M60' has a new Teledyne AVCR1790 engine developing 1,200hp with its variable compression ratio (VCR) pistons, compared with the 750hp of the standard AVDS1790. To take the increased engine output the Allison transmission is replaced by a German unit, the Renk Rk304, which can be used manually or automatically and has a torque converter with lock-up clutch. The new power pack necessitates some modification to the engine compartment and gives the tank 23hp/tonne power/weight ratio, allowing greater accleration and agility. This in turn needed improvement to the suspension, and a hydropneumatic suspension replaces the torsion bars.

Protection has been increased overall by adding high hardness applique armour all round, including top surfaces, and skirt armour. The result is a very modern look and four tonnes additional weight. The usual American M19 cupola has been dropped in favour of a new commander's cupola which is simpler, cheaper and lower. Teledyne's private venture is more akin to the modernisation programmes which have improved Centurions than to the virtually new designs of OTO-Melara and the ROF Leeds, but if the cost of the M1 Abrams rises too much the US Army may well adopt the Teledyne plan in order to keep its remaining M60s up to front line standard.

Left: Chieftain 900 is a development by the Royal Ordnance Factory at Leeds. It includes a 900hp Rolls-Royce Condor engine and Chobham armour. The increased angle of the glacis plate allows the driver to operate 'head out' even when the turret is traversing. *ROF Leeds*

Above: The Teledyne Super M60 with applique armour and lacking the usual commander's cupola has a modern look which supports its improved effectiveness. *Teledyne Continental*

Right: The Leopard ancestry of the OTO-Melara OF-40 Lion is given away by the turret shape, the exhaust louvres and the Wegmann type smoke grenade dischargers. *OTO-Melara*

OF40

One of the more successful private venture MBTs, in terms of sales, is the Italian OF40. This is a derivative of the Leopard 1, produced as the combined effort of OTO-Melara and Fiat, with a design weight of 40 tonnes.

OTO-Melara have been building Leopard 1 under licence for many years, under a contract for 1,000 for the Italian Army. In the mid-1970s they approached the German government on the subject of sales to non-NATO countries, but were not allowed to do so. In order to capitalise on their production experience with Leopard, they set about designing a 'new' MBT which they could sell with the blessing of the Italian government. In order to circumvent any possible objections from Britain, in respect of their 105mm L7 gun, the Italians designed a 'new' gun which could still fire the British and American 105mm ammunition, which is manufactured under licence in Italy for the Italian Army Leopards.

OF40 is a conventional tank using major components of, or directly derived from, the Leopard 1. The hull and turret are of spaced, welded steel plate. The hull sides are vertical, for ease of production, rather than sloped as Leopard, and the glacis is at a flatter angle.

The engine of OF40 is the same MTU MB838 diesel as in Leopard, though later models may have a Fiat engine as an option. The ZF transmission is offered as standard with an Italian made optional gearbox. Suspension and track are the same as Leopard 1 and performances would seem to be very similar. Only in the turret is there much difference, though it is shaped exactly like that of Leopard 1A3. As mentioned earlier the 105mm gun is designed by OTO-Melara, to fire the same range of ammunition as the British 105mm/51 calibres L7, but the Italian gun is longer by one calibre, which can impart a marginally higher velocity. The tube is fitted with a fume extractor and thermal jacket. The fire control system is all Italian, with ballistic computer and optics from Officine Galileo and LRF by Selenia.

Known sales of OF40, or Lion, as it was named originally, are 30 to the United Arab Emirates and 100 to Libya, with another 100 on order. This seems to prove the value of engineering the cooling and filtration systems specifically to the requirements of hot, desert countries, instead of to the conditions of the central front of NATO. It is believed that much of the expertise gathered during the trials of Leopard in Australia was utilised in the design of Lion.

TAM

Germany has, in fact, produced a private venture tank of its own, though the TAM is really in the medium class. Provided the customer is prepared to accept limited protection, it makes sense to build a tank with excellent mobility and firepower equal to a MBT. When you already have a set of components that have been well tried as an APC, and which are readily available, then you have a very marketable proposition. Thyssen-Henschel of Kassel in West Germany had a design team and the basic hull and components of the Marder MICV, so it was logical that they should accept a development contract, awarded in 1974, from the Argentine. It was for a battle tank of medium (30 tonnes) weight and a cannon-armed APC on the same basic hull.

The TAM (Tanque Argentino Mediano) and the VCI (Vehiculo Combate Infanteria) were developed and the components and prototypes tested in Germany, except for the turret and gun, which were constructed at the Rio Tercero plant in Argentina. Sets of components for the hull were shipped out and the whole vehicle put together at Buenos Aires. The planned production was for 200 TAM and 300 VCI mounting a Rheinmetall 20mm cannon.

The hull of the TAM is modified from the Marder, but the powerpack and running gear are substantially the same, though a more powerful (720hp) engine is used in production units. With a battle weight of 29.5 tonnes and a power/weight ratio of 24hp/tonne, the TAM has considerable agility.

Argentina makes under licence the French 105mm gun as used in AMX30. This is a medium velocity weapon and therefore the lower weight of the TAM is able to cope with the recoil loads. It does mean, however, that the FCS must have high accuracy in range-taking, in order to attain a good first round hit probability. The FCS electronics are also made under licence in Argentina, though the components are all of European design. The newest system includes a stabilised gunner's sight, LRF and thermal imaging night sight.

Some 150 TAM have been built and are in service replacing the ageing Shermans which Argentina has had since the end of WW2, and an unknown quantity of VCI. They were not deployed in the Falklands and have not been battle tested.

The Argentine TAM tank — based on a modified Marder hull and built by the Argentines from kits supplied by Thyssen Henschel. *via C. Foss*

2 Reconnaissance and Light Armoured Vehicles

Belgium

FN 4RM/62F

The Belgian weapons manufacturer Fabrique Nationale (FN) of Herstal, near Liege, built an armoured car in the mid-1960s, based on the parts of the military trucks which they made for the army. It was a 4×4 design, with a six-cylinder petrol engine developing 130hp (gross) giving 16.44hp/tonne. Transmission was through a four-speed manual gearbox and two-speed transfer box and a maximum road speed of 110kph was claimed, but cross-country mobility was limited by the beam axles mounted on semi-elliptic springs and the 9.00×20 tyres.

The armoured hull had sloping armour all round which protected against small arms AP rounds. The driver sat centrally in front and had access through a small square hatch; the steering wheel could be removed to allow the driver to pass the hatch. The commander and gunner were in the turret, commander on the right, with a dome-shaped cupola carrying eight episcopes. There were two designs of turret. One mounted a 90mm gun and coaxial MG. It fired a low velocity HEAT round at 649m/sec to an effective range of one kilometre. The other type of turret carried a 60mm mortar and 7.62mm GPMGs. Smoke dischargers were mounted on both.

The FN 4RM/62F AB was a simple vehicle destined for the Belgian Gendarmerie, who bought 62. They were not used elsewhere as they had little virtue as fighting vehicles and could not compare with the French AML, just coming on to the international market.

SIBMAS

The next Belgian-designed AFV was much more sophisticated and owed something to the experience gained in production of the Scorpion in Belgium. The SIBMAS 6×6 is described variously as an APC and as a fire support or reconnaissance vehicle. It is a large machine, with great versatility, and can be adapted to all these roles and many others, according to the armament and equipment fitted. This is the modern trend, and it makes it difficult to classify the SIBMAS.

The engine, axles and transmission are all standard commercial parts from the MAN range of trucks, which makes logistic support easier for overseas customers. The layout is simple, with the two rear axles grouped together, all being on coil spring suspension and having lockable differentials. The engine is situated in the left rear of the hull. It is a 320bhp MAN diesel, with a turbo-charger, and it is installed with four quick-release couplings for the systems so that an

FN 4RM armoured car with 90mm gun was designed for the Belgian Gendarmerie. This prototype was built in 1962 and followed by 62 production vehicles. *FN*

engine change can be accomplished in only 30 minutes, in the field. The gearbox is a six-speed ZF fully automatic commercial type with torque converter and hydraulic retarder, for improved braking. There is a separate drive from the engine to the two propellers which enable the SIBMAS to use the water drive and wheel drive simultaneously, which makes entry to and exit from water much easier. The maximum road speed is 116kph and 10kph in the water, using the propeller drive.

The monocoque steel hull is furnished with a door on each side and another on the right hand side of the rear plate. This enables the infantry — nine can be carried — to embark and disembark in a very short time. They sit facing outwards and are able to use seven firing ports, three on the left and four in the right, above each of which is a vision block. In the roof over the corridor at the right rear of the hull is a hatch and mounting for a GPMG.

But the versatility of the SIBMAS comes mainly from the variety of weapons which can be installed in the turret, which is carried just behind the driver. At the lower end of the weapon scale the APC version could have a small turret with one or two 7.62mm or 12.7mm MGs. Cannon of 20mm, 25mm, 30mm, 76mm or 90mm can be mounted in turrets by several different manufacturers. The most powerful example, which has been accepted by the Malaysian forces, is the Cockerill 90mm gun and turret, but Alvis

Left: The SIBMAS 6×6 in the reconnaissance role is armed with a 60mm gun/mortar, a 20mm cannon in a separate mounting, and a 7.62mm MG. *SIBMAS*

Below: SIBMAS as a gunboat. Well, almost, since it can only fire canister rounds from its 90mm Cockerill gun while swimming. The recoil effect of a normal round could be upsetting. *SIBMAS*

Right: The Belgian VPX5000 is the latest development in the line that started in the 1950s with the VP90 (Voltigeur Patrouilleur). The basic hull is offered with many different armaments, as APC, anti-tank vehicle or as a light tank. Its armour is said to keep out small arms fire and splinters, but its combat weight is only 5,800kg. The engine is a six-cylinder BMW, producing 180hp and the machine is lively enough on its rubber band tracks. Its most likely use would be in support of airborne troops, but it has not yet been adopted by any army. *Lohr*

turrets with 30mm or 76mm guns are also offered.

As with most other modern AFVs, the SIBMAS can also perform the roles of mortar carrier, AA vehicle, ATGW, command, ambulance and recovery vehicles, according to the needs of the user. It is one of the best examples of the comparatively inexpensive wheeled AFVs that proliferate on the market today, and which are being used to fulfil so many operational roles.

Brazil

Until the 1970s Brazil relied entirely on imported AFVs, including M4 Shermans, M47s, M3A1 Stuarts and some 250 M41 Walker Bulldogs. These last were powered by a Lycoming gasoline engine which the Brazilians considered unreliable and a fire hazard; so much so that crew members were forbidden to smoke in their tanks for fear of brewing up. (British AFV crews, who have always been banned from smoking in their vehicles may wonder at the discipline which permitted smoking in other tanks which were not so much of a fire risk.) The Brazilian M41s were reworked, the engines being replaced by a 400hp DIN Saab-Scania turbo-charged diesel made locally in Brazil. This necessitated re-siting the radiators in an armoured extension to the hull, but the results were worth it in terms of range (600km against 180km for the original installation) and reliability, while full life costs have been dramatically reduced.

As the Brazilian defence industry emerged during the 1960s, alongside the expanding and inventive automotive industry, moves were made towards the production of indigenous AFVs. Engenheiros Especializados sa (Engesa), of Sao Paulo, had been building a range of tactical trucks with a good cross-country performance. The main features were a simple transfer box of welded plate, which could easily be adapted to a multitude of drives and loads, and a walking beam rear suspension, with a wheel travel of up to 50cm. This gave the Engesa trucks a positive multi-wheel contact with the ground at all times.

EE-11 Urutu and EE-9 Cascavel

In 1970 work started on the design of an APC, the EE-11, later named Urutu. The hull is a simple welded structure, with a composite steel armour of a hardened outer layer laminated with a softer inner layer, to shatter attacking projectiles and to absorb the shock on the inner layer. The driver sits to the left front of the hull, with the engine to his right. Just behind him is a circular hatch in the roof which is the standard position for the commander. It can be replaced by a variety of turrets and mountings for MGs and cannon. In the rear of the hull roof, over the troop compartment, are six small hatches in two rows of three each, opening outwards. These provide the only means of firing personal weapons from the vehicle.

The suspension is the same as for the trucks, with independent, twin-wishbone front wheel stations on coil springs and the 'Boomerang' walking beam rear suspension on double leaf springs. Tyres are 12.00×20 low pressure, with run-flat inner tubes of the Hutchinson pattern. The engine is a six-cylinder Mercedes Benz diesel which develops 175hp (DIN), driving through a manually operated five-speed gearbox and the two-speed Engesa transfer box, with a power take-off for the optional propeller drive used for swimming. This is used on the version for the Brazilian marines, who wanted a vehicle for operations in the open sea, rather than the inland waters which the standard version could accomplish. The Urutu for the marines has two shrouded propellers and a large splashboard on the bows, with four schnorkel tubes which can be erected at the sides of the troop compartment. In this configuration the Urutu is said to be capable of negotiating 3m waves.

The first prototype of Urutu was delivered in July 1970, after which development continued. Alongside the APC, Engesa designed an armoured car armed with a 37mm gun. This EE-9 Cascavel (all the Engesa AFVs are named after local poisonous snakes) had the same type of transmission and suspension and the same engine, but this was placed in the rear of the hull in conventional fashion. In 1972 Engesa were given a production order for 10 Cascavel for the Army

and a number of Urutu for the marines. The pre-production vehicles were delivered in 1973 and the first production units in 1974. Urutu has also been sold to a number of foreign clients, including Qatar and Libya.

Later Cascavels built for export were fitted with the French H90 turret with the DEFA 90F1 gun, as used on the Panhard AML90. Later still Engesa built their own version of this gun and turret. These are far more effective than the

original 37mm guns which had been stripped from old Stuarts. Fitting the 90mm turret necessitated widening the hull roof slightly, and subsequent vehicles have a longer wheelbase.

Urutu can carry a crew of up to 15 men at its combat weight of 11 tonnes; the Cascavel weighs 10.8 tonnes in battle order with a crew of three. Both these are outweighed by the third Engesa AFV, the 18tonne Sucuri. This is

Above: The Cascavel has conventional rear-engined layout, with the turret set in the centre of the hull. This model is armed with the Cockerill 90mm gun and has a LRF mounted externally on the top of the barrel. *Engesa*

Left and right: The Urutu layout has the engine at the right front of the hull, next to the driver, leaving the rear hull empty for a large, unobstructed troop compartment which allows ample space for 12 troops; there are doors on left and right sides and at the rear, and four large roof hatches. Personal weapons can be fired from four ports in the left side of the hull, and from three on the right. *Both: Engesa*

Above: This view of the Engesa Sucuri fire support vehicle shows the extent of the travel of the 'walking beam' suspension. The FL11 oscillating turret of French design mounts a 90mm gun. *Engesa*

Left: The EE-3 Jacarara uses solid axles and semi-elliptic leaf springs suspension; a four-cylinder Mercedes diesel engine of 120hp (SAE) drives through a conventional clutch and five speed synchromesh gearbox and two-speed transfer box. *Engesa*

Above right: The X1-A2 light tank is made by Bernardini SA. Its suspension and running gear give it a superficial resemblance to the American Stuart M5. Main armament is the Cockerill 90mm gun. *Bernardini*

designed as a tank hunter, armed with the French FL12 oscillating turret mounting a 105mm rifled gun which fires the same Obus G shaped charge projectiles as the AMX30 tank, though at a slightly reduced velocity. The layout of the Sucuri is the same as the Cascavel, but the turret is set slightly further back on the longer hull. The latest from the Engesa range is the Jacarara, a small four-wheeled scout car, built like a Ferret, but with a crew of three and able to take various MG or cannon armaments. It weighs 5.9 tonnes and has a top road speed of 90kph.

X1-A and A1-A2

There has been an earlier attempt to design an AFV in Brazil, in the late 1960s. At least one prototype was built, and it was on the lines of the French Lohr VP90, with a very low hull, standing only one metre high on five small roadwheels.

The tracks were extremely narrow and the ground pressure, even with a projected combat weight of 2.72 tonnes, must have been quite high. The engine and transmission was at the rear of the hull, while at the front the driver and commander sat under a small shield and had a MG as armament. Two more crew were to sit facing the rear in the open-topped compartment behind the driver. It is not surprising that nothing more was heard of this extraordinary little vehicle.

However, the Brazilian Army had a store of old Stuarts, and the firm of Bernardini sa, also of Sao Paulo, had an idea for making use of them. They had considerable expertise in the working of high quality steels, in their normal trade of making safes and strong rooms, and had already gone into the production of bodies for military trucks. By 1972 they had progressed to the complete refurbishment of 80 M3A1

Stuarts for the Brazilian Army. They incorporated many modifications including replacement of the Continental radial engines by locally built Scania Vabis truck diesel engines, improvements to the volute spring suspension, improved tracks and a new, Bernardini-designed turret, mounting the French DEFA F1 90mm gun. This rebuild was called the X1-A and is in service with the Brazilian Army.

With this experience Bernardini went ahead with the development of a longer hull, with a number of new features. The belly of the hull was double-skinned to resist mine blast and the angle of the glacis plate reduced. The increased length was enough to take a third, two-wheeled bogie unit, and the idler, instead of being the large, trailing wheel of the Stuart, was reduced in diameter and raised to the conventional position, to give a better departure angle. The new Scania engine of 300hp gives a maximum road speed of 60kph and a ratio of 16hp/tonne, which permits satisfactory mobility over most sorts of ground.

The armament of this new model, designated X1-A2, is the Cockerill 90mm gun, made under licence in Brazil by Engesa. The new tank carries 66 rounds of 90mm ammunition, 24 of them in the turret, conferring a formidable anti-tank capability. There is a coaxial 7.62mm MG and the commander has a pintle-mounted .50cal Browning on the turret roof. This shows considerable initiative in using the old Stuarts. The Brazilians even extended the use of these old hulls by bringing out a bridgelayer, the XLP-10, based on the early modified hull with the standard length and two bogie units. It carries a 10m long duralumin bridge which can be laid or recovered in three minutes, using a horizontal launching beam technique. Another variant on the same hull is the XLF-40, which carries three Avibras X-40 unguided surface to surface tactical rockets with a 60km range.

Below: The XLP-10 Bridgelayer is based on the Bernardini X1-A1 light tank, which has a large trailing idler, like the Stuart M3 and M5. The hull is supported at the front by hydraulically operated feet and the bridge launched on an extensible beam. *Bernardini*

France

The traditional role of long range recce had been carried out during WW2 largely by wheeled vehicles. They had the virtues, as against tracked AFVs, of longer operational range, higher speeds and less noise under most circumstances. In the later stages, as more and heavier tanks became available, so the lighter tanks were more often used in the close recce role, usually as part of tank formations. The American M3 and M5 Stuart, Russian T-70, German PzII and British Cromwells all played this part, but wheeled vehicles were far more numerous.

In postwar formations the same trend continued and the same wartime vehicles soldiered on into the 1950s and 1960s. Daimler armoured cars were in use in the Arabian Gulf in the 1960s, and a few AEC Mk 3 served in Lebanon alongside Staghounds. American M8 armoured cars are still in use in some South American states. These bridged the gap until the next generation of wheeled AFVs appeared.

EBR75

The first French LAV was, in fact, based on a prewar design, resurrected, modernised and built by France as the Engin Blindé de Reconnaissance (EBR75). It was an 8×8 design, with a long, low hull housing a driver at each end, with duplicated controls. The 12-cylinder Panhard engine was horizontally placed in the middle of the vehicle under the turret. This permitted a very low hull of only 1.03m from floor to roof. On this was the turret, of the oscillating type, with a 75mm medium velocity (600m/sec) gun, fixed in the top section. The FL11 turret of the original EBR and the subsequent 1954 model did not have automatic loading, but the later FL10 turret, with a much higher velocity (1,000m/sec) 75mm gun was fitted with an automatic loading system. The new turret also increased both height and weight. From

2.24m to 2.58m overall and from 13 to 15 tonnes. Eventually all EBRs in French service were retro-fitted with the FL11 turret mounting a medium velocity (750m/sec) smoothbore 90mm gun, the HEAT rounds of which, it is claimed, can penetrate up to 320mm of armour. The other interesting feature of the EBR was the power train. The flat-12 engine produced some 200hp and drove through a small diameter, multi-disc clutch to a four-speed primary gearbox. From there the drive went to a second gearbox, just behind the front driver, giving a total of 16 possible ratios. Only four speeds are normally used for cross-country and six on the road. The secondary gearbox incorporates a lockable differential and from there the drive is taken by two propshafts to the front pair of wheels and via bevel boxes and four more shafts to the other six wheels. Since all four wheels on each side of the hull are positively linked by propshafts, it was though necessary to have another differential between the front and second pairs of wheels to eliminate tyre scrubbing and transmission wind-up; these are just outboard of the secondary gearbox.

The two centre pairs of wheels can be raised for on-road running and lowered for cross-country. Since they would not normally be in contact with the road surface, these wheels were furnished with steel grousers rather than tyres, but there are rubber blocks between the alloy rims and the wheel disc which allow a small degree of resilience. To attain its minimum turning radius of 3.962m both front and rear pairs of wheels were steered, though only the front were used for normal road running.

The EBR was an advanced design for the time and offered a good road speed and range combined with excellent cross-country performance. It had two major disadvantages: the air-cooled engine tended to overheat the crew and the turret had to be removed to carry out any major work on the engine or transmission. Because of its size, cost and com-

plicated systems, the EBR did not meet the French requirements for Algeria, so in 1956 a specification was issued for a smaller, lighter (and cheaper) Auto-Mitrailleuse Legere (AML). Panhard produced their design No 245, which was accepted in 1959 and in service by 1961.

AML

The AML became the progenitor of a family of AFVs unsurpassed in variety. It is powered by a four-cylinder horizontally-opposed air-cooled engine, giving sufficient power for a maximum road speed of 90kph. As with the EBR, the AML features three differentials, all of the limited slip cam type. Thus there can be relative movement between wheels on each side and between front and rear wheels, but no single wheel or pair of wheels can spin. The drive line is a modified H layout, from the transverse gearbox, via a line of four shafts each side which follow the side of the hull. The final reductions are incorporated in the trailing arm suspension. Thus no space is wasted under the turret floor. The engine is at the rear of the hull, which makes maintenance easier than on the EBR.

Entry and exit are far easier than in most small AFVs, owing to the provision of a large hatch in the wall each side.

Left: The Engin Blindé de Reconnaissance with a 90mm gun in the FL-11 oscillating turret. There is a small ring sight in front of each turret crew member, for quick laying of the gun. This picture shows the centre tractor wheels in the raised position and steering on the front wheels only. *ECP Armées*

Below: The Panhard AML90 is built under licence in South Africa and called Eland 90. The usual French Hutchinson tyres have been replaced by Dunlop Trak Grip Run Flat tyres made in South Africa. Note the very tall mounting for the commander's Browning MG. *H-R Heitman*

Above these doors the hull widens into a circular flange on which the turret is mounted. This allows very little space in the turret basket, compared with the full width of the turret above the turret ring. The original turret mounted a 60mm breech-loaded mortar and one or two MGs. The profile was low and the turret sides beautifully curved.

In the French tradition of 'something for every occasion', the variety of weapons which can be carried on the AML is bewildering. A 12.7mm MG or a 20mm cannon could be substituted for the 60mm mortar, which itself could be replaced by an 81mm mortar. In a later model the 90mm smoothbore gun made another appearance, the overall weight rising from 4.8 to 5.5 tonnes. Another version carries a 30mm Hispano Suiza cannon and coaxial MG. The curved sides of the original turret had to give way to flat welded plate in later turrets, to accommodate the larger weapons, and the height of the vehicle increased from 1.89m to 2.07m. A specially designed turret of bulbous and top-heavy appearance can be mounted in place of the standard turret, carrying twin 20mm anti-aircraft cannon. Another special turret carries four HOT wire-guided ATGW. Other ATGW, the SS-11 and the earlier Entac, have been mounted externally.

Some 30 countries have adopted the AML in its many varieties and it is still, after 20 years, a front line vehicle. Apart from those made by Panhard in France, an unknown quantity have been built under licence in South Africa, where they are known as the Eland. A unit of AML90 was deployed in East Falkland, during the 1982 war, but they do not appear to have been engaged, being captured undamaged and fully armed.

Sagaie and Lynx

The success of the AML family led Panhard to design and produce its successors, Sagaie and Lynx, in the late 1970s, hoping to repeat the earlier market triumph. The object was

to provide a cheap but powerful vehicle for the armies of the Third World. The main criteria of the design were light weight, good cross-country performance and a powerful weapon system. They have achieved this with a 90mm main armament on a 6×6 hull with a combat weight of 7.4 tonnes.

The hulls and running gear of both Sagaie and Lynx are almost identical. The Peugeot six-cylinder gasoline engine and the six-speed Panhard gearbox are at the rear. The centre pair of roadwheels can be raised for road operations, as in the EBR, and there are optional Dowty-Messier hydro-jets for water propulsion in the amphibious version. Maximum road speed is quoted as 100kph and the operational range as 950km.

Both vehicles are armed with a 90mm gun, but here they differ in operational concept. Sagaei carries a long-barrelled 90mm smoothbore firing the same range of ammunition as the CN90F3 gun of the AMX13 tank destroyer. The FS-HEAT rounds is fired at 950m/sec, which is much greater than the earlier guns in EBR and AML, and therefore offers a higher hit probability at a longer range. An APFSDS round is also available, but guns firing this ammunition must be equipped with a larger, rolled steel, double baffle muzzle brake. The APFSDS round is fired at 1,350m/sec and can penetrate the NATO triple target at 2,000m. Only 20 rounds of 90mm are carried in the turret, but this can be increased to 30 rounds by altering the stowage and deleting some items of kit. As is usual these days, a whole range of options can be exercised in the FCS, with day and night sights, LRF and thermal imagers available according to the length of the customer's purse.

Sagaie can be identified by the long barrel of the gun, the aluminium thermal sleeve and the single baffle muzzle brake. Lynx, on the other hand, has the same H-90 gun as in AML90, with the CNMP-Berthiez turret slightly modified.

The barrel is shorter and there is the same twin baffle muzzle brake. Only 21 rounds of 90mm can be carried, as well as 2,000 for the coaxial MG. Sagaie has the same secondary armament. Both vehicles have a crew of three; driver, gunner and commander. Although the Sagaie was designed for export only, one of the first purchasers was the French Army, which will use them to equip the Rapid Deployment Force based in France and the airbase defence units in Dakar, Ivory Coast, Gabon and Djibouti. Other customers are the Ivory Coast government, Mexico and the Argentinian Marines. The last two will buy the Lynx version, of which the higher turret roof permits greater elevation angles.

AMX10RC

The other candidate for the heavy support weapon system for the RDF was the much more sophisticated and expensive AMX10RC, mounting a 105mm gun. It is a much larger vehicle, of 15 tonnes combat weight with a crew of four, and was developed from the tracked AMX10P. By using many components and assemblies from the tracked vehicle a high degree of standardisation has been achieved and considerable economies.

The basic hull is almost the same width, through not having to allow space for the wheels to steer. The AMX10RC is skid steered by using the same technique as for a tracked vehicle; slowing down one side and speeding up the other. This does, however, produce problems of tyre wear, and steering on soft going can cause the wheels to dig in more than usual. Steering is controlled by disc brakes operated by levers. The hydro-pneumatic suspension can be used also to vary the height and attitude of the hull, which gives more scope to the elevation of the main armament, from −8° to +20° in its mounting. Mobility is better than the tracked vehicle; road speed is a maximum 85kph and the road range

Left: The Panhard Sagaie carries a formidable load of ammunition. Shown here are 81 rounds for the 81mm Brandt gun-mortar, 16 belts of ammunition for the coaxial 7.62mm MG and four smoke pots for the launcher tubes carried on the sides of the turret.

Above right: The AMX10RC is the replacement for the EBR, but with greater firepower. The 105mm gun has a muzzle reference sight fitted behind the muzzle brake. The light alloy thermal sleeve on the barrel is in two sections which telescope on recoil. The suspension is adjusted, in this picture, to give maximum ground clearance. A skid steering system is used, so there is no loss of hull space to allow for turning the wheels for steering. *ECP Armées*

Right: The AMX10P uses a hull very similar to the AMX10RC, but with tracks. The grille on the rear hull is the inlet for the water propulsion system. These two vehicles are armed with a 20mm cannon with selective AP or HE dual ammunition feed. There are no firing ports for the personal weapons of the crew. *ECP Armées*

is 800km. The vehicle is fully amphibious driven by water jets as with the AMX10P.

The AMX10RC is a very heavily armed reconnaissance vehicle. The French philosophy is for recce units to be able to tackle the mass of enemy armour as far ahead of the main positions as possible. Therefore the AMX10RC carries a TK105 turret fitted with a 105mm gun firing fin-stabilised HEAT rounds at 1,100m/sec, with a 7.62mm coaxial MG. The turret's low profile belies the elevation range of the gun. The COTAC fire control system includes LRF, ballistic computer and sensors for ambient temperature, side wind and atmospheric pressure. The gun is slaved to the main sight which the commander can orientate separately from the gunner's sight, and with which he can lay and open fire, overriding the gunner. The sights are not stabilised.

The gun has a recoil load of only 13 tonnes compared to the 25 tonnes of the 105mm F-1 fitted in the AMX30, although it has no muzzle brake. There is also an HE round with a m/v of 800m/sec and there was to have been an AP round with a m/v of 1,500m/sec, attained by a small rocket fired after leaving the barrel. The project was put in abeyance in 1976, on grounds of cost, and has not yet been revived.

The gun barrel is 5.04m long and sticks out about 3.5m ahead of the hull, which may cause a few problems when turning in close wooded country or in narrow streets. AMX10RC is in service with French Army units in Europe, and is still in production. Morocco has ordered 108, but the French Army production programme is to be halted after five reconnaissance regiments have been equipped with 48 each.

Germany, Federal Republic of

Spähpanzer 2 Luchs
In a surprising return to the large vehicle concept of the 1940s, the Germans have brought into service their new eight-wheeled Spähpanzer 2 Luchs, or Lynx. The first of 408 vehicles ordered from Rheinstahl Wehrtechnik was delivered in September 1975, giving the Bundeswehr their first home-designed reconnaissance vehicle since the end of WW2. The recce companies of armoured divisions were then equipped with tanks and APCs, much on the American model, and for the same reasons — because they had not got any suitable modern recce vehicles. But while other members of NATO

have reduced the size of their recce vehicles as far as possible, the Germans built a 20tonne, eight-wheeled armoured car, which, at a quick glance, is of the same family as the SdKfz231 and SdKfz234 used in 1944-45.

Luchs is a lightly armoured and lightly armed vehicle with a four-man crew, which meets all the German requirements for tactical mobility, low noise level and good communications. The main reason for its huge bulk is to give it the inherent buoyancy it needs to be able to swim Germany's many rivers without preparation and at any state of the weather. All that is necessary for swimming can be done on the move, by the driver. The bow trim vane can be erected by a simple hydraulic ram, bilge pumps switched on and the Luchs can enter the water, powered by two steerable propellers driven from the main engine. It can reach 10kph in the water and is very manoeuvrable.

On land the Luchs can reach a maximum road speed of 100kph. The Daimler Benz OM403 10-cylinder engine was designed to be multi-fuelled and develops 390hp on diesel oil and 300hp on gasoline. It is unit-mounted with the automatic gearbox and ancillaries and the whole powerpack can be disconnected and removed in very little time. The engine can be test run outside the vehicle if necessary. The German operational requirement laid great stress on low noise level and the exhaust system has been carefully designed to give away as little as possible in decibels or IR radiation. The fuel tanks are bullet proof and are fitted with an automatic fire extinguisher system.

Above left: The Radspähpanzer 2 Luchs in all-wheel-steering mode; this permits a turning circle of 11.5m radius as against 19.4m with four-wheel steering. The beam axles and coil spring suspension are clearly seen. *BdV*

Below left: SPz 12-3 reconnaissance vehicle with 20mm cannon. This vehicle was used in the recce role until Spähpanzer Luchs became available. *US Army*

Below: The Ratel is used as a recce vehicle and APC by the South Africans. The turret carries a 20mm cannon, 7.62mm MG in coaxial mounting and French type smoke pot throwers. The three weapon slits on the side are each surmounted by a vision block. *H-R Heitman*

The gearbox provides four ratios in each direction and there is steering control at each end of the vehicle, with the rearward facing radio operator driving in reverse. The drive goes from a central transfer box under the hull, by four separate propshafts to the four beam axles. These axles have central differentials which are lockable and all have facility for steering. The driver can select the four front wheels, the four rear wheels or all eight wheels for steering as required. Eight-wheel steering gives a turning radius of 11.5m, which is better than might be expected of a vehicle with an overall length of 7.743m and a wheelbase of 5.165m. The axles are located by coil springs and radius rods, and altogether there is a forest of metalwork hanging under the hull, all of which would appear to be vulnerable to mine damage. However, with eight wheels, the Luchs has a very good getting home capability.

The armoured hull of the Luchs gives protection against small arms, splinter and blast and the sides are further protected by the boxes between the wheel stations being filled with a bullet-resistant and buoyant material.

For such a large and impressive vehicle, the Luchs appears ludicrously impotent. The two-man turret is fitted with a 20mm Rh202 cannon and no coaxial MG, though there is a 7.62mm MG mounted on a ring at the commander's hatch, which can be fired from the head and shoulders out position. Both commander and gunner have periscopic sights linked to the cannon and there are 12 episcopes for observation. Four Wegmann type smoke grenade dischargers are fitted each side of the turret. All this is consistent with the German philosophy of reconnaissance by stealth and of fighting only to get out of trouble.

Israel

As the production capacity of the Israeli defence industry has increased, so the emphasis has been placed more and more on exporting to obtain foreign currency. Designers used the great experience that had been acquired by the armed forces and have produced some very good weapons. One that was introduced in 1975, at the Paris Air Show, by Israel Aircraft Industries, was a small reconnaissance vehicle of unique design.

It was called the RBY Mk 1 and was obviously intended to

appeal to the impecunious countries which had a guerilla problem. A subsequently modified version was called the RAMTA the name of the company that built the hull and then shortened to RAM. The RAM is a four-wheeled vehicle with an open-topped armoured body giving some protection to the crew of up to eight men (driver, commander and six 'gunners'). The engine and gearbox are at the rear of the chassis, with propshafts driving both axles. The appearance is very much 'a wheel at each corner', for the front axle is placed far out in front of the main hull, with a wheelbase of

3.4m in an overall length of 5.023m. This is in order to minimise mine damage and to preserve the crew, a most important consideration in any piece of Israeli equipment.

The underside of the hull is shaped so as to divert mine blast away from the crew compartment, in which the driver and commander sit side by side at the front, with observation flaps of armour covering the windows. The rear crew compartment is open, giving no overhead protection to the men who man the MGs mounted at each corner, covering all sectors. A spare wheel is carried over the front axle and the ensemble resembles an extended, armoured dune buggy. Power comes from a Dodge petrol engine and commercial parts are used in the gearbox and axles. While the *Military Balance* lists RAM as being in use by the IDF, there are no records of any being sold abroad, yet.

United Kingdom

The British Army had traditionally used wheeled AFVs for reconnaissance since 1914 and still did so in 1945, though light and medium tanks were used in recce troops of armoured regiments from late 1944 onwards. Regiments for the recce role were equipped with a variety of armoured and scout cars, many of which were wartime expedients of doubtful value. The better vehicles survived the test of battle and soldiered on in the postwar army. Armoured car regiments served in Palestine (until 1948), Libya, Egypt and Malaya as well as with the British Army of the Rhine, in Germany.

The main equipments were Daimler armoured and scout cars, and the AEC Mk III, armed with a 75mm gun in the support troops. American Staghounds and Humber

armoured cars were phased out in the late 1940s, though Humber scout cars were issued to Divisional Reconnaissance Regiments until 1952, and there were some anomalies such as the odd troop of White Scout cars left over from Palestine. (Some 40 Humber Mk IVs are still on the strength of the Burmese Army and are the subject of an annual spares demand which is very hard to meet!)

The British armoured cars were all of four-wheeled configuration, the old six-wheeled Lanchesters and Crossleys having been abandoned long since. But the superior performance of six and eight-wheeled vehicles had not been lost on the British, and they had some experience with American M8 and Boarhounds and with the Marmon-Herrington Mk VI. So when the GSOR (General Staff Operational Requirement) was issued in January 1946, it called for an improvement in performance over the Daimler.

Saladin

The original intention was to continue with the 2pdr (39mm) gun, which had been in service since 1938, using a projected APDS round, fired at 1,295m/sec, and capable of penetrating 85mm of armour at 30° at 914m (1,000yd). The 2pdr could also fire a HE round but the effect of this was

Above left: Japanese Type 60 APC, used in the reconnaissance role, armed with a .50cal Browning MG on the roof and a .30cal Browning in a ball-type bow mounting. It carries a crew of two and a section of eight men, but its height to the top of the cupola is only 1.70m, compared to a minimum height of 2.02m for the M113. *Japanese MoD*

Left: The Fiat OTO-Melara 6616 armoured car has a low profile hull and inherent buoyancy, with water propulsion by the wheels at up to 5kph. The Rh202 20mm cannon can be elevated to +35° to give an anti-helicopter capability. *OTO-Melara*

Right: Daimler armoured car. *IWM*

Below right: AEC armoured cars armed with 75mm gun and coaxial 7.92mm Besa MG were used in the support troops of armoured car regiments. The chassis was developed from the AEC Matador 4×4 gun tractor. This vehicle is sealed and fitted with an exhaust extension for wading trials. *AEC Ltd(BL)*

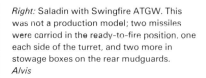

Left: FV601 Saladin negotiates a ditch.

Right: Saladin with Swingfire ATGW. This was not a production model; two missiles were carried in the ready-to-fire position, one each side of the turret, and two more in stowage boxes on the rear mudguards. *Alvis*

too small and a larger gun was desirable. A number of alternatives were discussed, from what was then available, but it was decided, in principle, to adopt a new design of 76mm gun being designed at RARDE. Meanwhile prototype work continued with the high velocity 2pdr until it was dropped in 1949.

It had been intended to keep the weight and size of the new vehicle down to the same level as the Daimler, but with the decision to use the 76mm gun this was clearly impossible. The turret, and hence the turret ring, needed to be bigger, and the hull wider, to accommodate it. The weight looked as though it would be at least 10 tons, so it was necessary to have a more powerful engine, needing a longer engine compartment.

As each part of the compromise proceeded, it became obvious that the larger hull and greater weight needed at least six wheels in order to get a ground pressure within reasonable limits and good cross-country performance. It may be coincidence, but the eventual configuration and dimensions of the new FV601 are almost identical to the American M38 six-wheeled armoured car. This was developed by Chevrolet from the T19 to replace the M8. It had three equally spaced wheels each side and carried a 37mm gun. The M38 never went into production owing to the change of policy in the US Army, which dropped wheels in favour of tracks for reconnaissance vehicles. Alvis Ltd, of Coventry, were given a contract, in October 1947, to build two prototypes of FV601, but owing to the priority given to production of the FV603 Saracen APC, sister vehicle to FV601, these were not delivered until 1953, and six pre-production vehicles built by Crossley Motors of Stockport, took a further two years. Thus it was mid-1958 before production finally started of the FV601C, now named Saladin. There had been numerous changes en route, in the A and B versions. The three-man turret crew was reduced to two, with the gunner acting as radio operator and the commander loading the gun. The driver's hatch was enlarged to allow

access and his two side observation flaps eliminated (though the periscopes remained). An idea for the commander to have a contra-rotating cupola for target acquisition was dropped because of cost, complexity and the fact that if the commander was to load the gun he would not have time to use the cupola as well. Provision for the commander to drive when going backwards in emergencies was also dropped, though the small observation flap in the rear of the fighting compartment remains.

Saladin came out, therefore, with a three-man crew of driver (seated centrally in front), gunner (on the left of the turret) and commander on the right. The turret had only hand traverse, both gunner and commander having controls, with electric power assistance for rapid traverse. The elevating gear was only manual. The gunner had a periscope sight linked to the gun cradle and had responsibility for the .30in calibre Browning coaxial MG. The commander had four fixed periscopes in front of his hatch, and one in a rotating mounting behind. He could also fire the .30in Browning MG which was pintle-mounted externally on the turret roof.

Access to the 42 rounds of 76mm ammunition stowed in the hull was quite good, with 11 ready rounds in the turret basket and the remainder stowed vertically round the hull, 11 on the right, 12 on the left and eight on the engine compartment bulkhead, so that replenishment of the ready use rack was easy. Rounds weighed only 7.4kg so were easily handled in the turret. Four natures of ammunition were normally carried: HE, HESH, base ejection smoke and canister. This last was revived after the Korean war experience of massed infantry attacks, against which 76mm canister would have blasted 780 steel pellets at an angle of about 40° from the muzzle, with devastating effect. On the outside of the turret were two six-barrelled smoke grenade dischargers which could throw the No 80 white phosphorous grenade about 40m in a 90° spread. Twelve replacement grenades would be carried internally, and 12 of the propelling fuses. Reloading had to be done in comparative

peace, as the two wires of each fuse had to be threaded through a hole in the base of the barrel and then attached to a series of terminals. This was not a task to be attempted in a hurry or in bad conditions of stress or climate. It was, moreover, important not to lose the safety pins of the grenades, in case they had to be unloaded without firing.

The 76mm gun had a conventional vertical sliding breech block and concentric recoil system. The mounting allows elevation from −10° to +20°, giving a maximum range for the HE round of 5,500m. This gives Saladin a good supporting fire capability, while the HESH round, effective at any range at which a hit is obtained, can destroy opposing light armour and damage MBTs.

The driver's compartment was comparatively comfortable, with an adjustable seat and the steering wheel angled to allow quick movement in and out of the compartment. Power-assisted steering and a pre-selector gearbox added to the simplicity of operation. The forward/reverse lever, on the driver's left, operated in the natural sense. The power steering made Saladin light to drive, except when the engine-driven hydraulic pump was not working, for example when a casualty was being towed. The steering operated on the front two pairs of wheels, and the effort needed to turn the wheel without assistance was huge, so towing had to be by an A-frame, rather than by a single pole or rope, to avoid accidents. The brakes, too, were power-assisted and the combination of these two factors caused a modification on the 67 Saladins sold to the German Border Police (*Bundesgrenzschutz*). On these vehicles there was an additional hydraulic pump driven by the right-hand rear bevel box, so that when the vehicle was moving, even without engine power, there was still enough hydraulic pressure to operate both steering and brakes. It is surprising that this modification was not offered on the remaining Saladins but, like the limited slip differential which was an optional extra, it was never adopted by any other customer. The BGS Saladins could easily be identified

by the lack of provision for a coaxial MG. They also carried the German Wegmann type smoke grenade dischargers, rather than the British type.

The engine eventually chosen for Saladin was the Rolls-Royce B80 which developed 160hp. It was the eight-cylinder version of the B series and gave and effective net power/gross weight ratio of 11.94bhp/ton which left Saladin very much underpowered when compared with the AML or the German Spähpanzer Luchs.

The transmission was via a Daimler fluid coupling to a five-speed preselector gearbox and a forward/reverse transfer box, which gave five speeds in each direction. The transfer box turned the drive 90° to power the central bevel boxes and from there the front and rear bevel boxes were driven by propshafts, forming the classic H drive layout. At the bevel boxes the drive went via short drive shafts and Tracta-joints to the final epicyclic reduction in the wheel hubs.

At each wheel station the suspension consisted of upper and lower wishbones at the outer ends of which the stub axle could move up and down in a shallow arc while remaining parallel to the bottom of the hull. The upper wishbone link was splined to a longitudinal torsion bar, the other end of which was fixed to the hull, the whole bar being contained in a tube outside the hull armour. While this was more vulnerable to damage, it took up no room in the hull and was easily accessible for repairs. Each wheel was independently sprung and independently driven, with all three wheels on each side positively locked together and unable to rotate independently from the others. Thus, if the going was bad, it had to be bad enough for all three wheels on one side to slip at the same time. When this did happen, in Arabian Gulf sabkha (salt flats) for example, the vehicle bellied and had to be extracted with great difficulty, the lack of a locking differential between the two sides being felt keenly.

However, this suspension could absorb a lot of mine damage and still allow the vehicle to get home. Up to two wheels could be lost, provided that they were not both on the same side and that one front wheel remained, and the Saladin remained mobile. This was demonstrated by running one vehicle over a 'mine', usually behind some bushes. The spectators would see two wheels blown high in the air, then a Saladin would emerge from the bushes minus two wheels, to perform manoeuvres and drive away. The original vehicle would remain in concealment until the crowds had gone home. The main hazard in this exercise was dodging the wheels as they came down: they had a habit of bouncing!

The hydraulic system included three accumulators, with floating pistons which separated the oil from nitrogen gas under pressure. It was not always easy to obtain supplies of nitrogen in the field, and the power steering could behave in an erratic fashion if pressure in the accumulators was allowed to drop.

Saladin has served with distinction in 20 countries and, apart from the BGS vehicles, has remained unmodified. This is partly due to the fact that no other engine of suitable output would fit into the restricted engine compartment. A B81 was tried, but it necessitated extending the hull. Also it was probable that the transmission would have been unable to accept any increased loads, had a more powerful engine been available. Many proposals were made to fit other weapons, but none reached prototype stage.

Alvis built 1,177 Saladins between 1959 and 1972, when the production tooling was broken up. Saladin is still serving with 14 countries, which says much for the design, first conceived in 1947, and the workmanship. Apart from their normal roles of reconnaissance they have been used in the fire support role and even as artillery.

Ferret

The organisation of a troop in an armoured car Regiment had evolved during the war into two sections, each of one armoured car and one scout car. In the armoured car regiments of the late 1940s this usually meant Daimler armoured cars and Daimler scout cars. The latter — usually known as Dingos — were, mechanically, smaller versions of

the armoured car, with rear engine, H-drive with pre-selector gearbox and independent suspension all round. They were low, fast and manoeuvrable. Total production was 6,626 vehicles, and they found their way into most 'teeth-arm' units. (The name 'Dingo' was first used by Alvis Ltd for their unsuccessful two-man scout car in 1939. The name was transferred unofficially, for onomatopoeic reasons.)

The continuing demand for such a vehicle caused the Army to issue a requirement, in 1947, for a successor to the Dingo. A development contract was awarded to Daimler in October 1948 and they completed the first prototype in June 1950. It was given the designation FV701 and named Ferret. It went into production in 1952 and by the time it was superseded in 1971, some 4,409 had been built, in many variants.

The basic vehicle had a polygonal hull with an extension at the rear for the engine compartment. The original Ferret Mk 1 was open-topped and armed only with a pintle-mounted Bren .303 LMG or .30 Browning. The driver and commander sat in tandem, the driver having controls similar to the Saladin, including the inclined steering wheel and forward/reverse transfer lever. He sat very low in the hull, between the shafts driving the front wheels. Although the suspension was virtually the same as for the Dingo, the wheelbase was 31cm longer, which, with 10bhp/tonne more than its predecessor, gave the Ferret a much better cross-country performance. In fact it was almost too good in that the driver, seated low down and braced against his seat, often forgot the plight of the commander, who had to hang on grimly to turret, microphone, mapboard and binoculars to avoid being projected bodily from the bucking, bouncing hull.

The Rolls-Royce B60 engine was a six-cylinder member of the B series family and developed 116bhp (129bhp in its final form). It drove through a fluid coupling and five-speed preselector gearbox to the forward/reverse transfer box and then, by shafts to bevel boxes at each corner of the hull. Short drive-shafts and Tracta-joints took the drive to epicylic final drives in the wheel hubs. There was no provision for

reverse-driving controls, but two flaps in the hull could be opened to allow the driver and commander rearward vision.

Although the Ferret Mk 1, used as a liaison vehicle, was open-topped, the Mk 2 was fitted with a small, manually-operated turret with a .30 Browning MG, as a recon-naissance vehicle. This was virtually the only difference from the Mk 1 liaison vehicle, and the Ferret Mk 2/3 (FV701) was the most numerous version built. The gun was aimed by a periscope sight in the turret roof, linked to the gun cradle and provided with a simple circular aiming mark which was calibrated by lining it up with the strike of tracer ammunition at 400yd. The commander would lean his back against a shaped pad on the turret ring and swing the turret bodily, right hand on the pistol grip of the MG and left hand on a brake lever that helped control the momentum of the turret. There was also a small plunger travelling lock which was useful on which to hang the headset, when not being worn. The turret roof hatch folded forwards to rest on two brackets, forming a useful map board rest and an anchor for the commander's hands when going fast across-country. The turret rear folded down to form a seat for less strenuous periods of observation and rest.

The gun had elevation from −15° to +45° and a depression stop bar was fitted on the rear of the fighting compartment to prevent accidentally shooting at the engine exhaust louvres. The Ferret Mk 2/3 carried 10 liners of 250 rounds each for the Browning, and twin three-barrelled smoke grenade dischargers with at least one refill.

Ferrets Mk 1 and 2 carried a spare wheel on the left side of the hull and a large stowage box on the right. In sub-sequent marks the spare wheel was deleted and extra stowage provided. All tyres were, in any case, run-flats, capable of going 50 miles totally deflated.

The Mk 2 was developed to carry four Vigilant wire-guided ATGWs, two in launchers either side of the turret and two more in stowage boxes on the left side of the hull in place of the spare wheel. The turret was very like that of the Mk 2/3, with the same Browning .30cal MG, but in addition there was a missile controller's sight mounted on top in place of the original periscope. The Ferret Mk 2/6 with Vigilant was a useful addition to the strength of armoured car units and of the air-portable squadron in support of air-borne operations. Vigilant was a first-generation manually guided missile, taking a shaped charge warhead to a maximum range of 1,375m.

The Mk 2/6 (FV703) was a stop-gap until a purpose-built ATGW vehicle could be put into service. This was the Ferret Mk 5 (FV712) with the larger Swingfire ATGW. Four missiles were mounted, two on each side of a large, flat turret, in the middle of which was a 7.62mm GPMG, for self-defence, and the missile controller's sight. The turret was made of welded aluminium armour, as were the armoured boxes for two more missiles, one each side of the hull, under the overhang of the turret.

The Mk 5 was to have been the main ATGW vehicle of the Royal Armoured Corps, but in the event, only 50 were built. These were conversions of the Mk 4 Big Wheeled Ferret, which was armed in the same way as the Mk 2/3, with a single MG in a manually operated turret. However, the gun itself was no longer the ageing .30 Browning M1919, but the 7.62 × 51mm GPMG which had been accepted by the Armoured Corps for use as a coaxial weapon in tanks. The other changes in the Mk 4 were larger wheels and tyres (11.00 × 20 instead of 9.00 × 16) and the suspension units were strengthened and modified to take disc brakes. A floatation screen was fitted, and, with the new stowage bins which could be sealed to give additional buoyancy, enabled the Ferret Mk 4 and Mk 5 to swim at about 5kph, propelled by the wheels.

There are 1,429 Ferrets still in service with the British Army, which cannot do without this versatile vehicle, both for Internal Security and normal liaison duties. At least 1,000 more are in service with 24 other countries.

At least two attempts were made to up-gun the Ferret in the 1960s. BMARC of Grantham mounted a small conical steel turret in which the gunner sat sideways, facing the breech of a Hispano 20mm cannon, aiming through a 90° prismatic sight. In another conversion, prepared for a poten-

Left: Ferret Mk 2/3 in the rough, while a Mk 1/1 waits on the road in the background. The driver is leaning as far forward as he can to try to see where he is going. *RAC Centre*

Right: The Ferret Mk 2/6, with two Vigilant ATGW on the turret, was issued to the airportable armoured squadron in support of parachute units. Two reserve missiles were carried in containers on the left side of the hull, in place of the spare wheel. *RAC Centre*

Left and below: Attempts were made to up-gun Ferret with 20mm cannon. An Oerlikon was ring-mounted on the Mk 2/3 and in another experiment Bemarc of Grantham mounted a Hispano-Suiza 20mm cannon in a 360° traverse turret. Although firepower was significantly increased, in both cases the extra weight reduced stability and performance. *Both: Alvis*

Right: Scorpion of the 16th/5th Queens Royal Lancers on watch in Cyprus, during the Turkish invasion of 1974. *MoD*

tial African buyer, an Oerlikon 20mm was fitted on an open ring mounting. Neither were adopted.

CVR (T) and (W)

The Ferret was the acme of the scout car, whose object was reconnaissance by stealth alone. It was to be followed by equipments more able to fight and survive in the nuclear age which was foreseen. In the 1960s the role of Britain's Army was changing. No longer was the main commitment the policing of the more far-flung parts of the world, but a con-centration of strength in support of the NATO defence against a Soviet invasion of western Europe. All the roles of the armoured car units were now concentrated into a smaller area, and the need for long range recce considerably reduced. Much more work would be done off the road rather than on, and tracked mobility would have great advantages. When the army started the search for a successor to the Saladin and Ferret, therefore, tracked vehicles were con-sidered for the first time since the demise of the light tank in 1940.

There was still an important worldwide commitment in the role of 'firemen'; British forces had to have a strong air-mobile element which could be sent to the aid of friends in need, so air-portability was a prime requirement for the new vehicle. Since it would be the only heavy weapon available, it would need a good fire support weapon and it must be capable of movement in all types of terrain, in all climates, if it was to be fit for the job. The other prime requirement was that of anti-tank weapon, since the 'fire brigade' force would be mainly infantry, armed only with their light anti-tank weapons.

In the feasibility studies which followed, the two major constraints were size and weight, to attain the air-portability which was vital. The first proposal was for a 13.6 tonnes tracked vehicle called the Armoured Vehicle Reconnaissance (AVR), in which a three-man crew sat in a limited traverse turret at the front of the hull. This included the driver, which posed some problems of orientation and control. The main armament would be a 76mm or 105mm gun, and Swingfire anti-tank missiles would be carried in armoured boxes on either side of the rear hull.

The AVR would have to do everything itself, and with such compromises it would do nothing well. It was considered too large and heavy for air-portability and a parallel development of a wheeled vehicle with skid-steering suffered from the same fault. It was decided that no single vehicle could satisfactorily perform all the duties required of it, and that a family of vehicles based on common automotive components would be better, with the major role of each clearly defined. This pragmatic attitude should be com-pared with the American way, which was to seek the best and most versatile single vehicle. This resulted in the cumbersome and troublesome Sheridan and the costly abandonment of the ARSV project.

It was felt that there would continue to be a need for a fast, well-armed wheeled vehicle, both in the world commitment and in the European theatre, so the family would contain a new armoured car. The family name was Combat Vehicle Reconnaissance (CVR). The tracked vehicle was the CVR(T), known later as Scorpion and the wheeled version as CVR(W), or Fox.

The initial work on CVR(T) was done at FVRDE at Chobham. Trials had long been going on with the tracked test vehicle to prove the value of various components and theories. It had the front-mounted engine and transmission which was adopted for Scorpion. The original Rolls-Royce B60 engine was replaced by a 4.2litre Jaguar, as used in the successful sports cars of the era, with a Rolls-Royce gearbox and controlled differential steering unit. This was replaced by a much more compact combined gearbox and steering unit, built by Self-Changing Gears Ltd and being virtually a scaled down version of their TN12 transmission used in the Chieftain tank, which had just come into service. An experiment with hydro-pneumatic suspensions was not adopted, since it gave no significant advantage over torsion bars and was heavier and more costly.

Incidentally, it was at this time that the Americans initiated another attempt to find a solution to the reconnaissance problem, an attempt in which Britain, Canada and Australia at first had an interest. The FMC Corp was given a contract to design a light vehicle, but it turned out to weigh too much for the requested helicopter lift and was turned down by the US Army. FMC produced it as a private venture and sold it as the Lynx to Canada and the Netherlands. It weighed eight tonnes and carried three men and a .50cal MG.

In 1967 Alvis was awarded a contract to build 17 proto-types of CVR(T) and they delivered the first on schedule in January 1969. In 1970 the company received the production contract which signified the change-over from wheels to tracks. The production of Saracen and Saladin at Coventry was run down, ceasing in 1972, when production of CVR(T) got going.

The contract for the British Army was for over 2,000 vehicles, but not all were to be the fire support vehicle which was the first of the family. Other types would include APC and ATGW vehicles, command, recovery and ambulances, and another turreted vehicle with a 30mm gun. The Belgian Army had followed the development of CVR(T) with great interest, with the result that they placed a contract for 700 vehicles, in a co-operation programme that gave them about 25% production at Malines in Belgium, and final assembly of their vehicles. Not only did they make parts for their own CVR(T), but certain parts for all vehicles were manufactured in Belgium and shipped to Coventry for incorporation in vehicles for the British Army and other customers.

It was difficult to sell a vehicle under the designation CVR(T), and in any case, it was a British tradition to name their AFVs. Alvis wanted to continue the names beginning with an 'S', that had become their 'trade mark', and the Ministry of Defence agreed. One of those put up by a dog-loving officer was Setter, but this was vetoed on the grounds that it was not aggressive enough. Eventually the name FV101 Scorpion was agreed upon for the fire support basic vehicle of the family. The others, numbered FV102 and FV107, were Striker (ATGW), Spartan (APC), Samaritan (naturally, for the armoured ambulance), Sultan (command vehicle), Samson (recovery) and Scimitar for the vehicle armed with the 30mm cannon.

The hull and turret of Scorpion are of aluminium armour plate, welded under a shield of argon gas, to eliminate the impurities that might occur with open air welding. Alvis installed special new machines to allow welding the whole length of the hull in one uninterrupted flow.

The hull is a monocoque structure, sufficient rigidity being obtained from the thickness of the aluminium to do without internal members that are not essential for other purposes. The armour used is an aluminium-zinc-magnesium alloy 7039, which had already been used for the hull of the M551 Sheridan. It would give immunity over the frontal arc against 14.5mm AP, and against small arms fire and splinters over the rest of the hull and turret. Using the alloy gave a significant weight advantage and enabled the designers to meet the specified combat weight of eight tonnes. Nevertheless, it was a constant struggle, with people on the one hand wanting more and better equipment for sighting, vision, fire control, gun control, mobility etc, and on the other demanding that the weight be kept down. For example a large day/night sight had to be encased in armour, while power traverse was deleted on grounds of weight.

The Jaguar 4.2litre sports car engine produced 265bhp, but in its military form it was de-rated to enable it to use heavily leaded fuels and rated down to 195bhp. This, however, gives an impressive 24.32bhp/tonne, and contributes to the outstanding mobility of the vehicle. Drive is through a centrifugal clutch, doing away with the need for a clutch pedal, to the seven-speed, hot-shift, semi-automatic gearbox, which incorporates a triple differential steering system, giving steering radii according to the gear ratio selected. The drive goes then to the front sprockets and to the lightweight track.

The track was, itself, an achievement of FVRDE with the manufacturers. It had been shown in experiments with the TV15000 test vehicle that replacement of the conventional steel track by a lightweight one increased the top speed of the vehicle by a phenomenal 60%. The lighter track also helped the sought after weight reduction. But it took years of research and trials to get to the ideal solution, which was a skeleton steel link with rubber bushed pins and rubber pads, 432mm wide. Each link had a single horn running between the double aluminium roadwheels, five each side. This combination is very quiet for not only do the rubber tyred roadwheels run on a rubber wheelpath, with rubber pads on the road, but the idler is also rubber tyred and the sprocket is fitted with two neoprene rings which take the weight of the track over the sprocket and reduce the rattle as the teeth take up on the track. In conjunction with the well-muffled exhaust, Scorpion enjoys the reputation of being one of the quietest tracked vehicles in service.

The result of having this lightweight track is that the Scorpion can motor at 80.5kph (50mph) on a good surface and that its nominal ground pressure is only .345kg/sq cm (5lb/sq in), less than the average man, and a great deal less than the heavily laden infantryman. By comparison the ground pressure of the Sheridan is .49kg/sq cm: the M114 C&R vehicle had a ground pressure of only .36kg/sq cm, but it could only carry a 20mm cannon and managed to reach 58kph on the road. The significance of the Scorpion's low ground pressure was made clear in its first battle. Its mobility across the bogs and mountains of East Falkland surprised both attackers and defenders.

One of the constraints in the design of Scorpion was width. It resulted from the experiences of the Malayan Emergency of the 1950s, and the fear that Scorpions might have to be used in the rubber plantations of Malaysia again, so the maximum width was held at 2.1m, to enable it to pass between the rubber trees. This also had the effect of restricting length, since the length of track on the ground should not exceed 1.8 times the distance between track centres. In Scorpion the ratio is about 1.6, but despite the short length of track on the ground Scorpion does not pitch as much as could be expected. The torsion bar and trailing arm suspension of the roadwheels gives a very good ride both on and off the road. One of the hazards of riding in the turret of Scorpion is the over enthusiastic use of the brakes, which can cause the vehicle almost to stand on its nose.

The Scorpion driver is comfortably seated in a rather narrow compartment beside the engine, on the left of the hull either head out or closed down. In hot climates it is essential that the insulation of the bulkhead is in good condition. Steering is by two levers and the controls are conventional except that the clutch pedal is replaced by a gear selector pedal. By raising or lowering this with his foot, rather in the manner of a motorcycle, the driver selects the ratio required and to let him know which gear is in use there is a visual indicator. The only fault with this method is that the driver must go through all the gears to get from top to bottom of the range, so he cannot coast to a halt in top and then straight away select bottom gear to move off again. He has a forward/reverse transfer lever, and can use all seven speeds in each direction, which makes for quick backing out of trouble, though with no rearward vision the driver is entirely dependent on the commander for directions.

Commander and gunner sit in the fully rotating turret,

either side of the 76mm main armament. The commander, on the left, has a periscopic binocular sight of ×1 and ×10 magnification, and seven fixed periscopes round his rear-opening hatch, for all round observation. He is also responsible for loading the 76mm and the coaxial 7.62mm MG, and for clearing stoppages in the latter if necessary. The gunner is provided with a monocular day sight ×1 and ×10, and two periscopes on the forward arc. If the passive night sight is fitted, it is permanently mounted in an armoured casing to the right of the gun. The 76mm gun itself is essentially the same as in the Saladin armoured car, though it has been modified and lightened by replacing the concentric recoil system with an external one. Forty rounds of ammunition are carried and are the same as for the Saladin.

Some users feel that the anti-tank capability of Scorpion 76mm HESH is inadequate for their needs and for such customers the Belgian firm of Cockerill-Sambre have designed a 90mm gun of higher velocity. When this is installed in the Alvis type turret, the vehicle is then known as Scorpion 90. The retrofit or supply as initial equipment is not over costly; it requires minor alterations to the ammunition stowage in the hull and turret and the provision of a new gun mantlet and sighting system. With the greater weight of the gun it is essential to have a power traverse, which is not provided in the standard Scorpion. The Cockerill modification includes a Cadillac-Gage electro-hydraulic drive, which is efficient but introduces the complications of using oil at very high pressures. Cleanliness of the oil is vital so filtration must be of a very high order, wear in valves and other components is severe and the system must be warmed up and kept ready for instant use by using electrical power all the time, whereas an electrical system can be switched on and used immediately.

Among the options in the Cockerill 90 system is a range of day and night sights and a ballistic computer from OIP Optics of Ghent in Belgium. The ultimate solution consists of

a periscope sight which includes both day and night optics, laser rangefinder and coupled ballistic computer. With some little modification to the roof mounting this unit can be put in to replace the standard sight as an almost complete fire control system, needing only the addition of sensors for tracking rate, trunnion cant and such meteorological data as are deemed necessary.

Cockerill co-operated with PRB for the ammunition which is the other half of this system. Five service rounds are available, and a training round. These are HEAT, HESH, HE, smoke and canister, plus HEAT/TP. The ammunition, except for the canister, is fin-stabilised. The gun barrel imparts a low spin to the round, compatible with the efficient performance of the HEAT projectile; the fins are slightly angled which maintains the spin and aids accuracy. The tail and fins of the projectiles are fitted well down into the cartridge cases, so as to reduce the volume of the round. A HEAT-T round for example, weighs 7.5kg and is 652mm long. This is just about what the average soldier can manage in the confines of the Scorpion turret, though it is easier in the Cockerill-designed turret of a larger vehicle.

HEAT is fired at 900m/sec and HESH at 800m/sec, HE at 700m/sec and smoke at 690m/sec. The canister round contains 1,400 pellets of 1.7gm each, which reach a minimum spread of 20m at 250m distance.

The HEAT round is said to have a perforation of solid armour plate of 300mm and an effective range of 1,500m. Despite the higher muzzle energy of the 90mm the recoil loading is only 8.5 tonnes at the trunnions and the vehicle does not move excessively on firing. This is aided by the very

Left: Scimitar at speed. The 30mm Rarden cannon proved a valuable weapon in the Falklands, where one gunner of the Blues and Royals claimed to have brought down an enemy aircraft. *Alvis*

Below: Striker in a typical hull-down firing position. The rear of the flotation screen is lowered to allow for the efflux of the missile rocket motors. *Alvis*

Right: The Spartan APC carries a crew of three and a section of five infantry, plus a load of mines and other munitions. It can be armed with Milan ATGW. *Alvis*

efficient triple baffle muzzle brake and concentric recoil system.

Installation of the 90mm gun on the standard Scorpion hull increases the weight to 8.723 tonnes, which brings the road speed down to 72.5kph and the gross power per tonne to 22.44hp. This is a very insignificant degradation of performance, and still gives a ground pressure of only .373kg/sq cm.

Other modifications which can be offered on Scorpion are the Marconi Radar SFCS600 fire control system, a neodymium-YAG laser rangefinder by Barr and Stroud and a diesel engine option. This last uses a Perkins T6-3544 turbocharged six-cylinder engine which produces 155bhp at 2,600rpm. This installation needs a new input gear train to match the performance of the diesel engine, and raises the weight of the vehicle by 538kg, so there is no real increase in performance, but one of the major criticisms of Scorpion when it was first introduced was the lack of a diesel engine, and it was felt that this may have lost some potential customers who preferred the lesser fire hazard of diesel fuel. Now, after 10 years in service and one successful campaign, Scorpion may be said to have come of age.

The diesel engine option can, of course, be exercised in the other members of the Scorpion family. The one which is nearest to its parent in design is the FV107 Scimitar, where the difference lies in the main armament and ammunition stowage. Whereas Scorpion was designed as a fire support vehicle to serve mainly with armoured reconnaissance regi-

ments, Scimitar is for the recce troops of armoured regiments and is armed with a 30mm cannon capable of killing all opposing APCs and other light armour. The Rarden gun is described on page &&. It is mounted in the same basic turret as the 76mm, with the same elevation from −10° to +35°. The turret has normally only the two-speed manual traverse, but can be fitted with an electric power drive. Up to 165 rounds of 30mm ammunition can be stowed in Scimitar, and the preferred method of the single aimed shot engagement finds this sufficient, though a six-round burst capability is built in to the gun. The short inboard length of the gun makes the turret seem less crowded than that of Scorpion, and much less so than the Scorpion 90, which seems to be overflowing with gun. Mechanically and in performance Scimitar is the same as Scorpion, though its combat weight is slightly lower at 7.756 tonnes, reducing the ground pressure to .338kg/sq cm.

FV102 Striker is the ATGW vehicle, armed with the Swingfire wire-guided missile designed by British Aerospace. From the waistline upwards Striker is very different from the turreted vehicles. The hull roof line is raised to 1.727m and the glacis plate angled up to meet the roof just behind the driver's hatch. Instead of being a slightly domed piece swinging to the left, the driver's hatch on Striker is a flat plate hingeing forwards. Behind the driver, on the left of the hull roof, is the commander's No 16 cupola on which can be carried an externally mounted 7.62mm GPMG, which can be laid and fired from inside the cupola. The commander has all-round vision with a ring of eight periscopes and a ×1 and ×10 sight. To his right is the missile controller with another sight, which can be traversed 55° left and right. The missile controller also has a separate sight, stowed inside the hull, which he can take out as far as 100m away, leaving the Striker behind cover. On the rear of the hull roof is a launcher box for five missiles, which must be elevated before firing. Five more Swingfire missiles are stowed in the hull and must be taken out via the rear door to be loaded into the launchers.

Swingfire is a second generation wire-guided missile, with a maximum range of 4,000m. It carries a large HEAT warhead with a significant over-kill capability on anything except the new Chobham type armours — and maybe on that too. It has a useful facility in that it is automatically

gathered into the field of view of the controller's sight and can be launched at any angle from the direct line to the target up to 45°. With the separated sight, Swingfire can be launched from behind cover. It has a minimum range of only 150m, not much greater than that of the tube launched missiles such as HOT or Milan. With a complement of 10 missiles, Striker compares well with other ATGW vehicles for both killing power and mobility.

There is just one difference between Striker and Scorpion below the waistline of the hull, but it is not too noticeable until one looks at the roadwheels. There are five on each vehicle and they are identical, but whereas on Scorpion and Scimitar they are regularly spaced, on Striker there is a more noticeable gap either side of the third (or centre) road wheel. The hull of Striker is longer, the distance between sprocket and idler has been increased and there is 25.4cm (10in) more track on the ground. From the side the pivots of the trailing suspension arms are clearly visible on Striker, between the second and third, and third and fourth roadwheels.

This applies to all the other members of the family. The hulls are longer and the length of track on the ground is greater than Scorpion. FV103 Spartan, the APC, has a hull almost identical to that of Striker, except where Striker has the missile launchers there is a large double hatch into the troop compartment, and there is no missile site fitted. Spartan is not intended to be an APC in the same way as, for example, the M113. Instead of the full 10-man section of infantry, Spartan carries a section of five men in addition to the driver and commander. It also carries a large complement of mines and demolition explosives or light anti-tank weapons. There are two periscopes in the roof on the left of the hull, and one on the right, so that troops within can observe and orientate themselves, but they cannot use their personal weapons from under armour except through the roof hatch. If used as a surveillance vehicle Spartan can carry a ZB298 or Radar No 14, with the aerial on the roof and the display in the commander's position so that it can be easily monitored. There are many other uses for Spartan and a variant with the American TOW ATGW is being developed.

The other three members of the Scorpion family are supporting vehicles. FV106 Samson is the recovery vehicle based on the same hull as Spartan. It is fitted with two

spades, either side of the rear door, so that the capstan winch can develop its full 12tonne pull on the 229m of wire rope stowed on the drum. It has to use a 4:1 snatch block to do this, but it gives the Samson the power to recover any member of the Scorpion family in almost any conditions. The winch is driven from the main engine and the winch rope is led out through a pulley guide on the rear of the hull roof. A small A frame may be fitted at the rear to enable Samson to carry out lifting jobs. The only armament is a pintle-mounted GPMG on the commander's hatch.

FV104 Samaritan is, of course, completely unarmed, except from the smoke grenade dischargers common to all members of the family, which are mounted in two sets of four on the front of the hull. In order to accommodate four stretcher cases and the crew of driver and commander/medical orderly the hull roof has been raised even higher than on Spartan, standing 2.016m to the roof and 2.416m to the top of the stowage bin on the roof. The rear door of the hull is a single piece, full width opening through which stretchers can be loaded on to the racks at either side.

FV105 Sultan is the command vehicle for Scorpion-equipped units and uses the same high-roofed hull as Samaritan. Like Samaritan there is a large rear door giving access to the 'office'. The vehicle crew of driver and commander would be supplemented by additional radio operators and staff personnel as required, up to a total of five or six. The only armament is a pintle-mounted GPMG beside the commander's hatch. The interior is fitted with mapboards, additional radio sets and batteries which are charged from the vehicle system, but do not allow continual use of the radio to run down the vehicle batteries. A penthouse tent is carried, folded on to the rear of the hull, which can be extended to give double the accommodation. A good crew will acquire 'optional extras' to make life more comfortable and a command vehicle is likely to be hung around with more items than those for which the stowage was designed. One area which must, on all Scorpion family vehicles, remain inviolate, however, is the glacis plate, for there are the louvres which allow air to circulate over engine and transmission. On Sultan it is also the place where a special, high radio aerial can be erected, braced to the hull by poles.

Above: Stormer is a stretched version of Spartan, with another wheel station added, to carry 10 infantry in the true APC role. *Alvis*

Above right: The Samson ARV has its Marlow Kinetic Energy tow rope fitted ready for action. The stretch of this braided nylon rope stores energy which can jerk a bogged Scorpion out of trouble. The earth anchor spades are stowed each side at the rear. Weather covers are fitted to the engine compartment louvres. *Alvis*

Right: Samaritan has the same raised hull roof as the Sultan command vehicle, to allow space for four stretcher cases. The smoke grenade dischargers are the only form of armament permitted. *Alvis*

Below right: The penthouse tent of the Sultan Armoured Command vehicle doubles the effective space for operational HQ crews. Note the mapboard in the hull. *Alvis*

The variety of roles for which CVR(T) have been designed points out even more strongly the difficulty of trying to design a single vehicle to do all. The seven CVR(T) provide a versatile mix of vehicles all based on the same mechanical parts, and all with the same standards of protection and mobility. All are able to swim by using a floatation screen. The low volume of the vehicles, dictated by the small size and weight required, precludes sufficient built-in buoyancy, but the screen is not difficult to erect and provides a good freeboard which makes swimming perhaps safer than without a screen. Water performance is 6.4kph with track propulsion, but all vehicles can be fitted with an applique propeller kit attached to the sprockets, which brings water speed up to 9.6kph. These would normally only be issued for specific river crossing operations. Since they were designed to operate in the European theatre, on the NATO front, all vehicles are able to accept a NBC pack. Over 3,300 Scorpion family vehicles have been sold to 14 countries.

The other part of the CVR family was to be a wheeled AFV to replace both Ferret and Saladin. The parallel development to the Scorpion test vehicle was a six-wheeled chassis with skid steering rather than the conventional turning of the

wheels in relation to the hull. The advantage of this system is that the hull can be wider, since no space has to be given for the turning of the wheels. This project did not get very far as the disadvantages far outweighed the advantages. Tyres wore out rapidly, it was less stable on the road and it tended to dig itself in on soft going. Thus the replacement for Saladin was a tracked vehicle and it was decided to have another light wheeled vehicle for long range road operations.

Commonality of materials and components dictated that the new CVR(W) should be built of aluminium alloy and powered by the Jaguar engine. The design owes much to the Ferret and is really no more than a logical development of its predecessor's latest mark. Wheel and tyre size, track and wheelbase dimensions are identical to those of Ferret Mk 4, the 'Big-Wheeled Ferret'. It was named Fox and Daimler were given a contract to develop it. The first prototype was built in 1967 and 14 more by April 1969. In July 1970 Fox was accepted by the British Army and the production contract went out to tender.

By this time Alvis, Daimler and Jaguar were all part of the British Leyland group, so a very large part of the vehicle was, in any case, going to come from virtually a single source, since Alvis would be making the turret. Daimler had all the know-how and experience of wheeled AFVs, and put in a tender. But the Royal Ordnance Factory at Leeds also tendered, and made a lower bid than Daimler. The ROF had no experience of either aluminium armour or

wheeled vehicles, but their overheads were covered by Chieftain and they won the order. This had the effect of ending the involvement of Daimler in armoured vehicles, thus weakening the defence industry, and of delaying production of Fox for at least two years while the ROF sorted out their problems. Fox eventually went into service with the British Army in 1975.

The layout of Fox is no different from that of Ferret and its other Daimler forebears. The classic H-drive, the double wishbone suspension and rear-mounted engine are all there. The engine is the same Jaguar 195bhp unit as in Scorpion, and the same style of fluid couplings and five-speed preselector gearbox are used, up-rated to take the extra power of the engine. The hull and turret are of aluminium alloy armour, the turret being a particularly good ballistic shape. It is a beautifully curved ellipsoid, the side pieces of which are welded from two extrusions. Inside the two crew, commander on the left and gunner on the right, sit somewhat less comfortably than their counterparts in Scimitar. In order to leave room under the turret basket for the rotary base junction, which carries all the electrical connections between hull and turret, and for the transmission, the turret floor is not as deep as might be thought. In fact the crew sit with their heels almost on a level with their seats, in rather cramped conditions.

The commander also acts as loader and has access to 99 rounds of 30mm ammunition, stowed in clips of three

rounds each. He is also responsible for loading and clearing stoppages on the coaxial 7.62mm GPMG which is to the left of the main armament.

Since Fox is designed as a reconnaissance vehicle it is very well equipped with vision devices. The gunner has two fixed periscopes, one each side of his main ×1 or ×10 binocular periscope sight, coupled to the 30mm main armament. There is provision for fitting a Rank passive night sight, with an armoured casing on the mantlet. The commander has a similar ×1/×10 periscope in front of his hatch and a ring of seven fixed periscopes giving an excellent all round view, even when closed down.

Fox, too, is highly mobile, with a maximum road speed of 104kph, and 30bhp/tonne. It can climb a 50% gradient and is amphibious when using the floatation screen, driven at 5kph in the water by the rotation of its wheels.

There was to have been a variant of the Fox, called appropriately, Vixen. It was to carry driver, commander and two extra men as radio operators, seated one either side of the commander, who had a small turret with a single GPMG. To accommodate the two operators the hull was widened, and where the Fox carried stowage bins each side, on Vixen there was a pannier behind the wheels for one man, with a hatch in the roof and a single periscope. Vixen was cancelled owing to cuts in the defence budget in 1975, and Ferret soldiers on indefinitely.

Although no other variants of Fox were planned it was obvious that the hull was a useful basis for other weapon systems. The ROF at Leeds have offered the vehicle with alternative turrets as a cheaper, and more direct, replacement. Under the name Panga it was submitted to Malaysia for trials in 1980, fitted with a Peak Engineering turret mounting a single .50in Browning MG. Following the trials, during which the Panga was driven 16,000km without any major problems, it was fitted with a new one-man turret by the Helio Mirror Co. This FVT-800 is equipped with a .50in MG and a coaxial 7.62mm GPMG. An alternative FVT-700 has twin 7.62mm GPMGs and there is potential for mounting a 20mm or 25mm cannon.

The turret is of welded steel and is manually operated. It can be fitted with a variety of day and night sights and observation devices. One particularly good feature is the depression of the guns to −15°, which leaves very little dead ground around the vehicle, and elevation to +50° which permits an anti-helicopter cability. There will, no doubt, be more variants based on Fox, as more different weapon systems are requested.

There is a huge range of converted commercial vehicles and vehicles designed round commercial parts, that are now classified as AFVs. One of the earliest, the doyen of the British type, is the Shorland armoured patrol car. In the 1960s the Royal Ulster Constabulary asked Short Brothers and Harland, of Newtonards, Northern Ireland to study the problems of designing and building a light armoured vehicle which would be cheap enough for them to purchase and operate, yet give adequate protection and mobility for their Internal Security and border patrols.

Shorts took as the basis the existing 109in wheelbase Land Rover, of which many hundreds were in service with the Constabulary. They strengthened the suspension and axles to take a greater weight and modified the axle ratios to take advantage of the engine characteristics. They mounted on the chassis an armoured hull to take a crew of three, driver, commander and gunner, with a manually operated turret similar to that of the Ferret, mounting a .30in Browning MG. Protection was added round the engine and wheel arches and glass-fibre matting was used to give underfloor

protection. The Mk 1 engine produced 67hp at 4,100rpm, and had to work hard to move the Shorland, which had an all-up weight of about three tonnes. Protection was against .30in ball ammunition at that time, but events in the province soon showed that it would have to be improved. It was a popular vehicle with the police, and sold well to many overseas customers who wanted something cheap and cheerful to boost the morale of their police by offering mobility and protection at prices which police forces, always chronically short of funds, could afford. As a military vehicle the Shorland was under-powered and lacked sophistication.

Since then it has gone through many modifications and improvements and the latest model, the Mk 3, which weighs 3.4 tonnes loaded and can attain a top speed of 110kph, has a higher level of protection. Mechanically, apart from the strengthened parts, it is the same as the ordinary Land Rover, which simplifies driver training, maintenance and spares holding. It is still one of the most economic vehicles for simple police type duties. Shorland is a milestone in the history of light AFVs and continues to serve in over 20 countries.

USA

Although the US Army used light wheeled vehicles, both armoured and soft skinned, for reconnaissance in WW2, the doctrine was based on the need to be able to fight for information, in contrast to the British view that armour and weapons on a recce vehicle were there to get out of trouble and to fight to get the information home only if necessary. Both views have been proven in battle to have some validity. The American view has a very profound effect on the vehicles chosen to do the job; even MBTs are deployed in the current armoured cavalry regiment.

Since the end of WW2 the army has used whatever was available, while it sought to establish what it really wanted, then to obtain it. In the 1950s the old M8 and M20 armoured cars where phased out and sold, or given, to some 20 of the smaller and poorer countries of the world, where they continue to serve. They were replaced in the reconnaissance battalion by the M24 Chaffee light tank.

M24 Chaffee

The M24 saw combat in both European and Pacific theatres in the latter years of the war, and fought in Korea and South-East Asia. With a weight of 18.37 tonnes and a power output from its two Cadillac V8 engines of only 220hp SAE it was not over endowed, but could attain a top speed of 55kph on the road. Armament was a 75mm M6 gun, which had been adapted from the cannon used in a version of the Mitchell bomber, and had a concentric recoil system, to save space in the turret. It was phased out in the US Army in the early 1950s, but continued to serve elsewhere. In Norway the Thune-Eureka company carried out extensive modifications to 54 vehicles of the Norwegian Army. The main armament was replaced by the French D/925 low pressure, 90mm gun, for which 41 rounds can be stowed. The .30in coaxial Browning was replaced by a .50in and Wegmann type smoke grenade dischargers fitted, four tubes each side of the turret. The Cadillac engines were superseded by a single V-6 Detroit Diesel of 250hp driving through a fully automatic Allison transmission. While this has not improved the top speed by much, acceleration and reliability are better than the original.

Right: The M24 Chaffee saw action in World War 2 and continued in use with a number of armies after the Americans had phased the vehicles out of service in the 1950s. *via G. Forty*

Below: The Brazilian modernisation of the M41 includes replacement of the original armament by the Cockerill 90mm gun, made under licence by Engesa. *Bernardini*

M41 Walker Bulldog

Realising that the M24 would soon need replacement, the US Army started work after the war on a light tank designated T37. The first prototype was built in 1949 and production started in 1951. It was designated M41, and was known, to start with, as the 'Little Bulldog'; when general W. W. Walker was killed in Korea the name was changed to 'Walker Bulldog', by which it has been known ever since.

The M41 was armed with a 76mm M32 gun, with a performance greatly superior to the 76mm which had armed some of the later Shermans. In the production vehicles 57 rounds were carried, including a HVAP-T with a muzzle velocity of 1,260m/sec. The muzzle was adorned with a distinctive T-shaped blast deflector and a bore evacuator, the first on any American tank. Turret traverse was by electric power in early models, later changed to electro-hydraulic, which, it was felt, gave a faster and more positive response. Similarly the stereoscopic rangefinder was exchanged for a

coincidence type, with the automatic lead computer and ballistic corrector.

The M41 had a normally aspirated Lycoming gasoline engine, but later versions had first fuel injection (M41A1) and then, in the M41A2 and A3, a supercharged engine developing 500hp, which helped give the very respectable top speed of 72kph. Colonel Robert J. Icks writes that the M41 was the first tank to have been designed round a powerplant, and not having an engine found to fit. An auxiliary generating set was installed in the right front corner of the engine compartment. Colonel Icks also records (*AFV Profile 41*) that an automatic loader had been tried out, which selected a round of the required nature, loaded and rammed it, then caught the empty case on ejection and returned it to the appropriate place in the magazine. It was not adopted, since it must have been very complex and expensive, and probably slower than a human loader.

Apart from its value as a light tank, the M41 was the

basis for three SP guns, 105mm and 155mm howitzers and twin 40mm AA guns in the M42 Duster. But the most significant variant was probably the one-off M41 with an early Shillelagh gun/missile launcher, which was to form the armament for the AR/AAV (armoured reconnaissance/airborne assault vehicle) that became the M551 Sheridan.

M551 Sheridan

In many ways it was an unfortunate coincidence that the US Army had two, vaguely similar, requirements at the same time. In 1959 it was looking for a new vehicle for the cavalry role, in reconnaissance, and at the same time wanted an armoured vehicle which could provide anti-tank and fire support for airborne forces. The characteristics of these vehicles are in fact very much opposed. The cavalry needed a vehicle capable of carrying a useful sized gun, which implies a certain weight to absorb recoil, yet at the same time wanted to use the vehicle for reconnaissance. The airborne had to have a light vehicle, but needed two different sorts of firepower. The inevitable result of the compromise was that the M551 was large (for a reconnaissance vehicle) and yet had little more than immunity to small arms fire, while the airborne had a heavy vehicle, of which only one could be carried in their standard transport plane. Both versions suffered from a main armament that never came up to its expectations. It could be dropped by parachute but the normal method of delivery was to have the aircraft fly as low as possible and to allow the tank, fixed to a special pallet, to be dragged out of the aircraft by a drogue chute, and let it crash to a halt on the ground. The crew would be dropped by parachute.

The hull of the M551 Sheridan is made of aluminium armour, though the turret is steel, which helps to keep the combat weight down to 15.83 tonnes. It is amphibious, being almost buoyant enough without the floatation screen that is used to provide sufficient freeboard for operational use. The Sheridan is adequately mobile, having a top speed of 70kph and a range of 600km. The engine is a 300hp V6 Detroit Diesel, so the 18.9bhp/tonne power/weight ratio is not over generous. The torsion bar suspension provides for a reasonable cross-country ride, the bars for the right side roadwheels being behind those of the left, which sets the right roadwheels back about 10cm, and accounts for the slighly lopsided look from the side, under the hull.

The interesting part of Sheridan, and that which caused most of the problems, was the armament. The Shillelagh ATGW and the associated conventional rounds and gun/launcher are dealt with more fully on pp 117-8, but the effect of the choice of this weapon system on Sheridan was to delay production and entry into service and to give the vehicle a reputation for unreliability.

In July 1962 a Shillelagh turret was mounted on an M41 (see above) and extensive trials were carried out and 590 missiles were fired (*Janes World AFVs* by C. Foss). By the end of the year the first of 12 prototypes had been completed but it took three more years before the XM551 was classified as a Limited Production standard and a contract awarded to General Motors for production. It was not classified Standard A and dropped the X (for experimental) until 1966. Some 1,700 M551 Sheridans were built over the next four years, and during that time and subsequently there were continuous problems with the weapon system.

Possibly because of its poor reputation, but more likely because it did not fit in with any other nation's requirements, the Sheridan served only with the US Army. It must be the only American AFV not sold overseas since WW2. The Australians evaluated Sheridan for use in Vietnam, but rejected it. Sixty-four Sheridans were sent to Vietnam, but since the threat was people rather than AFVs, they were not used in the role for which they had been designed. In fact, no missiles were fired but use was made of the heavy HE round and canister. Even with these, there were serious problems. The combustible cartridge cases absorbed moisture and tended to break up and, when fired, they left more burning debris in the chamber than was safe. The recoil of the conventional HE round was too great for the weight of the vehicle and could shift the whole tank up to a metre. Another result of this shock was to create problems with the electronics and optics. The Sheridan crews were far more confident in the effectiveness and reliability of the M2HB .50cal Browning MG which was carried on the commander's cupola, and used it to good effect. However, that meant exposing the commander's head and shoulders, so it was common practice to add an armoured shield to the cupola, which could add as much as 70cm to the height of what was already, for a reconnaissance vehicle, a tall tank.

The canister round which was developed specially for Vietnam, was very effective; it had a range of 400m, so it could be used as an offensive weapon in ambushes along the Viet Cong supply routes. The troops in Vietnam disliked the Sheridan also for its habit of overheating when halted with the engine running, and for the high-pitched whine of the turbocharger, which could be heard for long distances by sharp-eared Viet Cong. (*Modern American Armour*, Steve Zaloga and James Loop.)

Perhaps the Sheridan would have been more successful in the European theatre, where its missile capability against tanks would have been very useful. We shall never know, for it was retired from front line service in 1979, being replaced by the ubiquitous M113 and the M60 tank in the cavalry units. Some Sheridans have found a useful role in the OPFOR (opposing forces) training programme in the USA. A number of Sheridans have been fitted with lightweight skeleton modifications (VISMODS, or visual modifications) to make them look like Russian PT-76 light tanks for training US forces in fighting a realistic enemy.

It is believed that a large number have been offered for sale, reworked with a 90mm gun.

Left: British Life Guards man a Sheridan during a reciprocal training exercise. *UKLF*

Below: M113A1 of the Canadian Army. *Canadian Armed Forces*

M2 and M3 Bradley

One of the problems that the US Army faces with any new concept for equipment is that only the best will do, even if it is very complicated and very expensive. This was exemplified in the case of the MBT-70 programme, which failed on both cost and complexity, to reach production. The same applied to the ARSV. It was plain that the M551 Sheridan and the M113 and M114 were not ideal for the reconnaissance role and that there was scope for improvement. Sheridan had powerful (if unreliable) firepower, the M113 could carry a useful squad for dismounted action and the M114 was not too large. The last two could swim without preparation and all had adequate mobility. (It is interesting that the smallest and lightest had the lowest top speed, 58kph, and the worst cross-country performance.)

The 'Recon' elements of the army wanted better reliability and performance all round and wrote an operational requirement that included a top speed of 80kph, a combat weight of 7.72 tonnes and a ratio of 35hp/tonne. Ground pressure was to be 4lb/sq in (.28kg/sq cm) and the vehicle was to swim with 22.5cm of freeboard when fully loaded. Armament was initially to be the existing M139 20mm cannon, but provision was to be made for the projected 20-30mm Bushmaster weapon system. All this within an envelope giving 'improved ballistic protection', which in practice meant immunity to 20mm AP over the front arc and to 12.7mm AP all round.

Six companies responded to the request for proposals. Ford, Condec and Lockheed chose the wheeled vehicle approach, Lockheed basing their proposal on the articulated-hull Twister. Chrysler, FMC and Teledyne Continental opted for a tracked vehicle, Teledyne offering a version of the British Scorpion, in conjunction with Alvis Ltd. At first this looked like a favourite contender; it met, as it stood, a high proportion of the requirement, and modified with a Teledyne engine and the US M139 cannon it seemed the Scorpion might well fill the bill. For one thing, it existed in metal, and the US Army was already privy to the trials and evaluation reports. It could be in service with the US Army in under two years, with the US modifications. This was very attractive to the men in the field, but the power of the US automotive

industry lobby and the 'not invented here' complex of the authorities combined to kill the Teledyne approach.

After a long drawn out evaluation of the concepts offered, it was decided to award further development contracts to the manufacturers of one wheeled vehicle and one tracked vehicle. Contracts went to Lockheed and FMC on 23 May 1972, each company to provide four complete prototypes and one ballistic hull for the next phase evaluation. At the end of this phase, which would be some two years, the companies would make specific proposals on price and production, and one of them would be selected to continue the process. All told, it would be 1978 before the first vehicle could a reach a unit in the field.

The Lockheed ARSV was a 6×6 vehicle with roll articulation between the front and rear hulls. The front section carried the fuel tank and the front differential and steering mechanism. In the larger, four-wheeled, rear hull were engine and gearbox, rear suspension and walking beams, the driver's station and the turret with weapon system. It was developed from the original 8×8 Twister, which also had pitch articulation between the hulls.

The combination of 25° of roll each side of the centre for the front hull, with walking beams at the rear which had a wheel travel of 50.8cm, meant that there should be no time at which all six wheels should not be in contact with the ground, making for good continuous drive. The engine was the Detroit Diesel GM6V53T, developing 300hp (SAE) at 2,800rpm. This gave a top road speed of 108.8kph and a power/weight ratio of 38.8hp/tonne. The tyres were large section run-flats, but the ground pressure was 6lb/sq in (0.422kg/sq cm). There was a swimming capability, driven by water jets, at 8kph. Altogether, mobility was very good, with the limited slip differentials preventing the wheels spinning, even in the worst conditions.

The driver was seated centrally in the fore part of the rear hull, strapped into a well-sprung seat and with 180° vision through glass blocks when in the closed down position. He needed to be strapped in because, even with the excellent articulation and suspension, he got a rough ride at speed over poor going. The two-man turret crew fared worse, since they sat higher up and were subjected to great moments. The commander (also acting as gunner) and the observer sat either side of the 20mm cannon, the observer on the left. They could change positions if required. Both had 180° field of view, so if the commander was firing, the observer could only scan half the battlefield, and half his sector was the opposite direction to the known danger. The observer could slew the turret for target acquisition, at the commander's direction. This does not seem to be a very good arrangement, but a fertile field for recrimination. The commander could take his revenge by ordering the observer to stand head and shoulders out of the turret to man the secondary armament of a pintle-mounted M60 MG. Only 500 rounds of 20mm and 2,000 rounds of 7.62mm were carried, which is not a lot for a 24-hour battle day. It is more in keeping with the concept of reconnaissance by stealth than with the method of fighting for information, which the US Army seemed to have adopted.

The Lockheed design was reckoned to offer a reduction of 40% in the life cycle cost of the vehicle when compared with the M114. Its layout would provide the crew with good survivability owing to the mine-sweeping characteristic of the front hull, but the armour plate cannot have been much more than 8mm on the sides and belly, to get within the all up weight of 7.7 tonnes.

FMC were able to base their design on work already done on successors to the M113. They used the same Detroit Diesel GM6V53 engine as in the Lockheed Scout, coupled to a new Allison X200 hydrostatic steering and transmission. The exhaust system was designed to reduce noise and IR signature. They experimented with both four and five roadwheels each side, deciding finally on four larger wheels to give the best cross-country ride. The track width was kept to 19in (48.26cm) so that the maximum hull width could be used. While this meant that maximum buoyancy was obtained from the hull, it raised the ground pressure to 4.4lb/sq in (0.3093kg/sq cm), which was slightly above the required figure.

The hull was of varying grades of aluminium armour, with the glacis sloped well for ballistic protection, while the sides

Left: The Lynx C&R (Command and Reconnaissance) vehicle is often known as the M113$\frac{1}{2}$, since its main power train and running gear components are derived from the M113. The Canadian version has the vehicle commander seated behind the driver, not on his right, as in the Netherlands vehicle. The armament is a single .50cal MG. *Canadian Armed Forces*

Above: M2 Bradley seen on static display during the 1983 Canadian Army Trophy: a large reconnaissance vehicle, but well served with a 25mm cannon and TOW missile launcher (note launcher on turret side). *Martin Horseman*

Right: FMC's M2 IFV and M3 CFV are the US Army's latest reconnaissance vehicles. Time alone will tell whether they perform the required role as well as the sales blurb suggests. *FMC via G. Forty*

and rear were vertical, giving maximum volume for inherent buoyancy. The turret also mounted a M139 20mm cannon, with an ammunition supply of 500 rounds. There was no coaxial secondary armament but a pintle-mounted M60 MG could be operated by the observer from a head and shoulders out position. The commander/gunner in the FMC turret was also on the right, but he had a 360° field of view through six episcopes and an articulated telescope day and night sight. The weapon station was stabilised by a GE electrical system, whereas the Lockheed vehicle had an electro-hydraulic system. It is doubtful whether either could have been effective at any speed, and represented an unnecessary complication and expense.

TACOM, the US Army Tank Automotive Command, were very hopeful of the extent and thoroughness of these selection procedures, involving no less than six prototypes with

parallel wheeled and tracked vehicle options. One engineer wrote, 'The US Army cannot fail to profit from such an ideal situation'. Such optimism was short-lived. Before the trials even reached a conclusion, before a selection had been made, the two main contracts, each worth $12 million, were cancelled and the cavalry were ordered to join with the infantry in the MICV programme, for which a joint MICV Task Force was formed in 1976.

The object was to develop the XM723 MICV into a vehicle suitable for the purposes of both branches. Basically, the requirements of each side were almost diametrically opposed, except in the armament, where both sides agreed on a cannon/TOW mix. The infantry needed a vehicle big enough to carry a squad of nine or ten men, who could fight from under armour if required, and who would have as much armour protection as could be carried. The cavalry wanted a small, fast vehicle, with lightness and mobility as the highest priorities. A 20tonne MICV or an up-armoured AIFV were the last things they wanted. They had already got the M113 ACAV and ITV configurations, and it was those very things they were trying to better.

The XM723 MICV came through trials with success and was going to be adopted as the infantry fighting vehicle (IFV). Reluctantly, in order to get something in metal, the cavalry accepted the same basis as their new reconnaissance vehicle. The term 'scout vehicle' was dropped and the new machine became the cavalry fighting vehicle (CFV), with some slight modifications from the IFV. While it made economic and logistic sense to have two almost identical vehicles, it meant a very radical change in the reconnaissance requirement of the cavalry. They would have to adapt tactics to equipment, instead of the reverse, which they had spent the last decade seeking.

The new machines were named Bradley (after the American WW2 field commander in Europe, under Eisenhower) and designated M2 IFV and M3 CFV (Steve Zaloga, in his book *Modern American Armour*, reveals that the M3 may be named Devers, after the commander of the US 6th Army Group in Europe, 1944-45.) The manufacturer is FMC, and their sales description of their vehicle runs, 'Bradley Fighting Vehicles have outstanding mobility to
● accompany the Abrams MBT
● move troops rapidly in the combat area
● increase its own survivability'.
Nothing is said about the ability to go ahead of the MBT, or to remain undetected on the battlefield. Its survivability would be enhanced by reduction in size. In short it is a most unsuitable vehicle for the reconnaissance role that the US Army had previously envisaged for the ARSV.

The cavalry have revised their scout requirement to adapt to their new mount. The M3 weighs 23.285 tonnes, more than twice that of the ARSV, and has a ground pressure of .54kg/sq cm. With a gross ratio of 20.62hp SAE/tonne, it can attain a top road speed of 66kph, which is just acceptable. It is buoyant, but needs a screen to have sufficent freeboard to swim at 7.2kph. Both versions have an identical hull 645.3cm long and 230cm wide. Both stand 297.2cm high to the top of the cupola. The hull is armoured to withstand 23mm fire over the frontal arc, which, FMC claim, can defeat 91% of all the weapons likely to be encountered on the battlefield. (If the vehicle was smaller it would, perhaps, not be so likely to be hit by 91% of the weapons encountered.)

The firepower of the Bradley is excellent. The cannon plus TOW armament gives it the ability to fight MBTs and APCs, like Striker and Scimitar. The M3 CFV uses one less man to do this than Striker and Scimitar together, but it keeps its five-man crew in one large hull, making a better target; it can engage only one target at a time, and it weighs 38% more than the Alvis pair. While cost is likely to be about the same, the effectiveness for reconnaissance is halved.

Instead of a three-man crew in the ARSV, the cavalry now have to find five; the normal driver, gunner and commander, plus two 'scouts', who are designated for dismounted reconnaissance, though one suspects that they are there primarily to look after the back of this large vehicle and to justify its size. One suggestion for utilising the space available was to carry a motorcycle in the rear compartment, for use in scouting. The 'dirt bike' was dropped, not on grounds of noise, but because its unprotected fuel tank would be a hazard. Whereas in the M2 IFV the troops in the rear of the hull are provided with special M231 firing port weapons (which are basically cut down M16s) with which to spray the neigh-

bourhood, the two scouts in the M3 have only their M16s, and the firing ports are blanked off. The manufacturer says that the 'M3 Cavalry Fighting Vehicle (CFV) has greater armour protection than that of any dedicated Cavalry Vehicle', also that 'these weapon systems are a major determinant in winning force-on-force simulations in combined arms scenarios'. It is not clear whether this means that they are any good as reconnaissance vehicles, or whether the cavalry might still be seeking their ideal equipment.

Cadillac-Gage Commando

Until now only one LAV has been used by the US forces in any numbers since 1945. This is the Cadillac Gage Commando, a four-wheeled, amphibious and very versatile vehicle, with a long history and many imitators. It is one of those wheeled AFVs which it is very hard to classify, since it can perform so many roles quite well, though none of them perfectly. The Commando was conceived in 1962 by the Cadillac Gage company of Warren, Michigan and therefore is one of the progenitors of the type. The first prototype came out in 1963 and production started a year later. Since then the Commando has been produced in four basic sizes and dozens of configurations and weapon fits to fill innumerable roles.

The original Commando V-100 was adopted by the US forces under the designation M706 and served extensively in Vietnam with the Army, Air Force, ARVN and Thai forces. Since then it has been purchased by some 20 countries and has been copied by others. In Portugal it is made by Bravia under the name Chaimite, though they deny the plagiarism, even hinting that their original design was 'acquired' by Cadillac Gage. Almost every light, wheeled general-purpose AFV since the 1960s owes something to the Commando.

The concept was to use readily available commercial components in a simple welded structure which would have the possibility of being adapted to a multitude of roles and weapon systems. It is doubtful, however, that the designers, when they started, had any idea of the extent they would eventually reach.

The hull of the Commando is of welded steel, which has been improved over the years as has been necessary to resist bullets of higher penetration. When the M16 rifle came out, with 5.56mm rounds, many light AFV manufacturers were caused to revise their immunity claims, and to improve their protection. The waistline of the hull is rectangular and the sides, front and rear slope inwards, both up and down, to give good ballistic angles. Beneath the hull, and outside the armour protection, are two beam axles with central, lockable differentials. The large tyres (14.00 or 16.00 × 20) are in wheel wells in the lower hull sides but are unprotected by plate. They are normally run-flat type, with deep cross-country treads, though wider sand tyres have been used in desert countries. There are three doors in the hull, one each side and one in the right hand side of the rear. The top half of the side doors swings out in normal fashion but the lower half drops to form a step; the top of the rear door lifts instead of swinging. There is a vision block and a firing port in each upper half door.

It is a tall hull, 1.96m high, and bulky to look at. However, this bulk gives it sufficient buoyancy to swim and propulsion in the water is by the wheels, so it achieves only 4.8kph. This utility hull makes it easy to carry a number of different turrets and weapons systems and to adapt the interior for many roles. It has been used for police and escort duties without any turret weapons, and in the same configuration as command, ambulance and recovery vehicle. With a raised superstructure, open at the top, it can carry a mortar, and

Right: Cadillac Gage Commando equipped with the Cockerill 90mm MkIII gun. *Cockerill*

Below: The 8×8 version of the Mowag Piranha won the contract for the LAV-25 for the US Army and USMC. Armed with a 25mm cannon and two 7.62mm MGs the LAV-25 carries a crew of three and a section of six troops. There is power-assisted steering on the front two axles, with coil spring suspension and torsion bars on the rear pairs of wheels. Swivelling propellers allow a top swimming speed of 10.4kph, while the top road speed is 100kph. The LAV-25 weighs 12.84tonnes in combat order. *General Motors of Canada*

use it on the 'shoot and scoot' principle. With a turret the Commando carries from a single MG to a 90mm cannon.

From the original V-100 model the Commando was developed into the larger V-200 model with a bigger engine, and later into the intermediate V-150. The latest version is the Commando V-300, which is a 6×6 vehicle. Its longer wheelbase makes it more stable when firing the larger calibre guns, such as the Cockerill 90mm. The earlier Commando, with a French 90mm, took some time to come to rest after firing, while firing at 90° to either side could only be attempted on level ground. The Commando was not intended to act as a gun-boat, even though it has two bilge pumps fitted. It was also essential to check that the drain plugs were properly fitted before swimming the vehicle. Singapore was one user who learned this lesson the hard

way. Although the Commando was used by the US Army as a convoy escort and patrol vehicle in considerable numbers in Vietnam, it was never acepted as a standard equipment, but rather as a stop-gap. It was regarded as too big for a good reconnaissance vehicle (though smaller than the vehicle with which the cavalry have ended up) so it was logical for the manufacturers to bring out a successor which was dedicated to the reconnaissance role.

Cadillac Gage Commando Scout

In 1978 the Cadillac Gage company brought out a light four-wheeled AFV named the Commando Scout. It weighs 6.123 tonnes when combat loaded, and has a two-man crew. It is roughly a quarter bigger all round than the Ferret, and has a better and more versatile load capability. The hull presents

Above: The Canadian Army Grizzly is armed with .50cal and coaxial 7.62mm MGs and has a crew of three, with the capacity for 4-6 infantrymen. The Detroit Diesel 6V53T engine and Allison transmission are common to all the family. *General Motors of Canada*

Left: Another member of the Mowag family produced by General Motors of Canada is the Husky 6×6 Maintenance and Recovery Vehicle. Armed only with a single MG, the Husky is equipped with a 650A HIAB hydraulic crane of 3.5tonnes lifting capacity and an 8tonne winch. It is fully equipped with workbench and tools and spares and has a crew of four. *General Motors of Canada*

good, well-angled plates all round, and is immune to small arms AP. The long glacis plate has a higher rating, and the sharp nose is said to enable the vehicle actually to 'cut its way through sand, dirt and underbrush'. It is not inherently buoyant and cannot swim, which may be why the US Army has not seen it as the right vehicle for its front line reconnaissance forces. The engine is a Cummins V-6 diesel, of 155hp, driving through an Allison four-speed automatic transmission, which gives it a top speed of 97kph. The driver sits on the left of the hull, next to the engine and in front of the turret, which is placed over the back axle.

The Commando Scout can carry a variety of turrets and weapons, as long as they can be controlled and fired by one man. Versions have been proposed with 20mm and 30mm cannons, TOW and 106mm recoilless rifles, as well as any requested mixture of MGs. All the turrets have the same type of commander's cupola, with a ring of eight vision blocks, and can be power operated. Mobility is said to be very good, aided by lockable differentials and large run-flat tyres. The Scout would seem to be an attractive proposition for forces which have a long range reconnaissance role in desert or similar areas, and whose organisation permits of two-man crews. Now that the Americans have accepted a five-man crew and a large tracked vehicle for reconnaissance, it would appear unlikely that the Scout, or any similar vehicle, could be accepted until the M3 Bradley has been disproved.

LAV

Both the US Army and the USMC have formulated a require-

ment for LAV (light armoured vehicles) for the restructured light infantry divisions and the 7th Marine Amphibious Brigade allocated to the RDF, an American 'fire brigade' for action anywhere in the world. The Army has plans for 2,550 LAV of various configurations and the Marines plan to buy 744. The defence budget for 1982-83 included $122million for LAV.

The main agreed parameters for the LAV are that they should be small enough to be carried by the heavy lift helicopter and to be air-portable. An amphibious capability is desirable for both services. The design must be flexible enough to perform all the tasks required of an independent unit, anywhere in the world.

Naturally, the requirements of the services do not coincide. The army envisages having 550 mobile protected guns of medium calibre, 400 TOW vehicles and 1,500 squad carriers, to carry 11 men and a .50cal MG. The USMC wants a nine-man vehicle with a 25mm Bushmaster cannon system, with assault gun, mortar, anti-tank, command, recovery, air defence and logistic variants.

In April 1981 the USMC asked a number of manufacturers to submit proposals, the intention being to eliminate the wasteful development and trials phases and to acquire existing designs and off the shelf production. In September 1981 this was reduced to four competitiors. Alvis Ltd, with Martin Marietta Inc, offered the Scorpion 90 and the Stormer APC with the Arrowpoint 25mm cannon turret. General Motors of Canada offered the Mowag Piranha 8×8 vehicle made under licence as the Cougar and Cadillac Gage submitted the Com-

Right: The PT-76 is a large vehicle now some years old. Amphibious and mobile its 76mm armament made it a useful recce vehicle particularly for the river crossing role anticipated in NW Europe. *via C. Foss*

mando 4×4 V-150 and the Commando 6×6 V-300. Each contractor delivered three vehicles for testing, two being APCs and the third an assault gun variant with the Cockerill 90mm though this was not necessarily the final choice of gun.

The US Army leased 15 of the GM of Canada Grizzly (Piranha 6×6) and a Husky recovery vehicle to carry out tactical operational and doctrinal evaluations. Although they performed well generally there was criticism of the exposed suspensions and brake lines which tended to get damaged by tree stumps and barbed wire. In October 1982 the contract for LAV was awarded to GM of Canada for the 8×8 Cougar version of the Mowag Piranha. The vehicle will be suplied supplied in a mix of configurations, and may include a fire support version with the Cockerill 90mm gun.

USSR

At the end of WW2 Soviet tank brigades and regiments had sub-units designed for 'combat security' or 'combat support', but their real duties were those of the reconnaissance units in western armies, including flank protection and rear area security. They were composed of armoured and infantry troops, mainly equipped with T-34 medium tanks, Lease-Lend White scout cars (M3A1) and some BA-64 armoured cars. As the organisation of the Soviet Army has developed since 1945 the reconnaissance role has been taken over by a divisional reconnaissance battalion in both tank and motor rifle divisions, along with the more esoteric duties of chemical and radiation surveillance and radio and radar intercept.

The scale of motorised recce in conventional operations is up to 50km in front of the FEBA, while in nuclear war this could be doubled. The specialised recce units in a division are equipped with amphibious light tanks and scout cars, supported by specially trained infantry in amphibious APCs and by motorcycle units. Tank regiments also have a recce company with three light tanks and four scout cars which are employed on more local recce, some 5-10km in advance of the regiment or on flank guards etc.

The divisional reconnaissance battalion has a tank company with two platoons of three light tanks and one HQ tank, and a scout company of 19 scout cars and 13 motorcycle combinations. The long range recce company may have wheeled APCs or trucks for its five sections. The radio and radar intercept company would be in soft skinned transport. The main tools of the specialist reconnaissance units are the PT-76 light tank and the BRDM scout car.

PT-76
The PT-76 was developed in the 1950s from an unarmoured

arctic exploration vehicle called Pinguin. The PT-76 has a large volume welded steel plate hull with a long, upward sloping bow and flat sides and rear. This gives sufficient buoyancy for the 14tonne tank to swim well in inland waters and calm seas, with a freeboard of 17.8cm. To aid the swimming capability a trim vane, or splash board, is added to the bows. This prevents water surging up the glacis plate and pushing the bows down into the water. The driver can see over the top of the trim vane through the middle one of his three periscopes, which can be elevated for this purpose. Water propulsion, at up to 10.2kph, is by two hydrojets driven by the main engine, the outlets for which are an obvious feature of the back plate of the tank. There are three bilge pumps to take care of minor flooding through the turret or louvres.

The turret is a simple truncated cone shape with a flat roof and no shot traps under the lower edge, where the turret sits very close to the hull roof. There is a single large hatch in the turret roof, with two shallow domes above the commander and gunner. The PT-76, although a reconnaissance tank, is not well provided with observation devices; the commander has three periscopes in his cupola, while the gunner has a single, rotatable periscope in the turret roof and his telescopic sight.

The main armament is a 76.2mm D-56T gun with multi-slotted muzzle brake, or a D-56TM, with a double baffle muzzle brake and fume extractor. There is a coaxial MG to the right of the main gun, on the same side as the gunner, who is, therefore, responsible for loading and clearing jams. The commander acts as loader and has 40 rounds of 76.2mm ammunition available. These include HEAT, fired at 325m/sec, and HVAP at 965m/sec, as well as HE and APHE, from the same range as the gun on the T-34 tank. Turret traverse is manual or electrically powered, while elevation is always manual. Some PT-76 have been fitted with stabilisation, but this is not standard.

Power is from a six-cylinder 240hp diesel engine, which is, in effect, one bank of the V-12 engine used to power the T-54 tank. It drives through a multi-plate dry clutch and five-speed manual gearbox to the rear sprockets. The six road-wheels are hollow, for additional buoyancy, and have torsion bar suspension. There are no return rollers, so the top run of the track rests on the top of the roadwheels. The main fuel tank takes 250 litres, which gives a road range of 250km, but only 70km in the water; mixed going, with swimming, reduces the effective range drastically. To rectify this two additional fuel tanks can be carried externally, on the engine deck each side; these are normally used for the approach march and discarded for combat.

The PT-76 is not fast, at 44kph, but it is tactically mobile and agile. The 76mm gun is adequate for a reconnaissance vehicle to get out of trouble, but the armour is nowhere

The BTR-40 resembles the American M3A1 and was superseded in the late-1950s by the BRDM.   *via C. Foss*

thicker than 14mm and is vulnerable to shell splinters and small arms AP rounds. PT-76 served in Vietnam, where they were found vulnerable to air attack, and in the Indo-Pakistan war of 1971, when they performed a useful function in the delta of East Bengal. More recently they have been employed by the Iraquis in the Shatt-el-Arab, against Iran.

The PT-76 stands higher than the turret on the AMX30 and has a longer hull. The Russians, like the British, see no advantage in reconnoitring with a big and bulky machine when smaller and more discreet ones will do the job. The PT-76 may well be replaced by a special recce version of the BMP.

BRDM

The other armoured vehicle of the recce units is the BRDM, a light, four-wheeled scout car of great tactical mobility and flexibility. It emerged in 1957 as the replacement for the earlier BTR-40, which was basically no more than an armoured truck, open-topped and resembling the M3A1. A fully enclosed version, the BTR-40K, was built at the end of the production run. The BTR-40 was developed into an anti-tank vehicle by the East Germans, who mounted launchers for the AT-3 'Sagger' (9M14M Malyutka) ATGW. The BTR-40 is not amphibious, and could not, therefore, keep up with the PT-76 tanks of the recce groups. Being open-topped it was very vulnerable to all kinds of fire and could have no NBC capability. The Egyptians copied the BTR-40 and produced it locally under the name Walid, using it as an APC.

Its successor, the BRDM, rectified most of the faults of the BTR-40. Although prototypes were open-topped, the production models had a totally enclosed superstructure with two firing ports each side, and roof hatches. The engine is at

the front of the BRDM hull, and drives both axles through a manual gearbox. The danger of bellying over ridges or soft going, which is inherent in four-wheeled vehicles, is virtually eliminated by having four small wheels (two each side) between the main wheels. They are chain driven and can be lowered when needed, to lift the hull and to reduce ground pressure. They minimise the effect of having the main wheels on beam axles with a conventional leaf spring suspension, which is cheaper to make and simpler to maintain than the double wishbones of the British wheeled AFVs.

The sharp bow and long, almost flat, glacis plate gives the BRDM a racy look which agrees with its mobility. The hull is buoyant and it can swim, with no preparation except raising a splash plate at the bow, at 9kph, driven by a single water jet propulsion unit very like that of the PT-76.

There have been several variants of the BRDM. Apart from the original scout car, it serves as an NBC monitoring vehicle in the reconnaissance battalions and in the chemical warfare companies as a decontamination vehicle under the designation BRDMrkh. But the most important variants are the 'tank destroyers', carrying launchers for all three of the first generation of Soviet ATGW. The first was the BRDM (2P27), armed with the AT-1 'Snapper' (3M6) wire guided ATGW. Three launching rails were carried in an array which could be raised to the firing position once the roof hatches had been folded down out of the way. This was succeeded by the variant with four launchers for the AT-2 'Swatter' radio-guided missile. Finally there was the BRDM with provision for six AT-3 'Sagger' wire-guided missiles. On this type the whole roof panel rose when the launchers were elevated, eliminating the delay while the roof hatches of the earlier versions were folded down, and keeping some protection against airburst. These vehicles gave the recce units a formidable long range anti-tank capability.

In 1966 a revised version of the BRDM was introduced, with the engine moved to the rear of the hull and the crew compartment moved forward and topped with a small turret, like that of the BTR-60, armed with a 14.5mm MG. In this model, which was 1.4 tonnes heavier, a more powerful GAZ-41 engine of 140hp was fitted, and performance improved all round. Maximum speed rose to 100kph, and 10kph in the water, and the operating range from 500 to 750km.

As with the earlier vehicle, the BRDM-2 was soon adapted for the anti-tank role, with a six-rail launcher for the AT-3 'Sagger' missile, and stowage for 14 more in the hull. A command vehicle was produced, with an additional generator to power the extra radios and a BRDM-2rkh followed the previous chemical decontamination vehicle. Further variants were revealed in 1974 (the BRDM-2 with SA-9 'Gaskin' surface-to-air missile) and 1977, when the latest ATGW was mounted. This was the AT-5, for which five launcher tubes are fitted on a traversable mounting. The AT-5 is a semi-automatic command to line of sight missile, like TOW or HOT, which requires only that the operator keeps his sight on the target, rather than having to 'fly' the missile, as in the earlier generation.

The Hungarians produced a version of the BRDM-2, modified to their own requirements, in the late 1960s. The vehicle, called the FUG, closely resembled the BRDM-2 scout version without a turret, but a turreted version appeared later. The FUG is in service with the Czechoslovak and Hungarian armies. NBC troop variants have been built of the FUG, too, while the Czechs have mounted some vehicles with an 81mm recoilless gun and have made an ambulance version. There do not appear to be any with ATGW yet.

3 Firepower

Main Armament

During WW2 all the combatants had taken whatever was most easily to hand for installation in tanks: field pieces, anti-tank guns, even the famous Flak 38 were adapted to become tank guns. With the coming of peace or, at any rate, a cessation of hostilities, the victors could devote time to the design of a gun specifically for tank use. The Russians, who had just introduced their IS-3 heavy tank with its 122mm gun, and the Americans with their 90mm, found no reason to alter their current programmes, but the British, having suffered grievously from being under-gunned throughout the war, reconsidered their approach to tank design.

The threat had changed and some hard lessons been learned. From a numerical superiority over the Germans in the later war years, the western allies now faced a greater number of tanks of not inconsiderable fighting ability. The previous split of roles between infantry and cruiser tanks was abandoned in favour of a universal tank, the main feature of which was to be firepower superior to any opponent. This could not be achieved immediately, and with the anti-tank role passed from the artillery to the Royal Armoured Corps, the British had an urgent need for stop-gap weapons. The successful 17pdr anti-tank gun had already been mounted in tanks (Sherman Firefly, Comet, Challenger) and self-propelled mountings (Archer, Avenger). It now became the main armament of the first universal tank, Centurion Mk 1.

However, good though its performance was, the 17pdr did not have the range to start knocking out the enemy at any great distance — its effective range was 800-1,000m. The huge assault tank, Tortoise, with its 32pdr gun, was too immobile and never went beyond prototype stage. However a US/British development of a 120mm gun with a potential range of 5,000m was available. The Americans used it in

Prototype Comet; virtually a 77mm gun in a new turret on a Cromwell hull. *Leyland Motors*

their M103 super-heavy tank and the British tried it out first in the hull of an infantry tank design, FV201, which had been shelved in 1949 as being too cumbersome and expensive.

After trials of the hull fitted with a Centurion Mk 3 turret, under the designation FV221 Caernarvon, the 120mm was mounted in a newly designed and very complex turret and named FV214 Conqueror. The big ammunition meant that, to be handleable, the charge and projectile had to be separate for the first time in a British tank. (The 32pdr ammunition in Tortoise was separate, but it was in prototype stages only, and never went into service.) The 120mm fired APDS and HESH only, but since its role was to support Centurion by long range attrition of the enemy armour, this was not a significant fault. Conqueror stayed in service until 1966 but the 120mm gun concept remained.

A French development of the same period was the AMX50 (qv), which also mounted a 120mm gun mounted in an oscillating turret. In 1954 the Americans tried the oscillating turret experimentally in the T54 tank, but it never went further than the one model.

But while they used the 120mm as a stop-gap, the British brought out their first purpose-built tank gun. Following the practice of describing the weapon by the weight of the projectile, the new gun was called the 20pdr. Its calibre of 83.4mm was smaller than the dreaded German 88mm, but it was almost twice as effective. It was the first British tank gun to be loaded from the left, allowing the loader to use his right arm for ramming. The ammunition was fixed, with electrically fused primers. The APDS round was fired at the very respectable m/v of 1,460m/sec (cf 88km KwK43 which fired a 7.3kg projectile at 1,130m/sec). Although originally without, the later model barrels were fitted with a fume extractor.

Mounted in Centurion Mks 3, 5, 7 and 8, the 20pdr has been in service for 30 years. It has had a successful record in combat, first in Korea, where it was able to kill all the enemy armour with ease. Later it was used mainly as a heavy

sniping weapon and gained an enviable reputation as a bunker buster, able to 'post' a shot through a weapon slit with consistent accuracy. It served, too, as an anti-tank weapon in the early 1950s. There were more 20pdr guns available than Centurions to carry them, but there were a large number of obsolete Cromwells. The 20pdr was fitted in a lightly armoured two-man turret and 24 rounds of ammunition were carried. The vehicle was named Charioteer and went into service with the divisional regiments of the RAC, providing anti-tank defence for the infantry divisions.

Charioteer was highly mobile, which helped to offset its lack of armour and the height of the turret. A major problem was that the muzzle blast caused considerable obscuration and, with the high m/v, the round would arrive at its target before the commander/gunner could observe fall of shot. To overcome this a fourth man was added to the crew, who normally travelled in the old hull gunner's position, but became gunner when the crew commander dismounted to observe and correct fire from a flank. Charioteer is still used by Lebanon.

Tortoise Prototype 1, showing the massive cast hull, in unarmoured mild steel for the prototypes. The Besa 7.92mm MGs are not mounted in the turret nor in the ball mounting in front of the gunner's position. *RAC Tank Museum*

During this period the firepower of American tanks in service had remained virtually static. The M26 Pershing, coming into use at the end of the war, was armed with a 90mm gun derived from a 3in anti-aircraft gun by way of a wheeled anti-tank gun. With improvements in fire control and ammunition, this gun remained in front line service until the 1970s. It is still used by many foreign armies and an unmodified M47 and M48 with the US National Guard. Its performance has barely improved. The original 90mm M3 on Pershing fired a 12kg shot at 1,021m/sec. The current HEAT-T M431 round is fired at 1,219m/sec but the AP-T round has a mv of 914m/sec.

On the other side of the Iron Curtain the 85mm tank gun was replaced in the new T54 tank by the 100mm D10T gun

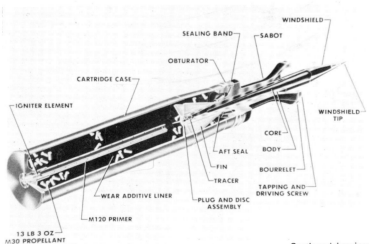

Sectioned drawing of a 105mm APFSDS round. Note the elongated peardrop shape of the core. *General Defense Corp*

which fired the same range of ammunition as the D10 anti-tank gun. A 15.4kg shot was fired at 900m/sec. The 122mm gun on the IS-2 and IS-3 had a much bigger punch; its 25kg shot was fired at 780m/sec, but the trajectory was much higher and accuracy lower. The Russian heavy tanks were gradually withdrawn to reserve divisions, but the Soviet threat to NATO increased in numbers of more effective tanks as the satellite armies re-equipped with the newer tanks.

Good as the 20pdr was, the British were looking for even better performance to extend the useful life of Centurion. In 1956 trials started on a 105mm barrel matched to the breech and mounting of the 20pdr. These were completed with user trials on the Hohne ranges in Germany by the 4th/7th Royal Dragoon Guards, who were most enthusiastic about the new weapon. It was accepted for service in the end of 1959 and put into production at the Royal Ordnance Factories at Cardiff and Nottingham. The first Centurion to be built with the 105mm gun as original equipment was the Mk 10, but it was retro-fitted back to the Mk 5.

The main anti-armour rounds for the 105mm are APDS, fired at 1,470m/sec and HESH at 730m/sec. A new APFSDS round is available, but the m/v is 'classified'. It is interesting that, while the APFSDS penetrator is only 0.21kg heavier than the APDS projectile, it is only half the diameter and therefore the mass of the 'long rod' is being applied to one quarter the area of the APDS core, with more than four times the energy.

The 105mm is the most widely used gun in the world outside the Soviet bloc. It is versatile, firing APFSDS, APDS, HEAT, HESH, HE, Smoke, canister and practice ammunition. Apart from retro-fitting to Centurions in foreign service, the 105mm was chosen to be original equipment on the German Leopard 1, Swedish Strv-103B S-Tank, Swiss Pz61 and Pz68, Japanese STB, American M60 and British Vickers Vijayanta. It is the first series main armament for the US M1 Abrams and is a standard retro-fit for up-gunning of M47 and M48. The Israelis, masters of the virtue of necessity, have standardised on the 105mm, not only in their fleet of Centurions and up-gunned Shermans, but in some 200 captured Soviet T-54 and T-55 tanks. It is also the main armament for the Israeli-designed and built Merkava MBT. In combat the 105mm has proved able to kill Soviet and American tanks and would doubtless prove equally effective against those of other manufacturers if required.

Twice British tank gun design has been influenced by the lucky chance of being able to examine opposing armour. In 1956 during the Hungarian uprising, patriots drove a captured T-54 into the compound of the British Embassy in Budapest, where the military attache was able to take a good look at it before it was returned to its (temporary) owners. The armour of the glacis plate was (erroneously) measured as being 120mm thick, at 60° and the 105mm gun was therefore required to be able to penetrate this thickness at 1,000 yards. In fact, the glacis is only 100mm at 54°, so there was a fortunate overmatch. After the Arab-Israeli war of 1973, western observers were able to get a close look at the latest Soviet T-62. This carried a smoothbore 115mm gun firing fin-stabilised rounds with a very high penetration, both kinetic and chemical energy.

After the failure of the German-US project MBT70, the Germans determined to go ahead on their own replacement for Leopard 1. They, too, chose a smoothbore gun, of 120mm calibre. They reasoned that HESH is no longer of value since there is so much use of spaced armour and external stowage, and the same argument applies to HEAT, so that a KE round is the essential for tank killing. Fin stabilisation allows use of a longer penetrator, with the more efficient application of energy to the target, and it is also more suitable for a combined shaped charge and HE or multi-purpose (MP) round. Thus, they thought, the smoothbore configuration gives the flexibility of attack and the possible extension of capability which a rifled tube would not. This is precisely the opposite view to that of British users and designers, who believe in the flexibility of a rifled tube system.

When the USA again tried to combine with Germany on use of standard components in their new designs of MBT, the Germans submitted their 120mm gun for the main armament. Eventually, after much argument and bickering the German gun was selected, instead of the improved British rifled gun which had also been a contender. Nevertheless, the first production run of the American M1 Abrams carries the 105mm M68, which is the British 105mm L7 made under licence in the USA. The Rheinmetall 120mm still requires much work before it is acceptable to the US Army.

On the other side of the hill, the Soviets followed their 115mm smoothbore in the T-62 with an even larger, 125mm smoothbore in their next MBT, the T-72. It is little different in construction from its predecessor, and its performance can only be conjectured from the 1,600m/sec mv of the APFSDS round.

France developed her own design of 105mm gun for the AMX30 MBT. It fires medium velocity spin-stabilised HEAT (1,000m/sec) and HE (700m/sec) rounds; these are not compatible with the 105mm L7. The French gun is lighter in construction than the 105mm L7, as it does not have to take the high chamber and tube pressures of the high velocity gun. It has neither bore evacuator nor muzzle brake, but it does have a thermal jacket on the barrel, which can be electrically heated to maintain an even temperature all over. The French gun is also mounted in late versions of the AMX13 and in the Austrian Steyr Kurassier Antitank SP gun, in which it is in an oscillating turret.

The Americans made a significant departure from the conventional when they combined the ATGW with the gun. Like most compromises the Shillelagh system brought out the difficulties in both sides, being successful in neither role. The object was to have a missile with a warhead of large enough calibre to be sure of defeating all known and

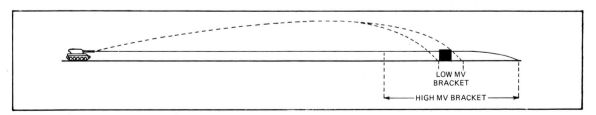

Fig 1 The trajectories of high and low muzzle velocity projectiles.

foreseeable enemy tanks. The missile was to be launched from the same tube as a conventional high explosive round, which meant that the HE round had to be of the same calibre as the missile. The missile was of 152mm diameter, and the HE round was therefore as big as a medium artillery projectile. The artillery handle such ammunition separately, but the tank round was built as fixed ammunition; it weighed 22kg and was 68cm long, too large and heavy to handle in the confines of a tank turret. It was also too big to be of tactical use. The tank commander would wish to use HE against soft targets or against an area inhabited by troops. For this he needs a number of fragmentation rounds spread over an area. With one 152mm round he could utterly destory one truck or one foxhole, but it was not an economical use of ammunition. Nor was it effective use of stowage space in the tank.

The HE round had other problems too; in order to avoid the problem of disposing of large brass cartridge cases from the turret, the propellant charge was contained in a combustible case which was burned up in the firing of the shell. The case material was not strong and tended to break under the tough conditions of stowage and handling in the turret. It was also liable to absorb moisture and become even less strong, and after firing it used to leave smouldering debris in the chamber, which could ignite the following round. To cure these conditions the rounds were stowed in nylon bags and the breech was scavenged by a blast of air, to blow debris out of the muzzle. This caused further problems in handling the ammunition and added another complication to an already complex system, without curing either problem. On firing the recoil could upset the optics and electronics of the tank.

The missile itself is 115cm long, weighs 26.76kg and carries a 6.8kg hollow charge warhead that can destroy any known MBT. It is fired from the tube by a small expelling charge, then boosted to 1,000m/sec by a solid fuel rocket motor. A tracking flare in the base of the missile is followed by optics mounted above the gun barrel and a computer translates deviation of the flare from the desired path into commands which are transmitted on an IR guidance link. This was sometimes found to be susceptible to interference from other IR sources on the battlefield, and natural ones such as the sun.

The Shillelagh missile has a dead zone of about 1,200m from the muzzle before the command system starts to operate, which means that it is useless for emergency anti-tank work, but it has a useful maximum range of over 3,000m.

The system was the main armament of the M551 Sheridan AR/AAV and the M60A2 MBT. It was proposed for the ill-fated MBT70 project. When the Sheridan M551 saw service in Vietnam the Shillelagh missile was not fired, only the HEAT and a canister round being used. Although M60A2s continue to serve in the US forces in Europe, it is likely that they will be the first to be withdrawn when replacement M1s become available. The US Army is disenchanted with Shillelagh.

Apart from larger bores and longer barrels, the most noticeable change in tank guns is the almost universal use of fume extractors, or bore evacuators. These are cylinders fitted round the main tube, sometimes offset, with a number of holes drilled through from the bore. After the projectile passes those holes a vacuum is created in the extractor cylinder which draws the remaining gases forwards, preventing the escape of large amounts of fumes into the turret when the breech is opened. Another visible change is the use of thermal sleeves on the longer barrelled guns. Most

are made of fabric, though the French prefer aluminium on their 105mm gun. The thermal jacket contains insulating material and covers the whole length of the barrel. It is designed to maintain an even temperature all round the tube. This prevents wind or rain from cooling one side of the barrel more than another, which could cause the tube to bend. This effect is greater with the long barrels of modern guns and can have a significant effect on accuracy. Chieftain tanks are fitted with a muzzle reference sight which allows the gunner to check any deviation from the true line of the bore without having to dismount and use a bore sight. This MRS must be an integral part of the gun barrel, as experience shows that 'add-on' sights can too easily be displaced by the continual shock of firing.

As guns became longer and pressures increased, so the weight of guns rose to the point when weight-saving became imperative. An important step in the elimination of the impurities which cause weakness in the structure of the metal is electro-slag refining. The process of auto-frettage is used in production to obtain a barrel of which the inside metal is in compression and the outside in tension. This allows higher pressures to be endured for a comparatively thin-walled tube. It is claimed that the fatigue life of the barrel (as opposed to the wear life) is greatly extended.

Light AFVs

Great improvements have also been made in the firepower of smaller AFVs. in 1945 armoured cars and reconnaissance vehicles were usually armed with 37mm or 40mm guns with limited AP capability and very little in HE. The larger armoured cars (AEC Mk III and SdKfz 243 for example) which were mainly used for fire support, carried 75mm guns of medium velocity.

British recce vehicles armed with a gun were Saladin and Scorpion, both having virtually the same 76mm gun with a fairly good anti-armour capability, owing to an effective HESH round. The contemporary French vehicles (EBR and Panhard AML) went from a 75mm to a 90mm gun, the latter firing fin-stabilised HEAT and HE projectiles (at velocities of 760m/sec and 650m/sec respectively) but no KE penetrating round. The American M41 Walker Bulldog light tank used a version of the 76mm gun which had armed the late model Shermans. (The similarity of calibre caused considerable problems for Ethiopia, who bought 10,000 rounds of surplus 76mm ammunution from India, only to find that it did not fit their guns. They had bought M42A1 instead of M352A1, both being 76mm HE.)

The French 90mm had some export success. It was fitted as main armament on the Brazilian Cascavel armoured car, part of the family designed by Engesa, and on the South African Ratel wheeled MICV. It is also to be found as optional armament on several fire support vehicles, APCs and armoured cars.

By the end of the 1970s many users felt that even light AFVs should be able to carry a weapon system of dual capability, able to destroy enemy armour at 1,500m and to use HE against buildings and soft targets at over 2,000m in the supporting role. The Belgian firm of Cockerill, the biggest steel company in Belgium, in conjunction with the ammunition makers PRB, designed a 90mm weapon system taking advantage of the latest technology. The barrel is of ESR steel and can take higher pressures for a given weight. The rifling consists of 60 shallow grooves with a 20ft pitch, the lands of which are slightly rounded. This reduces gas erosion on the rifling and the low spin avoids the 'drift' effect of spin-stabilisation. Cockerill designed a very effective three-baffle muzzle brake, which reduces trunnion pull by 40%, to about

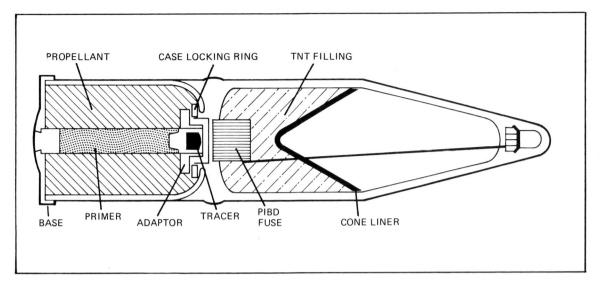

Fig 2   The 152mm round used in Sheridan. Conventional ammunition for the 152mm Gun/Launcher M81 was fragile and difficult to use. Rounds available were HE-T, HEAT-T and Canister, with a Target Practice round for training.

Dimensions	HE-T	HEAT-T	Canister
Weight, complete round	22.7kg	22.66kg	21.8kg
Length, complete round	625mm	688mm	488mm
Muzzle Velocity	683m/sec	683m/sec	683m/sec
Max effective range	8,950m	8,950m	85m
Filling	4.55kg TNT	2.86kg Comp.B	10,000 steel flechettes 0.84kg

The cartridge cases were made of combustible material and were fragile, easily ignited and hygroscopic. The ammunition was fixed, with the cartridge case attached to the projectile by an aluminium locking ring. The method of assembly was unusual. The cartridge case had a curved lip which fitted inside a similarly shaped rear end of the projectile. A locking ring clamped the two pieces together,

held in place by an adaptor and tracer assembly, which was itself screwed on to the projectile base. This meant that the cartridge case body was fixed to the projectile before it was filled. The propellant and the initiator were loaded in through the still open base of the case, and lastly the cartridge case base was glued on to the body. It did not make for a very strong assembly.

Each round was packed in a 'barrier bag' of neoprene or elastomeric (stretchy) rubber, with an outer fibre tube containing a desiccant. Finally each round went into a wooden case lined with polystyrene foam. The list of 'do's and don'ts' for this ammunition was formidable. Care in handling started with the wooden containers, which the crew must not 'drop, drag, throw, tumble, roll or strike'. They had to be extra careful not to knock against rounds stowed in the turret and to ensure that there was no contact with oil, grease or water. A loose or torn barrier bag on the round meant that it was unserviceable and initial inspection included feeling, through the bag, for cracks, damage or separation. Moisture, even on the outside of a barrier bag, was always a danger. When loading, the gun chamber had to be checked for damp and smouldering residue from a previous round. The barrier bag had to be removed just before loading the round; not easy to do in the confines of a turret.

8.5 tonnes. The concentric recoil system keeps recoil distance down to 300mm so that the gun can be accommodated in vehicles with small turret rings, as long as they are over seven tonnes gross weight. (Recoil loads of the French DEFA 90mm F1 and the Mecar 90mm are 5.5 and 5.0 tonnes respectively, but they fire at lower velocities than the Cockerill gun.) The barrel life is at least 2,000 EFC, which means at least 2,000 rounds of HEAT-T or 2,860 of HE-T. Cockerill have designed their own steel turret for the 90mm and it can also be installed in the aluminium armour turret of the Alvis Scorpion, in place of the 76mm gun. Another version of the Cockerill 90mm was designed to replace the 76mm in the M41 Walker Bulldog light tank. This gun fires a range of ammunition with slightly different characteristics, since the base vehicle is heavier and can take higher recoil loads.

As the performance of small calibre ammunition has been improved, there has been an increase in the use of 20mm-30mm cannon as armament for recce vehicles and APCs. In two cases a 20mm cannon was selected as secondary

armament for a MBT. The Mk 1 Centurion had a 20mm Polsten in a ball mounting to the left of the main gun, and the French AMX32 carries a coaxial 20mm M693 cannon. This can be disengaged from the coaxial setting and super-elevated to 40° for use against helicopters or low-flying aircraft.

Probably the most useful advance in the design of cannon used in AFVs is the development of the dual ammunition feed. Instead of having to use belts of mixed ammunition to cover all situations, the gunner is enabled to select, by the flick of a switch, the nature appropriate to the action in hand. With improved fragmentation of HE rounds and enhanced penetration of AP, this is an important advantage which gives the light AFV a better chance on the battlefield. A small cannon is quite easy to mount externally, raised above the level of the turret roof. The frontal area of the turret is reduced and the gunner less exposed. Such a mounting also gives greater scope for high angle fire than if the cannon is conventionally placed in the turret.

Another way of saving space inside a turret is by reducing

the inboard length of the gun; that is to shorten the distance from the trunnions to the rear of the breech. This is one of the virtues of the British 30mm Rarden cannon, jointly developed by the RARDE (Royal Armament Research and Development Establishment) and the RSAF (Royal Small Arms Factory) at Enfield. It was accepted for service in 1970 and chosen as main armament of the CVR(T) Scimitar and CVR(W) Fox recce vehicles.

The Rarden has two main roles, attack of armour and attack of soft targets such as transport and troops in the open, and a secondary role in attack of helicopters. It is not a fast-firing cannon like the Hispano, Oerlikon or Rheinmetall, but exemplifies the British philosophy of the single, aimed shot, though its action is fully automatic and it has a burst capability of six rounds at a rate of about 90rpm. The basic concept requires high accuracy, reliability and low weight. One cannot afford to waste ammunition, but its effect on target is very good. It is not possible to stow as many rounds as for a 20mm, but the accuracy of the Rarden means that more of its rounds arrive on target than from an automatic cannon firing bursts.

The Rarden ejects empty cases forwards, out of the turret, and there is no escape of fumes internally. There is a sliding breechblock, as in larger tank guns, which cuts down the length of the body, and the long recoil (the length of a round) takes place entirely within the enclosed body, so there is no wasted space in the turret to allow for recoiling parts. The recoil loading is only 1.36 tonnes; the overall length of the gun is 3,150mm of which only 430mm is behind the trunnions. Accuracy comes from the long barrel and the fact that it fires from a closed breech, there being no sudden transfer of weight during firing. The barrel is supported half way along its length to damp out vibrations during recoil. The two main rounds against armour are the APSE, fired at 1,070m/sec and APDS at 1,200m/sec, with a very flat trajectory. It also fires the Hispano range of 30mm ammunition. Reliability has proved high. All the working parts are contained within the body so there is little ingress of dirt. The weight of the gun is only 110kg, which is comparable with the 96kg of the 20mm Oerlikon and far less than the 30mm Hispano at 136kg.

Ammunition is stowed in three-round clips and loaded in threes. A total of six rounds can be loaded at one time, and once three rounds have been fired another clip can be loaded. Since the normal rate of fire is the single aimed shot it is reckoned that six rounds should be sufficient for one engagement and reloading is swift and simple, and does away with the necessity for complicated belt feeds from large magazines.

Secondary Armament

AFV firepower is incomplete without the secondary armament of a machine gun to take care of targets not worthy of a full calibre shell. This is usually mounted coaxially with the main armament and of rifle calibre, though American and Soviet vehicles have heavier 12.7mm guns on the turret roof or commander's cupola.

In WW2 tanks it was customary to have a hull gunner, next to the driver, with a MG covering the frontal arc and very useful for flushing snipers and Panzerfausts out of hedgerows and trees. While it was most useful to have another pair of eyes watching ahead, in close country, ready to hose down with prophylactic fire all suspicious points, the value of the fifth crew man was also in his help with maintenance, guards and refuelling. However, as more space in the tank was taken up by bigger rounds of ammunition the fifth man became redundant and the hull gun disappeared.

With the disappearance of the hull gun, more and more AFVs seemed to sprout MG mountings on the commander's cupolas. Although these guns added marginally to the firepower of the vehicle they had two disadvantages; they exposed the commander to more danger than necessary while firing and they distracted him from his primary function — commanding. The Russians and Germans got it right, by putting their extra MG at the loader's hatch. The Americans, in trying to rectify the fault of exposure, compounded the error by putting a Browning .50in calibre MG in a cupola with anti-aircraft capability, thus distracting the commander into yet another sideline, and raising the height of the tank once more. On those vehicles without the anti-aircraft mounting, commanders stood waist high out of their turrets to spray the Korean, then the Vietnamese countryside. When casualties of commanders mounted their reaction was not to tell the commanders to to get back inside their turrets and commmand, but to erect cosmetic screens around the erect figure — whereupon he would climb higher to see over the top. The M55 Sheridan, already

Left: M41 Walker Bulldog light tank rearmed with the Belgian Cockerill 90mm gun. This is the Mk IV version which uses a higher velocity round. *Cockerill*

Right: Cupola of an Australian Centurion in Vietnam. The Brownings were kept ready at all times in case of surprise attacks on the bases. *AWM*

Below: Compare the Chieftain cupola with that of the Centurion; it is lower and the episcopes are twice the size, each with its own wiper. The GPMG can be aimed and fired from within the turret. *MoD*

large for a reconnaissance vehicle, had a further two feet added in this way.

The weapons themselves change little over the years. The British Besa 7.92mm gave way to the more reliable .30in Browning, then to the Belgian designed GPMG, but it was still a rifle calibre gun, belt fed, firing a mixture of ball, AP, tracer and incendiary. The GPMG had the advantage that its empty cases were ejected forwards, out of the turret, cutting down fumes.

Recently the cupola-mounted MG has been fitted with remote control; this means that it can be loaded, cocked and fired from under armour. To reload or to keep the gun supplied it is necessary to remember to connect a new belt to the end of the old one before it passes through the gun.

The self-powered MG, ie one which uses the energy produced in firing to reload and fire, must, by the very nature of its operation, open the bolt at a time when the gas pressure in the barrel is high, thus allowing gases to escape from the open bolt. With the receiver and feed mechanisms inside the turret this means escape of noxious gases into the fighting compartment, to the discomfort of the crew, and necessitating an extractor system.

A development of the 1970s has eliminated this hazard, besides having many more advantages. The Hughes Chain Gun is an externally powered weapon, driven by an electric motor. This means that the rate of fire can be very easily controlled and adapted to the requirements of the situation. It does not rely on the energy of firing, so if there is a misfire the drive continues to function, and the misfired cartridge is extracted and ejected with no interruption. Since the gas produced by the propellant does not have to operate a piston there is no necessity to adjust its flow through ports, to keep the gun firing.

The Hughes Chain Gun was designed to use the standard 20mm round, but has also fired the 7.62mm cartridge and a 25mm cartridge. The weight of a belt of such a large round would, for a self-powered gun, mean that an electric motor would have to be provided to raise the belt to the gun. In a Chain Gun the same motor that drives the mechanism draws ammunition to the breech. A dual feed of two different types of round can also be more easily selected. The Chain Gun has a single barrel, making it more suitable for AFV installation than the multi-barrel Gatling type. Forward ejection keeps the turret clear of empty cases and of residual gases.

It is called the Chain Gun because the mechanism is driven by a simple 0.5in pitch roller chain on which is a bolt drive shoe. As the shoe moves in a circuit with the chain, it slides in a slot in the bolt and makes the bolt perform, in sequence, the functions of firing, unlocking, extracting and ejecting, feeding a new round and locking the bolt again. At the end of a burst the bolt always stops in the open position, thus avoiding the possibility of a 'cook-off' in the gun.

The rate of fire can be adjusted between 250 and 500 rpm in the 25mm version mounted on the M2 and M3 fighting vehicles, and could be up to a much higher rate if requested. During tests the 7.62mm version fired continuous bursts of 10,530 and 11,137 rounds, demonstrating a very high reliability. Should the vehicle power supply fail the Chain Gun can operate from a battery, and if all else fails it can be hand-operated at about 30rpm.

Smoke

Close smoke protection by throwing grenades had been established during WW2, and at the end of the war the British had a multi-barrelled unit which could throw up to 12 No 80 white phosphorous grenades to form a screen for immediate cover. The difficulty was that the grenades were propelled by an electrically fired fuse which had to be replaced after every firing. Two small lead wires had to be pushed through a hole at the bottom of each discharger tube, from the inside, then the fuse was pulled down until it seated in the tube. Then each pair of wires had to be separately connected to the electrical supply. But it was a far better screen than that from the 4in smoke candles lobbed from the large dischargers of the previous system; they took 10 to 15 seconds to produce a useful volume of smoke, which is a long time, when you are waiting for it.

The other method of firing smoke to a distance was with a short barrel 2in mortar fired through a hole in the turret roof. But this, too, took time to produce a screen. A new grenade discharger was brought out in the late 1960s and it has two major advantages over the first one. The propellant and initiator are contained within the base of the L8 grenade, which can be loaded quickly and simply into the tubes. The grenade body is of rubber, which can be seen to swell during flight, bursting and forming an instantaneous screen. The filling is red phosporous, which is less dangerous than white. This system has been bought by the Americans, and is being made under licence in the USA as the M239.

The Russian system was to drip diesel oil on to the hot exhaust of the engine, which produces a thick and lasting screen without the complication of phosphorous grenade and dischargers, but only behind the tank. This simple method is still used and has recently been proved to have an unsuspected technical advantage. Nevertheless, the latest Russian MBT appears to have grenade dischargers of the same configuration as the British type mounted on the turret.

Gun Control

Gun control is the method by which the gun is moved in azimuth and elevation. At the end of WW2 the most usual method involved handwheels with electric or hydraulic assistance, for traversing the turret, and handwheels with worm and wheel or rack and pinion for elevation. American M4 and M26 tanks were sometimes fitted with simple gyroscopic stabilisers in elevation only, but they were unreliable and often disconnected by the crew.

The first tank to be fitted with full stabilisation as original and standard equipment was the Centurion. From the Mk 2 (still with the 17pdr gun) onwards, all Centurions were fitted with the Metropolitan Vickers (Metrovick) stabilisation system, incorporated in FVGCE No 1 (Fighting Vehicle Gun Control Equipment No 1). Early Mk 3 Centurions had the FVGCE No 1 Mk 3/1, but after October 1950 the FVGCE No 1 Mk 4 was fitted.

Although the equipment was bulky by today's standards and liable to 'creep' when not closely watched, it was a tremendous advance over any other tank. Once the system was operating, any deviation from the original setting was sensed by two gyroscopes; the rate and direction of any deviation was passed to the metadyne and an appropriate correction sent to the traverse and elevation motors. Since there had to be an error before a correction could be made, the whole system was in a constant state of correction. Starting and stopping movement of the mass of gun and turret required large amounts of power on instant call. The Metrovick stabiliser system has proved effective and reliable under battle conditions.

In fact, although the gun barrel remains stabilised in space, the gunner has to make continual small corrections to compensate for movements of the tank hull, up or down hills, or sideways, relative to the point from which the initial stabilised lay on the target was made. He also has a trimmer

One of the latest developments in screening smoke for AFVs is the Schermuly Pains Wessex 'hot smoke' which produces a large cloud of infrared sources which blot out the IR signature of the vehicle to thermal imagers as well as screening the AFV from the naked eye. *Pains Wessex*

to compensate for the tendency of the system to correct more in one direction than another.

It was, in the 1950s and 1960s, an awe-inspiring sight when a line of Centurions moved across country, their hulls bucketing and turning and their gun barrels always pointing towards the target.

Argument started, and continues today, about the tactical value of firing on the move. The greatest value of a stabilisation system is that the gunner can keep his weapon laid very close to a target (within 0.5 mils with a modern system) so that there is only a minimal correction to be made when the tank halts to fire. This reduces engagement times and increases survivability.

Strangely the Americans did not fit full stabilisation into their tanks as a standard feature until 1970, when AOS (add-on stabilisation) was made a retro-fit for the M60A1. It is therefore true to say that the M1 Abrams is the first American tank to be designed with a stabiliser as original equipment. The Americans chose hydraulic control for turret and gun. Their system uses oil at about 3,000lb/sq in, giving quick responses and positive, fine control. The disadvantages are that using oil at such high pressures causes excessive wear in the control valves and needs absolute cleanliness. The slightest speck of dirt caught in a valve nullifies that part of the system and filtration must be of a very high order. In combat it was found that loosened joints or fractured oil lines could fill the turret with a fine spray of oil, while the sheer force of a jet of oil at high temperatures and velocities could cause severe wounds.

Modern improvements in solid state electronics now make a totally electrical stabilisation system more efficient and more attractive from the installation, maintenance and reliability angles. However, the most recent MBTs, the Leopard 2 and the Abrams, still use hydraulics. The Cadillac Gage electro-hydraulic system is used on the Leopard 1s of Germany and Belgium.

The latest American 'second generation' gun control system, from the National Water Lift Company, incorporates four gyros. Two monitor the usual traverse and elevation functions, while the other two read the pitch of the turret itself and the turning moment of the hull relative to the turret. The extra gyros feed the computer with information to anticipate commands from the gun gyros and give further accuracy to the system.

Fire Control Systems

In 1945 tank guns were aimed with the aid of nothing more complicated than telescopic or periscopic sights in which a series of graticules gave settings for range and lead marks for moving targets. The average range of engagement was under 1,000m partly because of the terrain and partly because the crews knew that their shot was ineffective at longer distances. Range taking was usually by the 'Mark One Eyeball'. When ranges were low and m/v fairly high, it was enough to get an estimate of range and make a correction on a quick second shot. However, when CE rounds fired at lower m/v came into use, the importance of accurate range-taking increased.

After WW2 the Americans were the first to use long (2m) base optical rangefinders mounted across the width of the turret. To start with they used the stereoscopic type, in which two images of the target are brought together 'in depth'. However, it was soon discovered that a high proportion of soldiers did not have the necessary stereoscopic vision ability and the rangefinders were changed to the coincidence type. In these two images are made to come together horizontally and the range is read off a scale when they coincide. These are much easier to use once one has got used to seeing the upper image inverted. Cross-turret rangefinders are bulky and take up a high volume in the turret; tanks so fitted are easy to identify by the armoured 'ears' on either side of the turret. The main disadvantage is that the accuracy of rangetaking is less with increasing distance, which is the reverse of what is really needed. Up to 1,000m the trajectory of a tank gun round is flat enough to get a hit by observation and estimation, over that distance the optical rangefinder is useful mainly in poor light conditions and in engagements when there is plenty of time to take several 'cuts'.

Some modern MBTs still employ the optical rangefinder. AMX30, Pz61 and Leopard 1, for example, have cross turret coincidence rangefinders, while in Leopard 2 the optical rangefinder can be used in coincidence and sterescopic modes at the choice of the gunner.

The Russian system was a stadiametric scale in their telescopic sights, consisting of an inverted V which covered the height of a 2.7m tank target at 1,200m. From this a very quick estimated correction could be made, provided the complete height of the target was visible. If not then another element of guessing came into play.

The only system of ranging that is accurate at all distances and does not depend on the gunner's eyesight is the laser rangefinder. Used in all modern MBTs and retro-fitted to many of the previous generation, the LRF can be built into a periscope or telescope sight or mounted separately on the turret or the commander's cupola, as in the Yugoslav ISKRA 22A conversion kit, fitted to Egyptian T-54s and T-55s.

The laser is aimed at the target and a pulse of light emitted which reflects from the target and is picked up by a receiving lens. The time taken for the pulse to reach the target and return is measured and computed into a range displayed as a digital readout. This is almost instantaneous and is acurate to ± 10m or ± 5m depending on the type. Accuracy is the same at all distances, which can be as much as 12-15km, far greater than the needs of a tank gunner. Most LRF have a 'gate' arrangement to eliminate or indicate spurious echoes caused by objects in the line of sight, such as trees, bushes etc.

Once the gunner has a range he can elevate the gun to compensate for it. This used to be by mechanical means, usually by turning a handwheel, but as stabilisers came into use more and more the handwheel became auxiliary to an electrically or hydraulically powered system, still under the direct control of the gunner.

With the appropriate aiming mark of the sight set on the target in traverse and elevation, the gunner of 1946 would have felt that all had been done that could be done to ensure a hit and he would have fired. If the tank was obviously tilted to one side and the gunner knew from experience that this could throw his shot off target perhaps he would have compensated by shifting his aiming mark 'uphill' a little. But he had nothing to tell him, until the American M103 became the first tank to incorporate a cant indicator and early mechanical ballistic computer. Now, with longer ranges and even greater need for first round accuracy, a trunnion cant indicator is incorporated in all FCSs which have a computer to work out the corrections.

As soon as guns had two or more natures of ammunition, high velocity AP and medium velocity HE, it was common practice to put two sets of aiming marks in one graticule, sometimes with a third for the coaxial MG. This was cheap and effective, but the necessity for the gunner to select the right scale, the right range and lead angle must have increased engagement times.

With the ballistic computer the gunner's work suddenly became easier. The correct nature of ammunition could be selected by a simple switch, which brought the relevant range table into play from those stored in the computer memory. The easiest method of storage is to have a memory card for each nature available. The computer displays the range as a digital read-out and is translated into the correct quadrant elevation, which can automatically be applied. All the gunner has to do is to keep the aiming mark on the target.

It is now unnecessary for the gunner to aim off left or right to hit a moving target. By tracking the target for a few seconds the computer can be supplied with sufficient information from a rate gyro on the traverse gear to compensate for target speed. The gunner looking through his sight will see the aiming mark change position relative to the target as the computer takes into account the information it receives from the sensors. He has only to move the gun and turret so that the aiming mark is again on the target.

With the solution to the problems of range, trunnion cant, natures of ammunition and moving targets in the computer, designers began to look at what other useful ballistic variables could also be compensated for. The temperature of the propellant charge can have a significant effect on the performance of the projectile; a sensor placed in the ammunition bins could provide this information. In practice it is not usual for this to be put in as a running correction. In some areas a variation of as much as 50-60°F occurs from day to night, which could make a significant difference to the performance of the propellant. But the change in charge temperature lags far behind that of the ambient air, particularly in well-protected storage bins. A charge that has cooled to 40°F at night may still be relatively cold at 1100hrs even in a hot turret in the desert; and though the air may be chill at 2000hrs in the evening the propellant may still be around 90°F. So real time sensing and entry to the computer could be very misleading.

It is common to put a manual correction in to the system twice or three times a day, depending on circumstances. The ambient temperature and humidity can also affect external ballistics and some people believe that it is worth the expense to take account of these variables. There is controversy on the value of compensating for wind speed and direction by means of a sensor on the turret roof. Will the wind be the same down range as it is at the firing point? In close country it is not unknown for the wind to be considerably different in direction and velocity only 1,000m away. But in the desert or similar terrain it can be the same for 100km. The argument is usually settled by consideration of the additional costs and complication and risk of failure. The author believes in simplicity and cost effectiveness.

In a typical modern MBT the basic sequence of engagement would be as illustrated in Fig 3. This is the system used by the Marconi SFCS 600 and is reproduced by kind permission of Marconi Radar Systems Limited, of Leicester. There are many other systems, varying in the complexity of their computers, the number of sensors, types of laser used and control. An important consideration for the designer of the MBT is the volume of the components and how they are packaged. The Marconi SFCS 600 has a control panel and a computer unit which would have to be placed on the turret wall, with the control panel at least near the gunner. The computer has a magazine for four or five printed circuit boards which contain all the range tables for a particular round, and which can be very easily changed if necessary. The laser is packaged into the gunner's periscope sight. The aiming mark is adjusted by spot injection; that is to say that

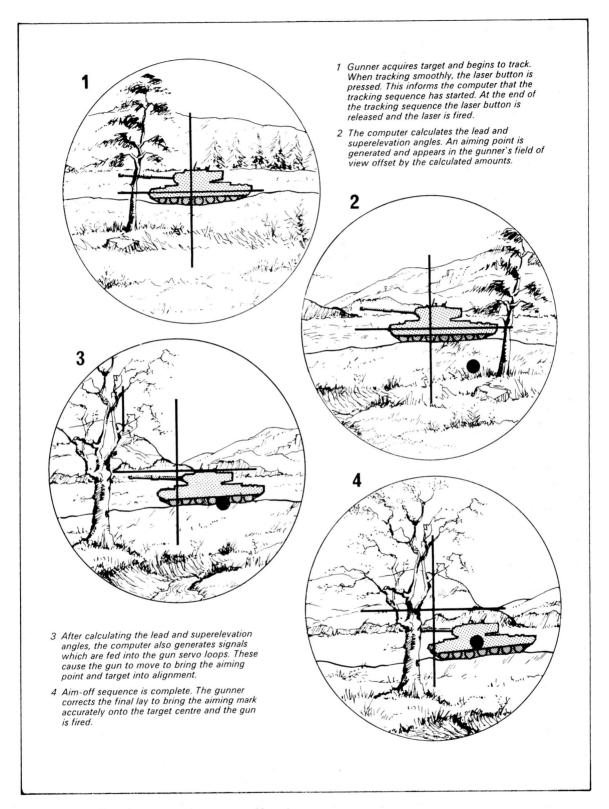

1 Gunner acquires target and begins to track. When tracking smoothly, the laser button is pressed. This informs the computer that the tracking sequence has started. At the end of the tracking sequence the laser button is released and the laser is fired.

2 The computer calculates the lead and superelevation angles. An aiming point is generated and appears in the gunner's field of view offset by the calculated amounts.

3 After calculating the lead and superelevation angles, the computer also generates signals which are fed into the gun servo loops. These cause the gun to move to bring the aiming point and target into alignment.

4 Aim-off sequence is complete. The gunner corrects the final lay to bring the aiming mark accurately onto the target centre and the gun is fired.

Fig 3 Marconi fire control system operating sequence. *Marconi*

the computer controls the movement of a spot of light in the sight picture of the gunner.

The Cobelda FCS, developed by SA Belge de Constructions Aeronautiques and Hughes Aircraft Co of California, shifts the aiming mark by servo motors moving a mirror, which alters the position of cross-hairs on the sight picture. In addition to the sensors for range, trunnion cant, wind and charge temperature and Cobelda FCS takes the ambient temperature and pressure, which can affect the external ballistics, and has a round counter to enable the computer to take wear in the tube into account.

In these systems the gunner has to re-lay using the displaced aiming mark after its position has been computed. In the French COTAC system the aiming mark is left undisturbed and the computer drives the gun control servos directly, reducing the possibility of human error. Basically it is easier to stabilise a light component than a heavy one. Inertia is less, responses are quicker and less power is required. For the gunner it means having a fixed periscope (he could not follow the gyrations of a moving sight) with head mirror array stabilised in two axes. The gun would then be slaved to sight, driven by servos controlled by the computer as it monitors the sight head. If necessary the gun firing circuit could be further controlled so that it could only fire when the bore coincided with the line ordered by the computer. The Swedish S-Tank has such a FCS, with a top section of the commander's sight stabilised in elevation and the sight itself in a cupola, stabilised in azimuth. The firing of the gun can be inhibited so that, on the move, it can only fire when it coincides with the line of the sight. The Leopard 2, and some retro-fitted Leopard 1s, have a stabilised panoramic commander's sight, and a commander's override which slaves the gun to the stabilised sight. The M60A2 has a commander's cupola stabilised in azimuth and the sight in elevation, though this seems a bit wasted when the armament is the Shillelagh missile, which is hardly likely to be fired on the move.

Fire control is largely the elimination of errors caused by variable factors inside and outside the tank, leaving only the final decision to the commander and gunner — to fire or not to fire. That is the only human decision in the system, and we must be careful that it remains.

Auxiliary power

Whatever gun control system is used requires a source of power, either electric or hydraulic. This is only a part of the power needed in an MBT. There are the normal mobility loads of starter motor, fuel pumps, lights, gear selectors and, possibly, ignition. Operational loads include crew intercom and radio, searchlights, passive night sights, FCS, gun control, NBC and, sometimes, automatic loading. Vision wipers, ventilating, cooling and heating, fire warning systems and navigational aids, even cooking, all take power from the electrical system of the tank and there are many more add-on systems that could add to the load.

The average electrical power consumption of a MBT, moving, or waiting to move, is 2-3kW, and can be as much as 5-6kW, depending on the equipments in use. Add to this the fighting load of about 6kW, which can peak at 18-20kW when everything is in use at once, and it can be seen that the electrical capacity of a MBT system must be able to deliver a considerable load.

A modern MBT will usually have a large battery capacity and a generator driven by the main engine to cope with this demand. This means that a certain amount of power is being diverted from the output to the tracks, diminishing the mobility of the vehicle. It also means that the main engine is

subject to higher fuel consumption and wear, since it will to be kept running all day, to keep the batteries charged.

Long periods of idling can cause fouling in the engine, and will produce noise, smoke and heat, all signs of the presence of a MBT. The latter is most significant now that thermal imagers are becoming more widespread in use. Alternatively it may be possible to run the main engine for short periods only. When on 'silent watch' an M60 must be started every 45 minutes, or risk running down its batteries. Another expedient is to restrict the use of certain equipments while the engine is switched off, to conserve power. Restricted use of radio, night vision and heating may be necessary, all of which can be detrimental to operational efficiency.

Typical of modern MBTs are the M1 Abrams, with six batteries with a total 300Ahc and a 650A engine-driven alternator, the AMX30 with a 125Ahc from eight batteries and Leopard 2 with eight batteries of 500Ahc and a 750A engine-driven alternator. Leopard 1 has a battery capacity of 400Ahc and a 9kW generator, but is also provided with external connections so that the batteries can be charged from a special trailer which can serve eight vehicles at a time.

The electrical power demands are beyond the capacity of the little, single-cylinder 'Tiny Tim' and 'Chorehorse' charging engine of WW2 tanks, though small charging units were retro-fitted to M48A2 and A3. The M60 has no auxiliary motor but the M1 Abrams now has a small auxiliary turbine generator.

The British solution was to carry an 18hp, four-cylinder Morris petrol engine in a corner of the engine compartment of the Centurion, driving a 3kW generator. The auxiliary engine had its own separate fuel and starting systems. It ran quietly, without the noise and heat signature of the main engine, but the space it took up reduced the fuel capacity of the tank and was partly responsible for the very low (90 miles) operational range of the Centurion.

In Chieftain, with even greater power requirements, the same idea was used, this time with a three-cylinder, six-opposed piston engine built by Coventry Climax, on the same lines as the Leyland L60. The H30 engine drives a 24V 350A dc generator to supplement the 150A generator on the L60.

The Vickers private venture tank, MBT Mk 3, used the same H30 auxiliary engine and generator, but the later Vickers Valiant has a 500A generator driven by the main engine to supply its 300Ahc batteries, and no auxiliary power source.

Soviet tanks have not been fitted with auxiliary generators, except the T-55, which is reported to have a 1kW auxiliary generator.

Tank Gun Design

When designing a tank gun system it is usual to start with the desired effect at the target and to work backwards from there, to the ammunition needed to achieve that effect, and then to the gun necessary to project that ammunition and the systems that control it.

Since a tank gun is primarily to kill other tanks, the effect would be stated as the measure of penetration of enemy armour, present and foreseen during the life of the gun, at a range dictated by the tactical philosophy of the users.

These days the choice of nature of ammunition would almost certainly be a high velocity, long-rod penetrator. This gives the maximum weight of projectile over the smallest area and therefore the maximum energy at the point of strike. Penetration of such a round is basically proportional to the velocity attainable and to the calibre of the gun from

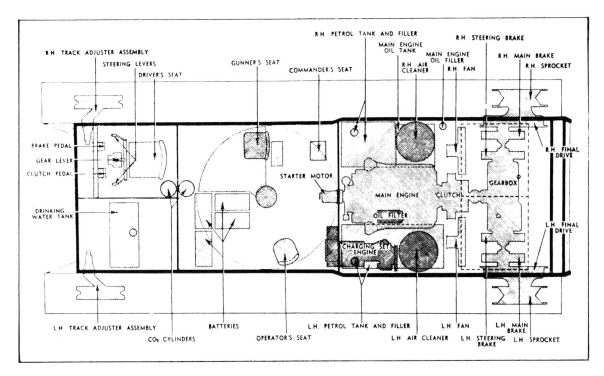

Fig 4 Layout of main components in Centurion: note charging set engine.

which it is fired: therefore the larger the gun the more penetration, up to the point where the advantages begin to be offset by the penalties of greater weight of gun, greater out-of-balance moment of the turret and the lower number of rounds that can be carried in a given volume. For example, it has been calculated that an increase of 5-10% penetration can be achieved by increasing calibre from 120mm to 130mm; but also that this would mean a reduction of 7.5% in the number of rounds carried in the tank. Is this worth it?

The pressure applied to the round in the gun is also a limiting factor. The higher the pressure, the greater penetration, but only up to the point where the increased pressure necessitates strengthening the sabot. It has been shown that the optimum chamber pressure is about 40 tons/sq in, which is already achieved in the British 120mm gun on Chieftain, using the materials and manufacturing techniques which exist. If the state of technology permits, future guns may well take higher pressures, and ammunition will then have to be redesigned in the light of these advances.

The length of the gun barrel also has an effect on penetration. The longer the barrel, the longer the round is in the tube and the greater the energy that can be imparted to the shot. For a given charge the accuracy also improves with barrel length, until the errors caused by vibration and droop outweigh the advantage. There is an obvious balance to be struck between kill probability and hit probability. For years it was a simple act of faith that penetration could be improved by increasing the muzzle velocity energy of a solid projectile. It followed that this could be achieved by increasing muzzle velocity for a given mass, and in the velocity range attained up to the 1950s this was largely true. However, there is an optimum m/v for each particular gun and shot, beyond which penetration deteriorates. The optimum m/v for most

modern guns lies between 1,400 and 1,800m/sec, though the newest smoothbores can get 2,000m/sec.

All these factors influenced the choice of guns for the American XM1 Abrams tank in the international competition of the mid-1970s. Britain, Germany and the USA carried out evaluation trials in 1975. The UK put up a 110mm gun that had been developed from the very successful 105mm, and, despite being a smaller calibre, was intended to perform as well as the existing 120mm. This Exp 14 M1 gun fired a long rod penetrator APFSDS that outdid both the US 105mm and the German smoothbore. Nevertheless it was agreed that a 120mm gun was the best solution and a further trial was arranged in 1971. The British entry was a new design of high pressure, rifled 120mm, the M13A. It used a stub cartridge for obturation as against the self-obturating breech of the L11 gun in Chieftain, and fired fin-stabilised HEAT and APDS rounds. The Germans entered their 120mm smoothbore and the Americans stuck to the 105mm M68, which is basically the British L7 made under licence, with a modified breech. The trials closed with each competitor convinced they had given the best performance, and there was considerable acrimony when the Americans decided to arm the first batches of the XM1 with their existing 105mm system. They announced, in January 1978, that they would use the German 120mm smoothbore gun in later batches, but this seems to have been influenced by the desire to offer some offset purchases, so that the Germans would consider the Chrysler/Lycoming turbine power pack for the Leopard 2. The American argument for retaining the 105mm gun was that their predictions of targets to come showed that the 105mm, with the improved ammunition that was being developed, would be able to perform satisfactorily on the battlefield for a long time to come, and that they would then have time to consider other installations, such as the 120mm.

Britain, at that time, stuck firmly to the rifled gun as the weapon for the future MBT80. This was to have 'the ability to defeat all types of Warsaw Pact tanks likely to be in 1(BR) Corps area during the lifetime of MBT80 at ranges out to 3.5km. These targets will be equipped with armour vastly superior to the current enemy MBT. To combat this the new gun will have to fire both KE and CE rounds. The present philosophy is to use APDS and HESH, as the latter is unaffected by spin stabilisation, but by using a slipping driving band it is equally possible to fire fin-stabilised rounds from a rifled gun. The driving band, made of a form of nylon, engages in the rifling to prevent the escape of gases past the round, but slips on the body of the projectile, imparting a very low spin. This allows the long rod and shaped charge ammunition to be fired from a rifled barrel with the same effect as from a smoothbore tube.

With either type of round, whether fixed or separated, a major consideration is wear in the bore. While such progress has been made in the use of harder wearing materials for gun barrels, including chromium plating, there is great scope for reducing the effect of the propellant gases. By using additives to the propellant, which are deposited on the wall of the barrel and have an insulating effect, and using charge cases of special combustible materials to form a cooler boundary layer of gases, barrel wear can be significantly reduced. At the same time, propellants are being improved to give greater muzzle energy. This may contribute to a smaller volume of propellant required, and to reducing the volume of stowed ammunition, but will require greater attention to bore wear.

Using bag charges has some advantages, but one aspect caused concern in the early stages of the trials of the 120mm. It was thought that the lack of rigidity of the charges would necessitate mechanical ramming of the projectile and a rammer was provided in early Chieftains. However, it was found to be unreliable, and was discarded when it was found possible to be able to do without it.

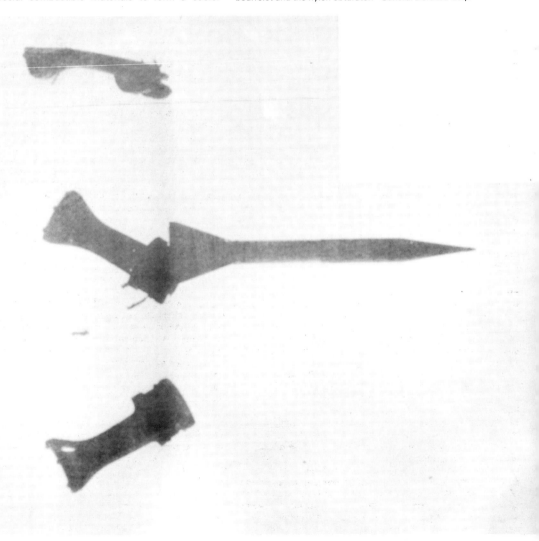

An APFSDS penetrator sheds its sabots. The three sections have peeled back like a banana skin as the air resistance built up in the forward section and broke the bourrelet, a ring holding the segments together at the front. The small pieces are from the bourrelet and the nylon obturator. *General Defense Corp*

Recent developments with fully combustible charge cases show that a rigid case can be made which, when burning, produces a layer of cooler gases. Such a case would be useful with separate ammunition, and with fixed ammunition, using a stub case for obturation.

Another development in Britain is the use of a split sliding block breech which combines the strength of the Crossley Pad type of obturator with the speed and ease of operation of the sliding breech. It has a pressure limit of 40 tons/sq in which is about the same as the current high velocity projectiles and would allow the latest and 'hottest' propellants to be used.

Ammunition

In 1940 most guns fired either AP shot or HE. The British 2pdr fired only AP; the German short 75mm fired only HE. The importance of versatility in tank armament was brought home in the desert campaigns of 1941-1943, and by the end of WW2 in 1945 the tank gunner had at his disposal three or four kinds of AP shot plus HE and smoke rounds. Since then the development of ammunition has matched that of armour, and overmatched it for much of the time.

From the solid homogeneous AP shot there evolved the APC shot with a cap of softer metal that prevented the shot shattering on impact and skidding off angled armour. This was followed by APCBC, with a ballistic cap over the first cap, to improve the shape of the round and maintain a higher striking velocity. Improved penetration came from the APCR (armour piercing composite rigid) shot in which a high density sub-calibre core was enclosed in a lighter, frangible casing that shattered on impact, leaving the core to penetrate the target.

All these were superseded by the APDS (AP discarding sabot) round which allowed the full calibre of the tube to be used to impart a high velocity to the sub-calibre core, while the sections of the 'sabot' flew off after leaving the muzzle. This is still the main KE round in use from either rifled or smoothbore guns and, because of its high velocity and flat trajectory, offers the best chance of hitting and killing the target. The latest development of the APDS round is the APFSDS (fin-stabilised discarding sabot). A spin-stabilised round can only be about six times as long as the calibre; this limits the weight of shot for a given size of gun. A fin-stabilised long rod penetrator can more than double that length without losing stability, allowing the use of more material with more striking energy over the same frontal area. The Americans have produced a penetrator of depleted uranium, the densest material available, but its cost makes it unlikely to be standardised. The main argument against smoothbore guns is that the rounds tend to lose accuracy after about 2,000m, but the proponents of smoothbore counter with the question 'Is it necessary to fire at tank targets further away than 2,000m?'

Since it is possible, by the use of slipping driving bands, to fire both spin and fin-stabilised rounds from a rifled tube it would seem that users of this type of gun have the best of both worlds, but the argument then centres on the effects of both types in the bore. The rifled gun is more subject to wear than the smoothbore, therefore having a lower barrel life.

Great advances have been made in the design of CE (Chemical Energy) rounds for tank killing. These are of two types (a) HEAT (HE anti-tank) which utilises the 'Monroe Effect' of a hyper velocity stream of gases from the explosion of a shaped charge, and (b) HESH (HE squash head) which allows a plastic explosive to form a pool against the target armour before detonation, the shock wave from which blows a 'scab' off the inside of the armour, causing great damage.

In order to develop its full effect a HEAT round must be detonated at a given distance from the armour, to allow the jet to develop. It is usually designed with an initiator standing well ahead of the body of the charge. The charge must burn from the back towards the hollow cone at the front, so the actual detonation is at the base of the projectile. The fuse used is called PIBD (point initiated base detonated). It consists of a Piezo-electric crystal which, when crushed by impact, generates a small amount of electricity to set off the detonator. The flame front burns towards the cone where it melts the material of the cone liner (usually copper) and merges into a jet of gas that penetrates the target, followed by the slug formed by the melted liner.

If the HEAT round were to be spin-stabilised for ballistic accuracy the centrifugal effect on the gases would tend to disperse the jet and reduce the penetration. It is usual, therefore, to fire HEAT from smoothbore tubes, with fin stabilisation. There are two ways of overcoming this limitation to smoothbore tubes for HEAT. The French 105mm gun on AMX30 is rifled, but the HEAT round, Obus G, carries the explosive charge mounted in ball bearings so that, although the casing is spun for stability, the inertia of the charge prevents it from picking up enough spin to degrade the effect. It is ingenious, but the diameter of the cone is less than it would be in a more conventional round, therefore penetration should, theoretically, be lower as well. Another method is to fire a fin-stabilised projectile from a rifled tube, using slipping driving bands of nylon (or a similar material) to act as gas seals. Very little spin is picked up by the projectile.

The shape of the HEAT round of the 1960s and 1970s was generally a flat nosed projectile with a long shaft sticking out from the front. The PIBD fuse was on the end of the shaft which provided the correct stand-off distance from the cone. One of the attractions of the HEAT round is that it does not have to be fired at the high velocities of the KE round, causing less wear in the barrel. The low velocity means a higher trajectory and greater accuracy is needed in ranging. Some modern HEAT rounds are therefore fired at higher velocities in order to obtain a better chance of a first-round hit. The extra barrel wear is acceptable as a trade-off against a kill. These rounds may have a more favourable ballistic profile, such as the 90mm Cockerill gun HFAT which is fired at 900m/s and has a sharply pointed nose for better ballistic performance. It has an effective range of 1,500m, can be fired from light AFVs such as Scorpion or SIBMAS and can penetrate 250mm of armour.

Though HEAT is the most popular CE anti-tank round, it has some disadvantages. It can be detonated outside the recommended stand-off distance, losing its potency before it reaches the main armour. When it does penetrate its effect is mainly directional along the line of attack and people or equipment out of the direct line of fire have a slight chance of survival, as was found during the Yom Kippur War of 1973. It was just as often found, however, that the jet of flame would set fire to ammunition and cause internal explosions sufficiently powerful to blow the turret of a T-62 more than 50m.

An alternative CE round, favoured more by the British, is HESH. The explosive charge is plastic and, when it hits a target, spreads out to form a pool. The detonator is in the base of the round, so that it does not initiate detonation until the pool is formed. The effect is to send shock waves through the metal of the target, which blow a scab of metal off the inside face, without making a hole in the plate. The scab, which in diameter is usually about 1.5 times the calibre of the round, flies round the interior of the tank, accompanied by smaller fragments, causing immense

Fixed Ammunition for Tanks, Cal. 120 mm, Smooth Bore Gun

Rheinmetall has developed new types of ammunition for the 120 mm smooth bore gun which — according to the tactical requirements — have a very high degree of effectiveness against soft- and hard targets. Two types of combat ammunition and matching practice versions are available: the multipurpose projectile (HEAT-MP) and the kinetic-energy (APDS-FS) — a fin stabilized subcaliber discarding sabot projectile.

The 120 mm ammunition has a partly combustible case with a metal base stub.

1 APDS-FS   2 HEAT-MP

Type of Projectile		APDS-FS *)	APDS-FS-P **)	HEAT-MP ')	HEAT-MP Practice
Cartridge Weight	kg	19	17	23	
Cartridge Length	mm	884		981	
Projectile Type		Discarding Sabot, fin stabilized		Full Bore Projectile, fin stabilized	
Projectile Weight	kg	7,1	5,6	13,5	
Dia. of Flight-Projectile	mm	38		120	
Prop. Charge Type		Bulk Propellant		Tubular Propellant	
Prop. Charge Weight	kg	7,1		5,4	
Case		partly combustible		partly combustible	
Priming		el. with Primer DM 72 A 1		Primer with radial ignition	
Scope		even over 2000 m against tanks	Practice firing	even over 2000 m against tanks and up to 4000 m against areal targets	Practice firing

*) APDS-FS = Armor-Piercing Discarding Sabot / Fin Stabilized

**) APDS-FS-P = Armor-Piercing Discarding Sabot / Fin Stabilized / Practice

') MP = Multi-Purpose

State: 1.1.1978

damage. Like HEAT, the HESH round is not affected by the velocity or the range to which it is fired, but also it is not adversely affected by spin stabilisation, so can be fired from rifled tubes. It is therefore more accurate at longer ranges and was chosen by the British for that reason, when they wanted to engage enemy tanks at 3,000m. The disadvantage of HESH is that it, too, can be detonated by skirt armour or stowage bins, wasting its effect.

The family of ammunition normally available for a tank gun now includes an AP shot and a CE round which may do double duty for a simple HE round in order to simplify the logistics. There is usually a smoke round and western tanks often carry a canister round. This is a modern development of the old fashioned grape shot, or canister, and is filled with several hundreds of small pieces of rod which spread from the muzzle of the gun like a big sawn-off shotgun, murderous at ranges up to 50-100m, and useful against the sort of mass infantry attacks experienced in Korea or ambush situations in the jungles of Vietnam. The other type of ammunition, possibly the most important, and which is fired more than any other type, is practice. Practice rounds have the same external ballistics as the service APDS or HEAT, and are fitted with a tracer, but they are inert, or contain only a smoke puff charge, and are made of cheaper materials than the service rounds, so that troops can afford to fire more. In the smaller cannon calibres the practice round is sometimes designed so that it breaks up shortly after leaving the muzzle.

Tanks may carry a smoke round to put down a screen some distance away, but they also carry smoke for their own immediate protection. Most western tanks, and now the latest Russian ones, carry tubular dischargers for smoke grenades. These are fired by a small propelling charge, in a spread to about 50m distance, and burst to form an instantaneous screen behind which the tank can make for cover. The British No 80 grenades used in the 1940s and 1950s used a white phosphorus filling and could cause nasty burns to personnel if any adhered to uniforms or vehicles. The modern L8 grenade has a rubber body, which can actually be seen to swell up like a balloon in flight and burst, has a less dangerous red phosphorus filling. Normal burning smoke compositions, such as hexachlorethane, do not react quickly enough to form a useful screen.

The physical size of tank ammunition is of great importance from the points of handling in the turret and the space needed to stow it in the racks or bins. A 105mm APFSDS round weighs 18kg and is 948mm in length, but this is not the biggest 105mm round. The Base Ejection Smoke round weighs 26.35kg, quite enough to handle in the confines of a tank turret.

Ammunition for the Cockerill 90mm gun is made by the Belgian firm of PRB, and they have found a good way of improving the handling in confined spaces; to keep the length of the complete round to manageable proportions the rear part of the projectile and all the empennage (tails and fins) is inside the cartridge case, with the propellant packed around the fins. This arrangement keeps the length of the HEAT-T round down to 652mm and the weight to 7.5kg, but even this is quite enough to handle in a Scorpion turret, very full of gun and crew.

Ammunition of 120mm calibre is a borderline case. The British view is that it would be too large and heavy to handle properly in the turret without an automatic loader and that the disposal of empty cases would be a serious problem. The British 120mm was put into service before the technology of efficient fully combustible cases was sufficiently advanced, so they use separate ammunition, with the bagged charges — easy to handle but marginally slower to load.

The German 120mm, developed 10 years later by Rheinmetall, uses a semi-combustible case with stub cartridge. The APFSDS round weighs 19.8kg and is 979mm long, and the HEAT round 24.5kg with a length of 981mm. This is very big ammunition and the Leopard 2, for which the gun was designed, was to have a semi-automatic loading system, which would move the round into the correct loading position no matter what the breech was doing. This would reduce the loader's effort and help prevent damage to the combustible cases. On the Leopard 2AV the gun is slaved to a stabilised primary sight, so it can be brought to a loading position between shots without slowing the rate of fire very much. It is regarded as an acceptable trade-off, but the loader still has to handle the heavy round.

The 125mm ammunition for the gun in T-72 would definitely be difficult to handle in the confines of that turret, so the tank has a fully automatic loader and separated rounds. The APFSDS 125mm is fired at over 1,600m/sec, and requires a hefty propellant charge. About 40 rounds of various natures are stowed under the turret floor in a sort of carousel, controlled by a computer, which keeps track of where each round is in relation to the loader. It must be awkward putting the projectiles into the boxes on the turntable, with the charges on top. The tank commander selects the type of round required, and the computer brings the nearest one of that nature to the automatic loader. With the gun barrel at +4° (and the breech lowered by the same amount) the box with the ammunition is raised until the projectile is in line with the breech, when it is rammed, the box lowered and the charge rammed. The loader then returns to the ready position and the barrel to its aiming position. This time consuming operation reduces the effective rate of fire to 4-5 rounds per minute.

Fig 5 Fixed ammunition for the Rheinmetall smoothbore 120mm gun. *Rheinmetall*

Comparison of 120mm AP shot — 1953 to 1983

The 120mm gun in the American M103 and the British Conqueror fired a solid AP shot which weighed 23kg. It was fired at a muzzle velocity of 1,066m/sec. This required 13.07kg of propellant which was loaded in a separate brass cartridge case 88cm long. The resultant energy hit the target on a frontal area of 113cm².

The latest 120mm gun to come into service is the Rheinmetall smoothbore in the Leopard 2. This fires an APFSDS round with a partly combustible cartridge case taking 7.1kg of propellant. The obturator is a brass stub cartridge. The muzzle velocity is estimated at about 1,480m/sec. The penetrator has a diameter of 3.8cm and a weight of 7.1kg. Thus the concentration of mass over the smaller frontal area results in more than three times as much energy being applied to the target per cm², giving greatly improved performance for the smaller round.

4 Anti-Tank Guided Weapons

The guided missile, as opposed to the unguided bazooka type of rocket, came into prominence in the early 1950s. It was the age of the missile for all purposes, from artillery rockets to anti-aircraft fire. The technology has been developed since the end of WW2 and the first ATGW in the field was the French SS-10, developed from a German design. The X-7 had not been operational by the time Germany was defeated in 1945, but the French picked up the design, and the expert personnel, and in 1952 the SS-10 was adopted by the French Army.

It was a solid fuelled rocket, flying at only 80m/sec, so it needed large wings. The maximum range was 1,600m and it carried a HEAT warhead of 164mm diameter capable of penetrating 400mm of armour. The weight was 15kg, so it was man-portable and it gave the infantry a significant addition to their anti-tank defences. Naturally, it was not long before the SS-10 was mounted on jeeps and other vehicles. Nearly 30,000 were made before production ceased in 1963.

The SS-10 was controlled by an operator with a small joystick, passing commands down a trailing wire link. The problem was that it took 500-700m (more usually the latter) for the operator to gain control of the missile, and some eight seconds of flight, during which time the target could have moved out of line, or worse, have come within the 700m range.

This problem was of considerable importance in the Indo-Pakistani war of 1965. The German Cobra ATGW, a slight improvement over the SS-10, had a minimum range of 600m and a maximum of 1,600m. Many were fired by the Pakistanis at the Indian Centurions, few achieved hits, as they were deployed in built-up areas and fired at short ranges. This was the first time that ATGW were used in action and useful lessons were learned. The French improved on their first efforts and brought out the SS-11, which had greater range and speed. It had the same method of control, however, and a minimum range of 500m. It was twice the weight of the SS-10 and had to be vehicle-mounted. This was no problem to the French, who produced ATGW variants of almost every AFV in their range.

Similar ATGW were introduced by Sweden (the Bantam) and Switzerland (the Mosquito). All those had acceleration control guidance systems and required time for the missile to reach speed sufficient for the airflow across the control surfaces to allow the operator to gather the missile and take control.

The first British ATGW came into service in 1962. It was the huge and clumsy Malkara, developed in conjunction with

Australia and named after an aboriginal throwing stick. It carried a 26kg HESH warhead, which would utterly destroy any contemporary tank unlucky enough to be hit. It was slow, flying at 100m/sec to a maximum range of 4,000m. It also had acceleration control. The trouble with Malkara was that it weighed, in total, 99kg and needed a vehicle to carry it. As it was too large for normal infantry use it was mounted on the lightly armoured Humber one-ton truck and issued to airborne troops as anti-tank support.

The next British ATGW was developed by Vickers-Armstrong and eventually built by BAC as the Vigilant. It was man-portable, weighing 14kg, and flew comparatively fast, at 136m/sec, to a range of 1,375m. The warhead was HEAT. The important difference was that it had an auto-pilot, with velocity control and reduced the minimum range to 200m. This was very important for what was primarily an infantry weapon, though it was also mounted on the Ferret Mk 2/6 scout car, in which role it took over from the Malkara Hornet system in airborne units.

The Russians had not been uninterested in the developments of the early 1950s, and produced their own counterpart, which entered service in 1962 and was code-named 'Snapper' by NATO. It was similar to other 'first generation' ATGW, having a minimum range of 600m and a

Left: Ferret Mk2/3 of the Australian Army with ENTAC ATGW mounted on the left side of the turret. Note the binocular observation device between the turret roof and the hatch. ENTAC was a joystick controlled first generation missile. A reserve missile is carried in the box on the rear mudguard. *ADA*

Below: Several alternative weapon systems can be carried on the Spartan APC. Here is a twin mounting for the Milan ATGW. Reloading is through the roof hatch. Ten additional missiles can be carried. *Alvis*

maximum of 2,000, moving at 89m/sec and having simple flying controls. Since it weighed 22.5kg it was vehicle-mounted, usually on a GAZ jeep or a BRDM scout car. It was followed by the 'Swatter', an improved version, which was radio-controlled and flew at 150m/sec out to a range of 2,500m. 'Swatter' was usually mounted on the BRDM scout car, and used in the anti-tank units of reconnaissance battalions. It is being superseded by the second generation AT-4 'Spigot' and AT-5 'Spandrel'.

Another Russian ATGW came to prominence in 1973 in the Arab-Israeli October War. The 'Sagger' is a man-portable missile of only 11.3kg, only 14kg in its container/launcher, which resembles a suitcase and so gave it the nickname of 'Suitcase ATGW'. Large numbers of these missile were rushed across the Sues Canal in the first waves of Egyptian infantry and provided an instant anti-tank screen which was very effective against the Israeli counter-attacks. 'Sagger' relies on the same methods of control as its predecessors, but has a range of 3,000m. In the open desert this was a great advantage and the minimum range of 500m was no great problem. 'Sagger' has also been mounted on many Soviet AFVs including the BRDM and BMP.

All the first generation ATGW have two important features. The controllers can be separated from the missile launcher by up to 100m and they must fly the missile all the way to the target. It means following, visually, a tracking flare on the missile and correcting when it moves away from the target. This means that it is possible (if not entirely practicable) to fly the ATGW over and around obstacles on the way to the target.

It would be simpler, of course, to have a sight which allows the operator merely to keep the crossed hairs on the target, leaving all else to semi-automatic control. This is the basis of the second generation, ATGW. It works by having a tracking device (goniometer) in the operator's sight array

which notes the position of the tracking flare in the base of the missile relative to the line of sight (LOS). When there is a deviation from LOS the computer works out the corrections necessary to bring the missile back on line and sends the commands down the trailing wire link. There is a continuous process of error and correction and the effect is that the missile flies 'down a tunnel' the axis of which is the LOS.

While this is simpler to operate, it requires more sophisticated electronics, and it means that the launch tube, sight, goniometer and the operator are on LOS to and from the target. Unlike the manual command to LOS first generation ATGW, which can be controlled from under armour, behind cover and up to 100m from the launcher, the SACLOS (semi-automatic command to LOS) second generation are more vulnerable to counter fire. Improvements have been made over the years and most can now be fired from under armour, but the direct LOS cannot be altered.

The first SACLOS missile on the market was, again, French. Harpon was little more than an SS-11 with a new guidance system; it still flew at only 160m/sec, had a minimum range of 400m and a maximum of 3,000m. The goniometer installation was behind a large and vulnerable glass window on the launcher pedestal. Harpon was replaced by the HOT (Haut-subsonique Optiquement Teleguide) ATGW, with greatly superior performance, from the Franco-German Euromissile consortium.

Aerospatiale and Messerschmitt-Bolkow-Blohm gmbh combined and started work in 1963 on two ATGW, one vehicle mounted and one man-portable. The vehicle mounted HOT has its missile packed in a sealed container which only has to be clipped to the launcher and fired out of the tube on to the LOS, when it is picked up by the guidance system. This gives a minimum range of 75m, and it flies at 260m/sec to 4,000m. The HOT is mounted on the German JagdPanzer Rakete and the French AMX. It still has large wings and the acceleration control system of the SS-11. The wings spring out after launching. The in-flight weight is 22kg and the HEAT warhead is of 136mm dia.

The Milan man-portable version has a range of 25-2,000m. The missile weighs 11.8kg and flies 200m/sec. The ground mounting for the launcher weighs 16kg, so it is not too heavy for the infantry. However, the warhead diameter is only 103mm and this is not considered enough to be sure of a kill on the frontal armour of an MBT. Nevertheless Milan has been adopted by some 15 countries, including most of NATO.

The Americans have their own vehicle mounted and man-portable systems. The M47 Dragon, which weighs only 14.6kg complete with sight and missile in launch tube, has a range of 25-1,000m. It was developed by McDonnell Douglas, with Kollsman Instrument making the tracker and Raytheon the missile. It became operational with US forces in Europe in February 1975.

The Dragon missile has a shaped charge warhead at the front and three spring-out fins at the rear. The centre-section contains 60 solid fuel rocket motors set to give thrust sideways and to the rear. On firing a gas generator pushes the missile out of the launch tube, after which the fins impart a slow roll to the missile. The rocket motors are fired, in pairs, as they reach the bottom dead centre of the roll, so that the missile flies on a continuous series of thrusts from beneath. Guidance is SACLOS, with the operator having to keep the cross-wires of his sight on target.

The larger TOW (Tube-launched Optically-tracked Wire-guided) system is used either from a tripod ground mounting or from specially designed launchers on AFVs, such as the M113 Improved TOW Vehicle or the TBAT-2 turret of the Bradley IFV. Its range is 30-3,000m (3,500 for the later, improved TOW) and carries a 127mm diameter HEAT warhead. It came into service in 1972 and did good work in Vietnam, often fired from helicopters, against both armoured and soft targets.

TOW is ejected from the launch tube by a small motor of 1.2lb of propellant which is expended before the missile leaves the tube, but it does make a considerable back blast which is not unlike a recoilless rifle and leaves a distinctive launch signature that can be dangerous, particularly to crews of TOW fired from the ground mount or from unprotected vehicles. TOW has four wings in the mid-section and four control surfaces at the tail, which spring into position when the missile leaves the tube. Having 'coasted' for about 12m the main propulsion motor ignites and carries the missile to the target. New TOW have an improved warhead with an extensible probe that activates the fuse at a more advantageous stand-off distance from the target. Another version, TOW 2, will have a warhead of 152mm diameter, the same as the Shillelagh gun-launched ATGW.

The British second generation ATGW is the BAC Swingfire, which came into service in 1969. It is not launched from a tube, but from a container which can be carried on armoured or soft-skinned vehicles, or even placed on a ground mount, as long as it is placed at roughly 35° of elevation and within 45° either side of the LOS. After launch Swingfire is automatically gathered into the controller's field of view, then flown to the target by the controller using a small joystick.

The Swingfire command system is by velocity control. The auto-pilot has two gyros, for pitch and yaw. If no correction is necessary the gyros keep the missile on course, but if the joystick is moved the gyros give a signal which alters the direction of the main thrust motor for as long as the deflection is ordered. When the joystick is centralised the course set is maintained until further correction. The automatic gathering of the missile after launch is completed at 150m and the maximum range is 4,000m.

These are the main ATGW in present service. The counter to a HEAT warhead is to increase the stand-off distance so that the jet of gas and metal cannot penetrate the armour. External stowage, skirting plates and composite armour all have a part to play in this defence. Other defences being investigated are using IR sources mixed with screening smoke to blind thermal imagers and the possible confusion of the tracking goniometer by putting up multiple decoy flares.

Left: A Striker of 'J' Sidi Rezegh Battery Royal Horse Artillery fires a Swingfire ATGW. *Alvis*

Below: The fate of an M48 hit by ATGW in Sinai in 1973. An internal explosion — probably of ammunition — must have lifted the turret.

5 Armour

The armour of early tanks was simple steel plate, bolted or riveted to an iron frame. It was thick enough (8-12mm) to keep out small arms fire and splinters, but was liable to 'splash' on the inside, where hit, and vulnerable to field artillery. During the interwar years the thickness of armour increased but little. In 1933 the British Director of Mechanisation stated 'For the moment we are contemplating armour for AFVs on an 11mm basis for reconnaissance vehicles and on a 14mm basis for fighting machines. I do not think we will ever go over one inch in thickness of armour for any future designs.'

However, by 1939 British Cruiser Tanks sported frontal armour of 30mm and the Infantry Tank Mk 1 had 60mm. On the continent, France had frontal armour of 40mm on the R-35 and Germany 30mm on the Panzer III. The material in all cases was homogeneous cast or plate steel, though many suggestions had been made for alternatives. These included spaced armour, composite layers of steel and rubber and spaced armour with the plates at an angle to each other instead of parallel. During WW2 the thickness of protection went up in response to improvements in attacking power. Skirting plates were added to explode shaped charge warheads beyond their effective stand-off distance, but the main defence remained solid steel. The German Panther had a front plate of 80mm at 55° and the Tiger 2 had a glacis plate of 150mm at 50°. On the Allied side the most widely used tanks were the Sherman with a maximum thickness of 75mm and the Russian T-34 which had a well-sloped glacis of 47mm at 60° from the vertical. The British Comet had a vertical front plate of 76mm thickness and was the last of this configuration.

The sloping of armour has the effect of increasing its relative thickness according to the angle of slope; more than that, however, the ballistic effectiveness of a sloped plate is of the order of three times its actual thickness, against KE attack. Against HEAT it is the slope angle which counts, but HESH acts at 90° to the plate, against only its actual thickness.

Modern AFVs are still mostly made of homogeneous plate or cast steel. Additives are used to enhance the tensile strength and hardness, those most used being nickel, chrome and molybdenum. This gives a metal of 300-400 Brinell hardness, to resist penetration, and a tensile strength of 11-12 tonnes/sq cm to absorb the energy of high velocity AP projectiles.

From 1945 to 1973 all modern MBTs had cast turrets, with the exception of the Vickers Vijayanta. This had a turret of welded rolled plate because there were insufficient casting facilities in India, where they were made. The advantage of cast turrets was that they could more easily be designed with the complex shapes and angles which give best ballistic protection. To get the same level of protection as rolled plate, castings must be thicker and heavier, but the advantages outweighed the extra amount of metal.

While early Leopard 1 had a cast turret, from the Leopard 1A3 onwards they were fitted with a new design of turret incorporating spaced armour, and made of welded plate.

Much research effort has gone into defeating attack by both KE and CE rounds. Many options have been tested and mostly found wanting in one respect or another. Face hardened plate could cause break-up of shot but was less effective in absorbing energy. Laminations of hardened and ordinary plate tended to come apart under the influence of shock waves at the joins. Hard steel rods and bars have been embedded in softer metals, with the object of deflecting shot and breaking up shock-wave effects.

The greatest single advance in armour protection is the development of a composite armour at the MVEE in Chobham, England. Known, therefore, as 'Chobham armour', it is a secret that has been shared with some of Britain's allies. The irony was that, at first, it was considered too expensive to equip British AFVs with the newly invented armour, but luckily circumstances changed and the Challenger is the first British MBT to have this form of protection. Before that, however, the German Leopard 2 and the American M1 Abrams both incorporated Chobham armour

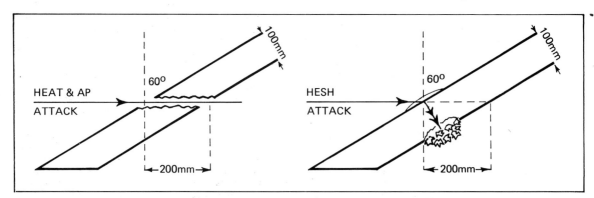

Fig 6 Penetration of armour by HEAT and HESH rounds.

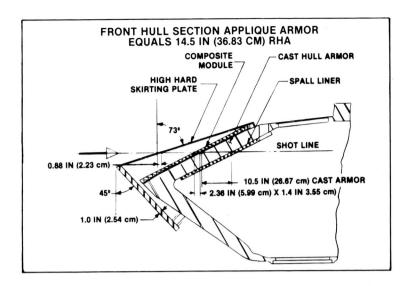

Fig 7 . The applique armour added to the Teledyne Super M60 glacis plate and front hull. *Teledyne*

FRONT HULL SECTION APPLIQUE ARMOR
EQUALS 14.5 IN (36.83 CM) RHA

COMPOSITE MODULE
CAST HULL ARMOR
HIGH HARD SKIRTING PLATE
SPALL LINER
73°
SHOT LINE
0.88 IN (2.23 cm)
10.5 IN (26.67 cm) CAST ARMOR
45°
2.36 IN (5.99 cm) X 1.4 IN 3.55 cm)
1.0 IN (2.54 cm)

in their initial designs. The configuration of the latest Russian T-80 indicates a similar development.

Chobham armour is a highly classified secret, but it is in essence a composite armour with an energy absorbent material sandwiched between two layers of high quality steel, possibly a titanium alloy. The interior filling probably includes a ceramic material, bonded by some man-made fibres on the lines of the Du Pont Kevlar which is used for body armour. The idea would be for the ceramic to deflect and disperse the high speed gas jets of HEAT and to absorb the energy of AP shot without breaking up too much.

Since Chobham style armour is many times thicker than conventional steel armour it takes up a great deal of extra volume. It is therefore unlikely to be used on light AFVs, where size is a more important factor. There has been a development of another metal which finds its best applications on light AFVs, rather than in MBTs.

Aluminium armour

In the mid-1950s American strategy required rapid reinforcement of its forces in Korea and it seemed likely that they might be called upon to intervene in the Middle and Far East and in Africa. Air-portability became a prime consideration and in 1955 the Chief of Staff directed that a family of lighter AFVs should be developed. FMC was awarded the development contract for a new APC. In the same period there was a drop in the demand for aluminium for the aircraft industry, so the manufacturers turned to other uses, including armour plate. The T113 prototypes were built of aluminium armour and the subsequent production contract established the M113 as the first APC to be made of the metal, as well as the most widely used AFV in the western world.

Aluminium armour is lighter, for a given thickness, than a steel plate. The specific gravity of aluminium armour is 2.66; that of steel is 7.85. Since the aluminium armour must be about three times thicker than steel to give the same level of protection, the weight of material needed is about the same.

However, the thickness of the aluminium plate brings another benefit. The aluminium plate, three times as thick, is also three times as stiff. This means that designers can use the armour as structural material, doing away with some purely structural items. Where components such as suspension, transmission etc had previously been mounted on steel supports, they could now be mounted directly to the thick hull walls. These changes resulted in savings of about 5% of the vehicle weight, compared to an equivalent in steel armour.

There are other savings too. Machining aluminium is easier and quicker than steel. Aluminium can be extruded in ready made sections, instead of having to roll and machine steel for the same purpose. The curved sides of the Fox turret are made from single extrusions, formed to a smooth radius. Some parts can be forged, such as the Scorpion nose plate, while the commander's cupola of the M551 Sheridan is an aluminium casting, though the rest of the turret is of steel.

The original Type 5083 alloy was used in the construction of the M113, M114 and M108 and M109 SP gun chassis. More recent vehicles such as the Sheridan use the newer Type 7039 material, which is an aluminium-zinc-magnesium alloy giving greater structural strength and superior ballistic performance. A similar alloy, X3034, was developed in Britain and is used in the CVR series.

There are, of course, disadvantages in the use of aluminium. Welding has to be very carefully controlled so that the heat does not lead to stress corrosion cracking of the metal. This was a problem with the early Scorpions. Exposed cut edges of plate are also susceptible to cracking and have had to be 'buttered' by covering the cut edge with welding material, a time consuming job, by hand. Before going into production with the Scorpion, Alvis Ltd had two years' hard work, changing from steel to aluminium and developing and learning new techniques. In the construction of the hull of Scorpion there are six long welds which run from one end of the vehicle to the other, uninterrupted, and very closely controlled for quality; this is almost impossible by hand, and a special machine was developed for the purpose.

Aluminium armour is used, so far, only for light AFVs. It does not give enough protection for any useful thickness to be used on MBTs. However, there could be a future for aluminium as the basis for composite armours. Steel or ceramic can be fixed to the outside of an alloy hull, or rods could be embedded in the alloy material to deflect projectiles.

6 The Future

The continuing necessity for mobility and protection ensures the future of the AFV in many configurations and for an increasing number of roles. It is the form of these vehicles and weapon systems that is in question. In the early 1970s a series of trials was carried out which indicated that the armed helicopter would be the master of the tank. After the 1973 Arab-Israeli war the ATGW was hailed as the king of the battlefield. Both theories forecast the demise of the MBT, but both were only partly right. The ATGW and the helicopter are, indeed, powerful threats to the tank, but neither are insuperable nor do they promise total mastery. It is still true that for every form of attack there is a counter and there are many different theories as to which counter is the most effective.

Though the MBT, created to perform a wide variety of roles, may disappear, there will remain the need for a tank, which is, in essence, a mobile, protected, direct fire, weapon platform. Only now has the technology evolved which will permit radical changes from the hitherto accepted norm of a hull, in which sits a driver, surmounted by a 360° traversing turret, with a three-man crew serving a large bore, high velocity gun. It is now possible to foresee a tank with a three-man (or even a two-man) crew, an externally mounted gun of medium 75-90mm calibre and super velocity, the whole being protected by composite armour within a combat weight of 30 tonnes. The automatic loader has gone through its first generation in the S-Tank, AMX13 and T-72, and is approaching the stage of reliability when it may be possible to dispense with emergency hand loading. If this becomes accepted, and there is great resistance to it among soldiers who have been let down by mechanical devices, then it is feasible to separate the crew completely from the ammunition, once it is loaded into the magazines. From there it is an easy extension to re-supply by pre-loaded containers which do not have to be handled by the crew at all.

If the main armament can be mounted externally, this releases the designer from the minimum hull width previously necessary to accommodate the movement of the breech in elevation and recoil. The upper part of the hull can be made narrower and the amount of frontal area exposed in the hull down position greatly reduced. It is possible to remove the gunner and commander completely from the gun, allowing sighting and observation by remote control from positions low in the hull, or in front of the gun/magazine compartment. If this compartment is made narrower then the hull itself can be narrowed, though not beyond the point where the ratio of track length on the ground to width between track centres is greater than 1.8:1, which would affect the steering ability. The space thus made available could be used for stowage or extra protection.

It is difficult to reduce the height of the hull itself, since sufficient room must be allowed for an average sized man to endure a battle day. Indeed, the hull height may have to increase somewhat as designers are forced to improve the defence of the roof and belly, which have been hitherto regarded as the least vulnerable areas.

Another advantage of the externally mounted gun is that it reduces the volume which must be protected by armour. The new composite and spaced armours are more bulky than homogeneous steel plate or casting, even if they do not weigh much more, so with a given size of hull, protection by Chobham armour leaves less space for the crew and components. A very important factor is transportability, which means that the width must be kept within the rail loading gauge and that the maximum weight must not exceed the available bridge classification. The British Challenger, at 60 tonnes, will be difficult to move in Germany, where the number of Class 60 routes is very limited. To get adequate operational mobility in future, the MBT should not exceed Class 40.

Modern powerpacks can be made smaller and lighter for a given output and can yet deliver a satisfactory power/weight ratio; 26-30bhp/tonne is as much as can be used with the suspension systems that exist or are likely in the future, so larger engines are not required, especially if combat weights can be brought down. The main criteria for future engines will be fuel economy and reliability. The gas turbine has a long way to go to catch up with the diesel in this respect, but it could happen in the next decade.

Main armament is still likely to be the high velocity gun, though there are still strong proponents of the guided missile, which has advantages of accuracy at ranges in excess of 3,000m. However, targets for tank guns at this distance are rare, and would, in any case, probably be the responsibility of the artillery, using CLGP. The smoothbore

From top to bottom:

Fig 8   The interior height of the turret is crucial to the amount of depression of the main armament.

Fig 9   The cleft turret allows greater elevation and does not interfere with depression as much as a conventional turret. It does, however, separate the turret crew and necessitates an automatic loader. A further advantage is that the breach of the gun can vent fumes direct into open air, rather than into the same envelope as the crew.

Fig 10   A possible configuration for the future MBT is this development of the Swedish Strv 103-B, or S-Tank. The gun would be mounted externally, on a pedestal at the base of which would be the gunner. Loading would be entirely automatic, ammunition being transferred from an armoured box magazine at the rear of the hull by a loading tray pivoting on the same pedestal as the gun.

Fig 11   Swedish designers have come up with an articulated vehicle which can be tailored to different configurations for various roles. The test rig for this XX20 concept performed very well in trials and could be the basis for a tank destroyer and an APC for the conditions of the far north of Sweden.

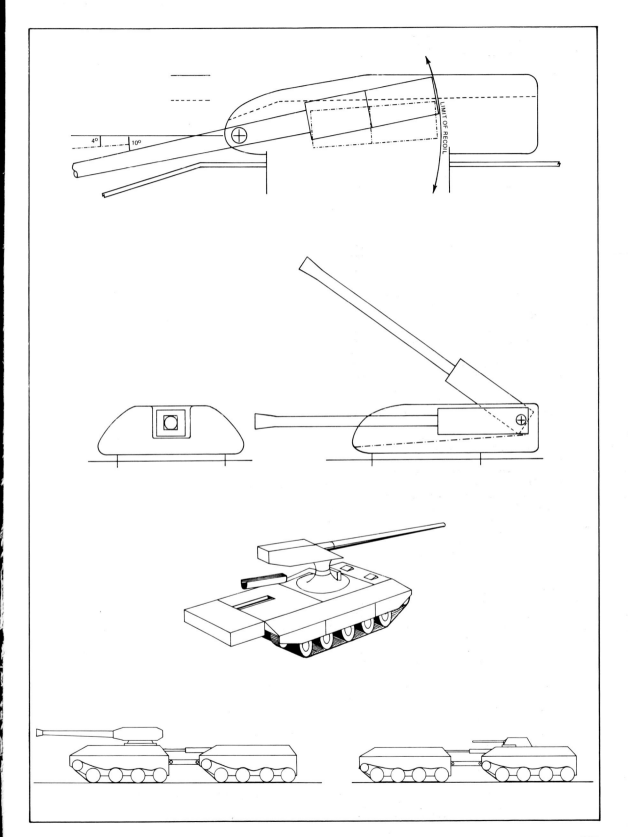

The High Survivability Test Vehicle (Light) or HSTV(L) achieves a hull height of 1.422m by putting the driver and gunner in semi-prone positions side by side in the front of the hull. Overall height, including the commander's 'hunter' sight, is 2.414m. The commander has all round observation through eight periscopes, except for the pedestal of the hunter sight, on his right. This sight is linked by TV to all three crew members.

The gunner's primary sight, which incorporates a CO_2 laser rangefinder, is stabilised and linked by TV to all crew members. The gunner also has a direct view optical sight in the hull, slaved to the main armament. The optical head can be seen between the crew hatches, under the gun. A Vidicon fixed view TV camera can give all the crew a rear view when required. Armament consists of a 75mm high velocity ARES cannon, a coaxial M240 7.62mm MG and another M240 on the commander's cupola. It should carry 60 rounds for the main armament, loaded automatically. Ammunition will include APFSDS, Multi-Purpose Fragmentation HE and Multi-Flechette round which can be used for air defence, taking advantage of the 45° elevation of the gun. It also has a phenomenal 17° depression over the glacis plate. With 30hp/ton from the AVCO Lycoming turboshaft engine the HSTV(L) is very agile, with a top speed of 80kph. It is a development model in the direction of a new generation of AFVs. *AAI Corporation*

tube, with hotter propellants (possibly liquid) and fin-stabilised long rod penetrators will be more widely used than the rifled tube. Muzzle velocities could rise to 1,500-1,600m/sec, and there are possibilities of achieving 2,000m/sec by using secondary propellant charges.

Apart from the additional killing power of the higher velocity projectile, the flatter trajectory will permit greater accuracy. This may allow simpler and less costly FCS, which would help to cover the extra expense of remote control of the externally mounted gun and automatic loader.

Much work has already been done to investigate these ideas and to prove or disprove their validity. In America a HIMAG (High Mobility/Agility) chassis has been developed to test the theory that agility on the battlefield can be an effective form of protection. The HIMAG vehicle is in the 29.5 to 41 tonnes weight range according to the amount of armour plate carried. It is powered by an AVCR-1360 diesel engine which was designed for the MBT70 and the GM version of the M1. It can develop from 1,000 to 1,500hp as required, so a great variety of power/weight ratios have been tested. Another feature is a hydropneumatic suspension, also like that of the MBT70, which enables the chassis to move very fast over poor going and to squat behind cover.

The HIMAG has been developed, too, into a High Survivability Test Vehicle — Light weight, or HSTV-L, with a low profile turret mounting a high velocity ARES gun. The HSTV-L is smaller than the HIMAG, only 1.42m to the hull top and 1.88m to the turret roof.

The turret is of the cleft type, with only the commander located in it; the gunner and driver are in semi-supine positions in the hull. There are two stabilised sights mounted on the turret, linked by CCTV to screens for commander and gunner. The gunner can engage one target while the commander uses his sight to observe and to acquire further targets. The gunner's sight incorporates a new CO_2 laser developed by the Raytheon Corp. The gun has elevation from −17° to +45° and it is claimed that it can penetrate most MBTs in service over the frontal arc. Its own protection can

be varied by applique armour, so that the HSTV-L can withstand hits up to 85mm. Up to now it does not use Chobam type armour, but this could further improve its immunity.

In 1976 TACOM awarded a concept study contract to Pacific Car and Foundry Inc to develop a gun pod using the Ares 75mm gun. This pod was mounted on a Sheridan tank hull in such a way that it could be raised bodily some 2m, enabling the tank to make very good use of certain types of cover. The Swedes have extended the concept of their S-Tank by adding a mechanism which raises the 105mm gun from its normal position in the hull, so that only the gun need be visible over cover. They have also fitted the same 105mm gun experimentally to a Marder, in an external mounting on the roof. The gun pod has also been suggested as a semi-expendable weapon system. When mounted on a well-protected, low profile and agile hull, an external gun pod could be easily replaced if put out of action, while the overall survivability of the tank and crew would be greatly enhanced.

During the last decade the APC has evolved into the MCV or IFV of the 1980s. It seems probable that costs will force most armies into accepting two standards of troop-carrying AFV in the future. The front lines MCV, with integral supporting fire weapons, will be supplemented by lower category vehicles in the rear areas, returning to the 'battle taxi' ideas of the 1950s.

Another return to old ideas could be the mounting of all SP guns on MBT chassis, in the interests of commonality and economy. SPs will take over from all but a very few towed guns for all roles, using CLGP with multiple warheads to extend the attrition range for engagement of enemy MBTs.

The next decade will see greater emphasis on survivability and reliability in order to get the most out of the limited funds. All arms are now equipped with AFVs and formations will become more integrated, to achieve the greatest effect with economy.

Appendix 1

Comparison of MBTs 1945-1980s

Year	Tank	Weight tonnes	Max engine DIN hp/rpm	Road speed kph	Cross-country speed kph	Road range km	Gun	Calibre mm	Muzzle Velocity m/sec	Type of round	Approx effective range m
1945	Comet	33.22	608/2,250	52.00	30-35	240	OQF 77mm Mk 2	76.2	793	APCBC	1,000
	M26 Pershing	41.82	506/2,600	40.00	25-30	160	90mm M3	90.00	1,021	APCBC	1,200
	IS-3	46.53	500/2,200	40.23	20-25	160	D25-M1943	122.00	780	APCBC	1,500
1955	Centurion	50.80	650/2,550	34.60	20-25	190	OQF 20pdr Tk	83.82	867	APCBC	1,800
	M48	46.74	650/2,800	51.50	25-35	258	90mm M41	90.00	884	APC-T	1,500
	T-54	35.40	527/2,200	50.00	25-35	620	D-10T 2S	100.00	1,000	APHE	1,200
1965	Centurion	51.80	660/2,550	34.60	20-25	185	L7A2	105.00	1,450	APDS	2,000
	M60	46.30	650/2,400	48.30	25-30	499	M68	105.00	1,458	APDS-T	2,000
	T62	38.00	700/2,200	50.00	45-50	450	U-5TS	115.00	1,680	APFSDS	1,500
1975	Chieftain	53.85	720/2250	48.00	25-30	500	L11	120.00	1,370	APDS-T	2,500
	M60	48.98	670/2,400	50.00	25-30	595	M68	105.00	1,458	APDS-T	2,000
	T-72	41.00	700/2,400	70.00	50-55	450	?	125.00	1,615	APFSDS	2,000
198-	Challenger	60.00	1,200/2,300	56.00	40+		L11	120.00	1,450	APFSDS	2,500
	M-1 Abrams	54.50	1,500/3,000*	72.00	48	440	M68E1	105.00	?	APFSDS	2,000
	T-80	48.50	700/2,400	60.00	40+	500	?	125.00	1,615	APFSDS	2,000

* Output shaft rpm

The figures in this chart are estimated when they cannot be confirmed.

Challenger of A Squadron, The Royal Hussars, during Exercise
'Eternal Triangle'. *Crown Copyright HQ 1 Armoured Division*

Appendix 2

AFV Chronology 1944-1980s

Year	UK	USA	USSR	Others
1944		T26E1 designated Heavy Tank		
1945	Comet in action in Germany A41 cruiser with 17pdr p/type	M26 standardised	IS3 seen in Berlin Victory parade	
1946	A41 enters service as Centurion			ARL 44 produced in France
1947	20dpr fitted in Centurion			
1948	Development of FV 214 Conqueror starts	M26A2 re-designated T40		
1949		T40 standardised as M46	T-54 first seen with 100mm gun	
1950		Hull of M46 with new turret standardised as M47		ARL 44 phased out
1951	FVRDE start study for future requirements	Contract for 1,348 improved tanks designated M48		Production of AMX 13 starts in France
1952		M48 standardised		
1953	Cromwell withdrawn and Charioteer introduced to service			
1954	Churchill phased out			
1955	Conqueror enters service Centurion Mk 5			
1956	Development starts of FV4201 Chieftain			
1957	Multi-fuel engines adopted by NATO			Criteria for new panzer published in Germany
1958				
1959	Centurion Mk10 with 105mm gun			
1960	Comet phased out	First batch of 180 M60 ordered		
1961			T55 introduced	Leopard 1 p/types built and comparative trials with AMX30
1962	Last Centurion gun tank built at ROF Barnbow			
1963		M48A3 with diesel engine Joint MBT70 programme with Germany		Germany joins with the MBT70 development with USA
1964		Work starts on mounting Shillelagh in M60A2		Germany orders 1,500 Leopard 1
1965		M48A5 with 105mm gun	T-62 shown in May Day parade with 115mm gun	First production Leopard 1 delivered
1966				OTO Melara up-gun M48 with 105mm gun in Italy
1967	Chieftain accepted for service	First lot of M60A2 turrets ordered		
1968		Add-on Stabilisation for M60		
1969				

Year	UK	USA	USSR	Others
1970		MBT-70 cancelled; data used for XM-803 study		Germany pulls out of MBT-70 programme
1971		Congress refuses to fund XM-803		
1972		XM-1 programme starts and further improvements to M60 considered		Germany authorises 17 p/types of Leopard 2
1973	Validation contracts for XM-1 to General Motors and Chrysler			
1974	Iran orders 1,200 Shir Iran	M60A2 with Shillelagh becomes operational		MOU between USA and Germany on MBT development
1975		Trials of tank guns for XM-1	T-64 in production with 125mm gun	
1976				Spain uprates M47 with new engine and 105mm gun. First p/type TAM built in Germany
1977			T-72 shown on parade for 60th anniversary of the Bolshevik Revolution	
1978	MBT80 concept study starts			
1979		Approval given for batch of 110 XM-1 from total order for 7,058		
1980	Announced that Challenger will supplement Chieftain in British Army	First production M-1 named Abrams		
1981			T-80 seen by western observers	
1982				AMX30B2 uprated MBT announced by France
1983	Challenger introduced to British Army			
1984				

Appendix 3

Weight Analysis of MBT Components

The weight of each component of a tank is of vital importance to the designer. It is interesting to see how the overall weight is broken down into components for different tasks. This analysis of weight refers to a Centurion 3.

Laden Battle weight	49,878kg	100%
Unladen weight	44,574kg	89.33%
Crew, stowage, fuel, ammunition etc	5,304kg	10.63%
Hull assembly, hatches, lourves etc	15,380kg	30.66%
Gearbox	982kg	1.97%
Final Drives	2,091kg	4.2%
Engine and frame	714kg	1.43%
Auxiliary engine and generator	191kg	.38%
Tracks	4,042kg	8.1%
Suspension units	6,528kg	13.1%
Driving sprockets	166kg	.33%
Radiators and header tank	306kg	.61%
Clutch	204kg	.41%
Turret, complete	13,118kg	26.3%
Turret less equipment	7,625kg	15.28%
Gun (20pdr)	1,300kg	2.61%
Gun mounting	1,300kg	2.61%
Elevating gear	191kg	.38%
Turret traverse gear and basket	383kg	.77%
Cupola	510kg	1.2%
Stowage and other items	2,660kg	5.33%

Armour protection accounts for 46% of the total weight of the tank, and automotive components 38%. Thus only 16% is dedicated to the crew and their weapons, which are the prime reason for the existence of the tank.